AN' IT'S CALLED A TAM-C

KENNETH WEST writes of his experiences during the twelve months of the Second Front in the Second World War. Not for him the strategy and manoeuvres of specialized services such as the Commando or Airborne units — his was the daily sight of strange surroundings, of holding on to ground just won, of digging in then moving off again to new objectives, just the regular daily grind of a private soldier. No — not just an ordinary private soldier, but one of the unsung heroes of an infantry battalion, a man, one among many who form the backbone of the British Army, or any army come to that.

This is not your conventional war story, although it is as true a record as one could find of the hopes and dreams of a twenty-one-year-old submerged in the horrors of war. And, too, it is a record of the humour which just had to be there — the ability to see the funny side of things which saved the spirit from breaking under the strain.

An' it's Called a Tam-o'-Shanter

Kenneth J. West

To Derek
Gunton 1993

© *Kenneth J. West, 1985*
First published in Great Britain, 1985
by Merlin Books Ltd., Braunton, Devon.
This edition published 1988,
by Kenneth J. West, 348 Humberstone Lane, Leicester.

To the memory of Derek Edmund Potter.
  'A voice from our household has gone,
  A voice we loved is still.'

CONTENTS

Preface	7
One — Just Another Day	9
Two — On the Move	14
Three — Ramps Down	21
Four — Follow the Cloud of Dust	28
Five — We Meet John the 'B'	37
Six — "Dig in .... we're moving"	44
Seven — The Phantom Dairyman	55
Eight — "Have you heard the rumour?"	61
Nine — Kybo	70
Ten — You Never Hear the One That Gets You	76
Eleven — Bleeding Heroes	86
Twelve — The Charm o' the Chanter	100
Thirteen — 'Rosie'	108
Fourteen — Reunited with the Fusiliers	118
Fifteen — On the 'Island'	127
Sixteen — The Little White Cottage by the Bund	133
Seventeen — Leave it to 'Ossie'	139
Eighteen — Secret Weapon	146
Nineteen — Silent Night	149
Twenty — Happy Hogmanay	156
Twenty-one — Betty	164
Twenty-two — The Bells of St. Mary's	170
Twenty-three — The 'Island Follies'	179
Twenty-four — Three Days' Leave in Brussells	185
Twenty-five — Drying Out	195
Twenty-six — Red Over Green	203
Twenty-seven — Over the Rhine	209
Twenty-eight — Awa' Doon the Road tae Amsterdam	215
Twenty-nine — Home Leave	226
Thirty — The Flowers o' the Forest	231

The Author
Brussels – February 1945

PREFACE

Many, many books have been written about the Second World War. The number of novels published may be counted in their thousands.

Autobiographies and memoirs by Generals and politicians of all nationalities, have dealt with the strategical and tactical manoeuvres and battles of every campaign, from 1939 to 1945.

Stories have been written, and rightly so, of the bravery and valour of men of the special services, such as the Commando units, Airborne detachments and many other specialized groups.

This book is somewhat different. It is about those unsung heroes of an infantry battalion who form the very backbone of all armies, no matter to what country they may belong. It is only on rare occasions that they make the headlines. They spend much of their time plodding on day by day, in unfamiliar surroundings, holding on to what has been won, then preparing again to advance to new objectives, mere names on a map that is part of some master plan.

This then, is the other side of the coin, as seen through the eyes of a young twenty-one-year-old private soldier. It contains his thoughts and observations of twelve hectic months, from the moment of hearing the announcement by General Eisenhower that Allied Forces had landed in France on the morning of 6th June 1944, to the eventual ending of the war in Europe in May 1945.

All events portrayed in this book are factual. Many persons named are the actual persons who took part in the activities recounted. In some cases, names have been altered, to avoid any possible embarrassment.

K.J.W.
December 1981

ONE – JUST ANOTHER DAY

The door of the Nissen hut was flung open by the Orderly Sergeant as he strode into the blacked-out sleeping quarters of trainee soldiers. Rattling his stick along the corrugated domed roof, he bellowed:

"Right me lads, let's have you . . . wakey-wakey, rise and shine . . . the sun's scorching yer eyeballs out."

I opened my left eye slightly and observed the red sash which lay diagonally across his back from his right shoulder to his left waist as he disappeared out of the far door to continue his way noisily into the next hut, as he had done every morning at 06.30 hours for the past few months. Somehow this particular morning he seemed unduly noisy.

"What's the matter with him this morning, George?" I called to my mate on the bunk above me. "Don't he like his bed?"

"Nah! The trouble with him, he's power mad," replied George, "they're all the same — give 'em a stripe and they think they're bloody Hitler."

"Never mind about him, what's the weather like?" I said to the pair of legs which dangled down from the bunk above.

The legs dropped down to the floor and the rest of the body joined them as they walked towards the open door.

"Oh, about the same as yesterday. Looks like we are in for another decent day again," replied George.

I opened the other eye and reached for my socks.

A quick wash and shave and then ten minutes later we were out on the path leading to the cookhouse. As we walked along the gravel drive, I noticed the lay-out of the grounds. The Nissen huts were dispersed amongst the stately trees within the grounds of a disused hall situated somewhere in the vicinity of Kingston upon Hull. The hall and grounds bore a remarkable resemblance to a hall which both George and I knew in our own locality.

"If it only had a brook running through under the main drive, it could be Barkby Hall," I remarked.

"Pity it's not," said George, "I'd have been round to the kitchen door a bit sharpish for a cup of tea with Kitty — and I'd have been all right for a good night tonight."

We walked on in silence towards the old stables which we now used as cookhouse and stores.

In Northern Command, all infantry recruits were required to spend one week participating in battle training in the field under as realistic conditions as possible. For this purpose, an area of Lincolnshire around the town of Louth had been chosen and was known as the 'Louth Circuit'.

The week long exercise consisted of forced marches in FSMO (Field Service Marching Order), which included every bit of kit one needed to go into battle, plus either a pickaxe or shovel. Everything we had been taught in our initial training was now put to practical use. Field-craft together with compass work and mapping, night operations, including a dummy attack on a small village, much to the consternation of the inhabitants. Bivouacs were improvised by the use of two rifles with the 'pull-throughs' for a ridge and then two groundsheet capes were draped over the ridge. They provided a dry shelter though they were a little draughty. On other nights, slit trenches were dug in the soft sandy soil of the area. Using pick and shovel, pairs of men dug a hole six feet long by two feet wide and three feet deep in which they later slept. For the dual purpose of testing the slit trench and the nerve of the occupants, a tracked vehicle was driven across the top of each one. This was also used to simulate an attack by German light armoured vehicles.

Two days were also spent amongst the bomb damaged streets of terraced houses in the town of Hull. Here the arts and crafts of house to house street fighting were demonstrated and practiced. Although this seemed a bit of a bore at the time, it proved to be of inestimable value in actual combat.

Following our sixteen weeks training at the Infantry Signals Training Wing at the Marquess of Zetland's stables near Richmond in Yorkshire, George and I had been posted as signallers to the 8th Battalion Worcestershire Regt, who were a holding battalion stationed at Usselby Hall Camp to the north of Lincoln. These holding battalions were used to give the recruit the experience of how a battalion worked during his final 8 weeks training prior to being posted overseas.

We had already completed our final training and so whilst awaiting posting, George and I were detailed to act as cookhouse assistants to the next batch of trainees at Usselby Hall who were to attempt the 'Louth Circuit'.

As we entered the cookhouse, the cook was pouring out the first pot of tea of the day. We slid our mugs silently on to the table to be filled.

George broke the silence.

"What's on the cards for today then, Charlie?"

Charlie walked across to the notice board.

"Let's see ... Wednesday, 6th June 1944 ... street fighting, Hull.
Breakfast — porridge, sausage and beans.
Tiffin — haversack rations.
Dinner — meat balls, potatoes and peas.
Then prunes and custard."

"Oh, bloody hell, prunes again," said George, "they mean to keep 'em on the move this week right enough."

"Shall we start the sandwiches, Charlie, whilst you carry on with the breakfasts?" I asked.

Charlie nodded his assent.

The remnants of breakfast had been cleared away and each man had been issued with his haversack rations for the day. Our next job was to check the 'spuds' which had been peeled on the previous evening by the men on 'jankers', after which we would load the large thermos containers of tea on to the 15-cwt truck ready for the journey to the wastelands of Hull.

The buckets of potatoes were in an outhouse attached to the rear of the washhouse away from the stables. Quickly our experienced eyes sorted out the half-peeled spuds and with a few deft strokes of our army clasp knives, they were despatched nonchalantly into the ever-filling zinc bath on the stone flagged floor.

Suddenly, we heard the sound of someone running through the washhouse. Charlie appeared at the door.

"Have you heard the news? The Second Front has started .... the lads went in at dawn this morning."

"Where's that rumour come from?" I asked, sensing that this was just another wild rumour like the others we had heard over the past few weeks.

"It's just been on the news on the wireless — an announcement from General Eisenhower's HQ saying that British, Canadian and American troops have landed in force in North-West Europe at dawn this morning."

We could tell by the look in Charlie's eyes that this was the real thing.

"Won't be long before we're posted now, Kenny lad. I bet it's bloody murder on the beaches. I wouldn't like to be in the first few thousand who landed," said George.

"I wouldn't like to be in the first 200,000," I replied.

"Well, Kenny lad, you'd better start polishing up your French — I bet we'll be over there within a fortnight."

As we stood against the ration truck waiting to serve the tea from the vacuum containers, we watched the street-fighting training. The news of the invasion had by now reached everyone. A lot of the flippancy was missing and the battle training had taken on a new kind of urgency. When that straw-filled dummy swung out of the doorway in front of the leading patrol, the rifleman was in with his bayonet in a flash, knowing that the next time it could be for real.

After dispensing the midday char, it was customary practice to return with the ration truck to the old hall and have a couple of hours or so free time. However, on the previous day we had arranged with Charlie to spend the rest of this afternoon in Hull and return by local bus in time to serve the late dinner.

The truck driver, George and myself were wending our way through the centre of Hull towards the YMCA with the idea of playing a few games of table tennis and to write a letter or two. We paused momentarily outside the theatre for a casual look at the poster, hoping that perhaps Phyllis Dixey might be in town.

"Excuse me boys."

We turned and saw a young woman, very neatly dressed, nice looking and about in her late twenties.

"Would one of you like to see the play this afternoon?" she asked sweetly.

We shuffled our feet awkwardly and thought quickly. Hull ... a port ... sailors ... ladies of the town — well they come in all shapes and sizes.

"Well, not really," said George, "you see we're just off to the YMCA Canteen...."

"Oh, I know what you must be thinking," said the girl, "actually, I have two tickets for the matinée today, but my husband cannot get leave. It is rather a pity to waste the ticket — are you sure one of you wouldn't like to see the play?"

"Plays aren't quite in my line," said George. He turned to me, passing the buck.

"You've been to see plays with your missus, Ken, why don't you go?"

We hemmed and hawed for a minute or two and then the driver said, "Go on mate, I'll square it with Charlie if you're not back, you might not get another chance like this till you get to Paris. Enjoy yourself."

So in I went with the girl, to take our seats as the curtain rose for the first act.

During the interval we adjourned to the restaurant for tea and cakes during which time Angela told me that her husband was a Lieutenant in the Royal Navy. He had been recalled from leave suddenly and presumably his minesweeper was taking part in the great invasion fleet somewhere in the English Channel.

I cannot remember the name of the play or much about the plot. I found it rather dry, but perhaps there were other things to think about.

Afterwards, in the auditorium, we talked for a time about the events of the day and as I shook her hand to thank her for the pleasant afternoon, I also wished that her prayers might be answered, that the war would soon be finished and we would all be reunited with our loved ones.

We parted, she to return to her bed-sit to await news of the Navy.

I went in search of George. He was still at the YMCA, in the writing room.

"How did you go on then, enjoy it?"

"Not so bad .... Nice girl though, her bloke's a Lieutenant on a minesweeper," I replied.

"Did you tell her that you're a private on a bloody 'tater-peeler'?" laughed George. There was no answer to that, so I sat down and wrote a letter to my wife Margaret, before we caught the bus back to the hall.

During the late dinner, the word was passed round that the pub just along the road had received a delivery of beer.

"I think we'll nip up the boozer for a celebration drink," declared my mate.

"Suits me," I replied.

The public house was buzzing with talk of the invasion. The local evening papers were being passed around and we saw photographs of the wounded already being brought home. We elbowed our way to the bar.

"Two halves please," I called.

"Sorry, regulars only," said the barman.

"Oh, come on mate, we only want two halves, we're being posted tomorrow," said George.

"Sorry, regulars only," came the reply.

We tried the smoke room, then the lounge and even the off sales, but all to no avail. It was strictly regulars only.

"Sod this for a lark," said George, "it's too late to go anywhere else — better go back and have a cup o' char with Charlie."

We talked of the day's events as we walked back to the billets. In the grounds of the old hall an owl hooted up in the trees.

"I see what you mean, Ken. It does put you in the mind of Barkby Hall. That road up from the main road is a bit like the Holt Road." He paused reflectively. "Ar .... I bet we'd have got a pint at the Brookside, I'm not exactly a regular there but they know me well enough."

We walked the rest of the way in silence, each with his own thoughts. There was no point in trying to raise Charlie. The cookhouse was in complete darkness, not a glimmer of light to be seen.

"I bet the old bugger is up at the boozer, knocking back the ale, in exchange for a bit of sugar and tea on the side," said George bitterly.

It was nearly eleven o'clock as we reached the hut. Checking that the black-out was in place, I flicked the light switch. Not a flicker.

"Somebody's nicked the bloody bulb," came a voice from the blackness of the interior.

We undressed in the dark and got into our bunks.

"Good-night, George," I said quietly.

" 'Nite Ken," came the voice from the bunk above, "I bet them poor buggers on the beaches would give a thousand quid to swop places with us tonight."

I lay there awake for quite a time as I thought about this special day.

It had started as just another day, rather humdrum, another day of repetitious training. Then the news of the invasion. A visit to the theatre with another man's wife, table tennis at the YMCA and getting worked up about a half-pint of beer. How incongruous it all seemed .... and on the sandy beaches of Normandy, young men who earlier that morning had hurled themselves gallantly against the great West Wall of Europe, lay where they had fallen.

They came first, they stayed last, for today was the sixth of June 1944. Today was D-Day.

TWO – ON THE MOVE

We did not have to wait many days before the order came to pack all kit in readiness for movement. By Saturday morning we had completed the week's 'Louth Circuit' and were once more at Ussellby Camp, to find the order posted on the notice-board awaiting our arrival.

All trainees will hand in to Company HQ, AB 64 part II., for checking, by 14.00 hrs.
All trainees will pack their FSMO forthwith and the remainder of their kit will be packed in kitbag.

After what seemed to be an interminably long weekend of conjecture and wishful thinking, the notice we were all expecting finally appeared on Monday morning.

A long list of names for the next draft were displayed for all to see. The names of both George and myself were included.

"This is it," said George darkly, "no more bloody Sunday-school outings for us."

"So much for not being in the first two hundred thousand," I replied.

All our FSMO was then unpacked, checked and duly labelled and marked with our names and army numbers, then carefully repacked, particular attention being given to boots.

Anyone within three months of their next innoculation or vaccination had to report to the Medical Officer and was duly jabbed.

After tea, a further notice was pinned up on the board.

All draft personnel will parade at 09.30 hrs. on Tuesday 13th June in FSMO with UXPDR (unexpired portion of the daily ration). Kitbags will be carried.

We turned from the notice-board and made our way to the billets in a rather sombre mood to write our letters to home. We were all confined to camp and so the rest of the evening was spent in the NAAFI where large amounts of tea and NAAFI buns were disposed of.

Tuesday was a bright clear morning with just a light breeze to stir the leaves of the silver birches which surrounded the company lines. A typically English summer's day had begun. Young sparrows chirped incessantly as they called for food and made their early attempts to fly. The brightly coloured cock chaffinches called with their distinctive 'chaff-chaff' to their mates. Blackbirds, as ever, sounded out their warning cries to protect their colonies from the danger of this unusual movement of humans.

Most of us were too preoccupied to enjoy the beauty of the morning. Weighed down with the full impedimenta of battle kit plus the white kitbag balanced precariously across the top of the big pack, one needed one's wits about one to negotiate the narrow raised slab pathways as one wended one's way amongst the trees towards the Company Office.

Names were carefully checked and we embussed in the long line of Bedford Troop Carrying Vehicles which awaited us at the camp gates.

The TCVs moved off to an accompaniment of ribald comments from the occupants directed mainly at those NCOs who had perhaps been a little over zealous during our stay with the 8th Worcesters.

The NCOs didn't mind the comments. They took it all in good spirits. Why shouldn't they? They were staying — we were off to God knows where.

The huge cathedral commands the city of Lincoln. Wherever you may be in that city, you feel your are being watched from that great edifice high on the hill in the very centre of the city. As the convoy of trucks whined its way down the hill towards the station we too were being watched, from the church and from the streets. News travels quickly in wartime and the troop train in the station was there for one reason only, to take reinforcements to the beach-head now firmly established in Normandy.

"8th Worcester draft this way," called a red-capped Military Policeman. We debussed and marched into the station and along to the far end of the platform.

"Eight men to a compartment," said a corporal with a black armband with RTO in bold red letters.

"Do we leave our kitbags here?" said George hopefully.

"Take 'em with you, son," replied the corporal.

"I must get a seat with my back to the engine," said my mate, just for the hell of it. "I don't want to be poorly on the journey."

As long as we all got a seat, nobody cared where they sat, and so George chose his spot as we waited for the other convoy from the Royal Irish Fusiliers from the nearby camp on Osgodby Moor. About an hour later all were entrained and the steam engine was coupled up.

We moved off — but in the opposite direction to the one we had anticipated, much to George's consternation. There was much light-hearted banter as he and I changed our seats. Finally he settled himself comfortably in his new position and enquired airily, "I wonder if there's a restaurant car on this train?"

Our journey proved to be very tiring. We travelled at a moderate speed between stops, which came at about every ten miles or so. Often it was to give right of way to supply trains or arms and transport. It was also very difficult to pinpoint our destination on the solitary railway map in one of the compartments, as the train veered first east, then west but always in a southerly direction. It was late evening before we eventually arrived at Bury St. Edmunds in Suffolk.

TCVs awaited us as we detrained at a siding. We were then despatched to a wooded area outside the town. Scores of khaki ridge tents were dotted amongst the trees and we were detailed off, ten men to a tent. George and I were together with a genial Irishman we knew from Limerick, who had been with the Royal Irish Fusiliers. We were to get to know Paddy even better in the coming months.

After supper, consisting of a large dollop of cheese and potato pie and a steaming hot mug of thick sweet cocoa, we settled down for the night and slept as we were, boots and all, on our groundsheets, wrapped in two grey army blankets. It was a cold, uncomfortable night.

Dawn broke on Wednesday with a heavy mist. This persisted well into the morning and added to the confusion a little as we had arrived in the dusk and had no knowledge of the layout of the camp. By midday the check had begun. Firstly it was weapons. Rifles and small arms. Yet another check on pay books and we were invited to fill in the rear page of part II, i.e., the page reserved for one's last will.

George and I demurred on this point and as we decided that we didn't own anything of any consequence, we had nothing of any value to leave to anyone, so there was no point in wearing out a perfectly good fountain pen. In any case we had no intention of letting anyone kill us.

However, we did make a pact to the effect that should either of us have the misfortune to 'cop a Blighty', the other one could have whatever was in his small pack, including his fags. I thought this a most generous agreement, considering the fact that I didn't smoke. Nevertheless we shook hands on it.

Confirmation of our destination came in the afternoon when we handed in our Field Service Caps, known popularly as forage caps, we received in return a khaki beret. This was now the official headdress of the British Liberation Army in North West Europe — and the BLA were in Normandy.

In the evening we were all transferred from whichever regiment we belonged, to either the Welsh Regiment, or the Royal Welch Fusiliers. Here George and I were separated, he to the RWF and I to the Welsh Regt.

All those with white kitbags had to hand them in and were in turn issued with either a black or brown one. Old names were stencilled out and ours were stencilled in. Personal kit was put in and our home address written on a label. These were then to be sent home. I have never found out to this day why it was necessary to send home our kit in a black kitbag instead of the one with which we had been issued.

We were to remain at this camp for just one more day and during this time everything must have been checked a dozen times, probably to keep us occupied.

An amusing event occurred in the morning. I was side-tracked by two fellows, older than myself, who had worked themselves up into a bit of a state, because after almost four years together in the same units, they had now been separated in this last transfer, one to the RWF and the other to the Welsh Regt. The one in the RWF pleaded with me to volunteer to swap places with him so that they could both be posted together. The cardinal rule in the infantry was never to volunteer for anything, but as my mate George was also in the RWF now, here was a heaven-sent chance to get back with him, so I agreed to accompany the two fellows to the Officer i/c transfers and after quite a lengthy discussion, he finally agreed. So within the space of 36 hours I was transferred again, lock, stock and barrel, to the Royal Welch Fusiliers. George grinned like a Cheshire cat when I told him the full story and lost no time at all in finding a spot alongside him in the tent.

Late in the afternoon the draft for the following day was posted on the board. Virtually the whole intake from our train load was named. We were required to attend a pay parade at 17.00 hrs.

Pay parades in the Army are usually stereotyped in the manner in which they are carried out. This one was to include a few surprises.

Firstly we were to be paid out in French francs, but not in those beautiful colourful notes of French origin. We were to be paid out in BAFVs (British Armed Forces Vouchers) of 5-franc and 2-franc denominations. These were very small in size, approximately three inches by two-and-a-half inches. On the face side the 5 francs were coloured blue, the 2 francs being green, whilst on the reverse was the tricolour flag of France. We were also handed out halfpenny and penny NAAFI tokens. These were twelve-sided pieces of plastic, dark brown in colour, for use only in overseas NAAFIs.

The biggest surprise was when everyone on the draft was deducted one shilling from their pay to meet the cost of 'blankets woollen – one – soldiers for use of'. When the first man queried this, he was told, "Before you go abroad, every man shall purchase one blanket. This will keep you warm whilst you are alive and will act as your shroud when you are dead. Any questions?"

There were no further questions, thank you!!

There was a feeling of some trepidation as we arose on the Friday morning. Apart from an acute attack of appendicitis, there seemed to be no chance of anyone missing the forthcoming trip across the briny. Breakfast was taken early. Blankets, woollen, one, was rolled in bandolier fashion and tied around the sides and top of the big pack.

As we marched to the TCVs we all looked as though we carried on our backs an inflated life raft. A Welshman summed up the situation adequately.

"I didn't think we'd be having to paddle across the Channel in our own coracles," he said, in that lovely lilting dialect of the Welsh valleys.

"Don't start giving 'em any bloody ideas," came the unmistakable voice of Paddy.

We entrained at the same sidings at Bury St. Edmunds where we had arrived only a couple of days before. As soon as all were aboard, a shout of "Mind the doors," followed by the sight of the train guard charging down the platform, frantically waving his red flag and blowing his own regulation whistle. The train ground slowly to a halt.

The driver and the guard then indulged in a heated argument lasting some minutes, before the driver realized that we had on board a comedian with a railway whistle. What he didn't know was that our friend Harry had also in his possession a green guard's flag. These two items of stolen property were to cause both havoc and much merriment at each stop along the route that day. At each stop Harry would call out all the station names from Aldershot to London and would end with, "This train is also going to Lasham, Hasham, Mashem and Bashem," which was followed by loud cheers from all on board.

The journey from Bury St. Edmunds started off with all the Welshmen singing 'Land of my Fathers' followed by 'Sospan Fach' and other well-known songs from the principality and it wasn't long before the rest of us from all over the British Isles were joining in the singing.

I don't know which way the train was heading, no one seemed to care particularly, the longer the journey, the longer we would be in England. Sooner or later we would arrive at a port, in the meantime we intended to make the journey as pleasant as possible.

London was reached by about midday. There were innumerable delays as we were shunted and shuffled through junctions and loop lines. Slowly we passed by bombed-out streets of houses, roofs gone, whole walls gone, wallpaper flapped in the breeze, doors and staircases opened out into space, but people still lived in those areas and whenever we passed over a bridge, children would be standing in the streets, shouting and waving as we in our turn threw our odd coppers amongst them and enjoyed watching them scramble for the coins. We stopped at one station and a porter passed a few copies of the daily papers to us. The headlines in most of them were about the new V2 rockets which were now being used against the city in addition to the V1, popularly known as the flying bomb or 'Doodle-bug', which was already causing so much damage. Questions were being asked in the House of Commons as to why they were not being intercepted. Maps of Normandy now showed that the beach-head was more than ten miles deep.

Our whistle stop tour of the Southern Railway network continued with, or without, the help from Harry and his band of enthusiastic helpers.

Suddenly there were seagulls to be seen among the other birds. The name Southampton was being passed around. It wasn't official. Harry hadn't yet included it in his list of stations, though there were cranes and gantries to be seen on the horizon. They became more clearly defined as we steamed slowly on, then stopped momentarily near to some houses.

"Is it Sarfamptan?" shouted Harry to a man leaning on his gatepost.

The man nodded and flicked his thumb in that direction. Confirmation at last.

There is an old saying that you can't get a quart into a pint pot. Southampton proved to all and sundry that this saying was no longer true. As we detrained and embussed on yet more TCVs, we could see that every spare yard of ground in and around the town of Southampton, was crammed with army equipment of every kind. Every street and causeway was packed nose to tail with tanks, DUKWs, armoured vehicles of every size, Bren carriers, 15-cwt trucks, 3-ton trucks, 25-pounder guns, anti-tank and anti-aircraft guns.

The TCVs had difficulty in squeezing between the lines of this vast conglomoration of arms waiting to be shipped across the Channel. We eventually debussed in a side street and were led to a small park which was to be our overnight stop.

Dark brown twenty foot square American marquees were pitched on this once green sward of grass. Scarcely a foot between each tent except for the pathways leading to the cookhouse or 'chow house' as the Americans called them. Each tent packed with troops. British, Canadian, American, Polish, all mixed up together, sharing the discomforts and the humour which abounds in those conditions.

The bright spot of this maze of tentage was the all nations canteen at the entrance to the camp. Here we were able to purchase tea, coffee, chocolates and candies from the American staff. We were unused to the generous rations of such goodies and we spent most of our last week's pay that night, indeed, some of us wished that we hadn't thrown so many coins to the youngsters in the streets of London. Despite the incessant noise of traffic, both vehicular and human, we did manage a few hours of fitful sleep.

Saturday 16th June was another gloriously sunny day. The early morning breakfast was eaten out in the lovely sunshine, on what small piece of earth we could find to squat. Washing and shaving took a lot more time to complete, the ablutions being swamped by half naked bodies who queued for thirty minutes at the wash-stand trying to complete their toilet before the bowl was yanked away to be filled by the next prospective user.

The camp area was contained within a chestnut fencing four feet in height. Here we spent most of the middle of the day chatting to various local inhabitants who were able to give us the latest news from the beach-head.

I well remember one dark haired woman of perhaps forty years of age who told us quite categorically that we would be landed on either Sword or King Beach.

"My Bill," she said, as she stood with arms folded across an ample bosom, "my Bill has been across every other day, and their ship has dropped the lads from this camp on one of those beaches — they'll drop you ashore from landing craft."

There was very little else to be gleaned from our newly-found friend other than the fact that we would be sailing at about six o'clock that evening.

At three o'clock we were called over the tannoy to embus on the TCVs which then wended their way to the docks. An American built Liberty ship was tied up alongside the quay. I never saw the name of the ship, we were much too busy picking our way along the quayside as we avoided the steel runways of the giant cranes, whilst at the same time making sure we were not the outside man who might be jostled over the edge.

As we made our way up the steep gangway, weighed down with our battle kit, the studded soles of our boots slipped on the wooden cross bars and lads stumbled and webbing harnesses became entangled. Loud curses and oaths of Anglo-Saxon origin filled the air as the unfortunates extricated themselves and continued their way to the top.

Crewmen, at the top of the stairways, directed us down to the interior of the vessel which hummed with activity. As we descended the stairs George turned to me and asked casually, "Ever been on a ship as big as this before, Ken?"

"No," I replied, "the only boat I've ever been on was a rowing boat on the Abbey Park."

"Same here. I ain't even been on the Isle of Wight ferry," chuckled George. "Let's see if they're selling return tickets."

THREE – RAMPS DOWN

We were aboard a Liberty ship, one of many such utility vessels produced by the Henry Kaiser shipyards in the United States of America. These ships were prefabricated in many parts of the USA and brought to the Kaiser shipyards to be welded together prior to launching. Because the shipyards were situated on a rather narrow river it was only possible to launch these particular ships sideways into the river, a rather revolutionary procedure in ship building circles. Also, as they were assembled in two halves and then welded together, there were instances where they had broken apart in the Atlantic gales.

Primarily used as a medium sized merchant ship, they quickly became a 'jack of all trades', ours, along with others being adapted as a Landing Ship Infantry (LSI) for use in the Normandy landings.

Our ship was crewed by American seamen and so perhaps there was a more free and easy atmosphere on board. Sensing this, George and I quickly stowed away our gear on to one of the bunks below deck and took the opportunity to get up on deck to witness the departure from Southampton.

Promptly at six o'clock the ship's siren sounded and we were on our way. No fuss and palaver, no cheering throngs on the dockside to send us on our way. Just another ship taking more reinforcements to expand the beachhead across the English Channel less than a hundred miles away.

We made our way slowly down Southampton Water, threading our way through the various craft which scurried about in all directions. The sentinel towers built in Napoleonic times to defend our fair isles against the French, now bristled with guns once more, to defend us as we sailed to bring liberation to the French people after four dark years of German occupation.

Soon we could see the Isle of Wight on our starboard bow, then shortly afterwards came the call for 'Blue mess' to assemble in the galley for 'chow'.

In the galley we were issued with a tray with various indentations of differing sizes. Into each of these shallow compartments was deposited the beefburger, peas, cabbage, potatoes, apple pie, custard and gravy which comprised the meal for that evening. We had heard that the Yanks ate their main course and sweet at the same time and now we were getting it confirmed in a very positive manner. Fortunately for us, it was a calm evening and so we were able to eat the separate ingredients, finishing with the sweet as I had always been taught by my mother.

One can imagine the effect that a rough sea would have on this type of catering arrangement.

Following the meal, we were ordered to stay below decks until further orders. Over the tannoy system we were given instructions on what procedure to take for a submarine alert — "Stay where you are!"

We were also instructed where to assemble should the order come to abandon ship.

Meanwhile, as the beefburgers and the apple pie rumbled inside, the smell of paint and fuel together with the thickening atmosphere of hundreds of sweaty bodies lulled us into a twilight haze during which we snatched a few hours' sleep.

Aaaeer . . . . aaaeeer . . . . aaaeeer . . . . aaaeeer . . . .

We were awakened by the klaxons sounding the submarine alert. It was almost 2.30 a.m.

Through the haze I estimated the distance to 'Assembly Point F', something like fifty paces.

An American voice over the intercom announced, "An unidentified submarine has been reported in the area. We are taking evasive action. Please stay in your mess areas."

For the next couple of hours I lay on the bunk listening to the throbbing of the ship's engines as we continued steadily on our way. I don't remember the stand down being called, I suppose by that time I had dozed off again.

"Blue mess will assemble in the galley for breakfast."

I was half-way to Assembly point F before I came out of my daze. The ship wasn't sinking, it was just the call for breakfast.

"Bloody hell," said George, "you were off like a whippet out of a trap. I didn't think you'd be that hungry," he said with a sly grin.

"I notice that there's no one else between us," I replied.

"Well, we've got to stick together, ain't we, mucker?"

The subsequent breakfast turned out to be quite an excellent meal of bacon, eggs, tomatoes, tea, and lovely white bread. We weren't aware at the time, but it would be a long, long time before we could enjoy another breakfast as good as that one.

Restrictions on deck were lifted and George and I took the opportunity to get a breath of fresh air. We were not prepared for the sight to greet us as we looked over the port side.

A vast armada spread over the sea. As far as the eye could see, there were ships of all sizes and shapes. Merchantmen, tankers, destroyers, cruisers, battleships, frigates, corvettes, tank landing craft (TLCs).

We crossed to the starboard. Once again hundreds upon hundreds of ships moving in all directions.

To the front, over the bows, we could see a faint line on the horizon. We were making our way slowly towards that direction. Some craft were making their way back to England. A couple of LCTs had wounded on board. Some waved as they passed, others, despite the bandages stained with blood, shouted words of encouragement.

"I'm all right mate, I've got a Blighty one."

"It's the only way you'll get back lads. . . . . "

"Don't worry about the ma'mselles — there ain't none."

George shouted back, "In that case, it's waste of time me getting off the boat."

Amongst all this activity, tugs could be seen towing huge structures of concrete towards the beaches. There was much speculation about these. What could they be used for?

George, being an old artillery man, came up with the answer.

"They're probably anti-aircraft batteries, to defend the beaches from fighter attacks."

At the time this seemed to be the most popular use for these huge blocks of concrete. What we didn't realize at the time was the fact that we were witnessing the assembly of Britain's secret weapon, the 'Mulberry harbour', which was to prove to be one of the turning points in the Normandy campaign.

As we edged nearer and nearer to the coast of France the sounds of gunfire become louder. Cruisers off shore were firing in support of the ground troops. Suddenly, about a mile to port came an almighty explosion. HMS *Warspite* had opened fire with her big guns. Even at that distance, the noise was almost deafening, but she and her sister ships kept up a steady bombardment during the rest of the morning. I also noticed a few splashes in the sea in between ships. The hot steel wasn't going just one way.

Overhead, planes whined as they sped hither and thither, each one with three white stripes under each wing. Mostly they were fighter planes, English and American, but also in evidence were rocket-firing Typhoons of the RAF. Not an enemy plane showed up. General Eisenhower was right when he said, "If you hear a plane overhead, don't bother to look up, it'll be one of ours."

The beaches could now be seen quite clearly. Obstacles were sticking up out of the sand and through the surf as each wave broke upon the shore. A column of black smoke would arise following an explosion on the beach as another mine was detected and blown up.

Small craft darted between the larger ships, messages flashed between crafts and ships. DUKWs and LCIs shuttled from ship to shore, transferring men and stores.

Suddenly we were ordered to return to our mess decks to await our call to disembark.

The call came at about three o'clock in the afternoon. By this time the Liberty ship was lying some mile or so off shore, broadside to the beach. On the starboard side we looked down to see scrambling nets hanging from the deck almost to the waterline.

LCIs were coming alongside, one at a time; they were being filled with thirty-six men and then off they went towards a large sign on the beach with the word 'KING' written on a huge signboard.

"Her Harry was right," I remarked to George, remembering our conversation with the lady in Southampton.

"Ar, the bloody civvies know more about what's going on than we do," replied George.

"Next party," called the Royal Navy Petty Officer. Now it was our turn to scramble down the netting. I swung my leg over the side and felt the net give slightly under my weight. Over went the other leg and holding on with both hands tightly I proceeded cautiously down two more rungs.

"Mind where you're putting your bloody feet," came a plaintive cry from below, "I can't hold on if you've chopped off me bleedin' fingers."

Apologies were not in order at that moment, I concentrated on the boots directly above my hands. I might as well learn by my own mistakes.

The net ended about four feet from the deck of the gently swaying LCI and I dropped the rest of the way and squatted on the right-hand side about half-way along the craft.

When all were aboard, we set off in a wide arc towards the sandy beach. I stood up and to the front I could see a large white building, rather like a seaside boarding house, right on the sea front. Although damaged, it looked pretty well intact. There didn't seem to be any other houses around that area.

"Get ready lads," called the Petty Officer. "The tide's on the turn, so we've got to keep backing off, but we'll put you down as close as we can but we've got to be careful, we had three craft stranded for twelve hours yesterday."

"Right lads .... ramps down."

The ramps were lowered and the first men walked off into the water, it was about ankle deep.

"Come on lads, the water's fine," called a wag.

A naval rating counted the men out. As number ten came on to the ramp, ten blankets were dropped across his shoulders.

"There you are mate — a blanket apiece to keep you warm tonight," joked the sailor.

The poor infantryman floundered in the water, then staggered ashore. I made a mental note and counted ten more blokes and placed myself about sixth in line after him.

We kept backing off from the edge of the waterline. Only two more to go now, then George, then it was my turn.

I reached the edge of the ramp. We backed off again. I jumped off the ramp and ... thump, 'ten blankets, woollen, soldiers for the use of', were dumped across my shoulders and I landed in the sea with the water up to my armpits. Staggering to my feet, I was pleasantly surprised to find the sea was quite warm. Having spent my childhood holidays on the east coast of England and remembering the ice cold water as we splashed about even in the heat of high summer, I had expected the immersion to come as quite a shock. However, here on the northern coast of Normandy the sea was pleasantly warm as I splashed on through the surf.

As we reached the beach I was conscious of the palls of black smoke we had seen from the exploding mines and I wondered if this part of the beach was free from mines. I made an instantaneous decision, all I had to do was to walk in the footprints of the chap in front and I would be all right. It never occurred to me at that time that if he went up in smoke, there wouldn't be much of me left either.

Meanwhile I hummed an old song to myself:
"I'm following in father's footsteps,
I'm following my dear old dad.
I don't know where we're going,
But when we get there, I'll be glad . . . ."

Walking just three paces behind the chap in front, the water drained from my soaked battledress, down both legs and into my boots. As I carefully trod in the footprints left by my comrade in front, the sea water squelched inside my boots and then spurted out through the eyelets. By the time I joined the rest of the party on the sand dunes, most of the water had been expelled.

I dropped the blankets on to the pile already there and sat down in my soggy clothes and equipment.

We'd got there – and I was glad.

We turned and looked out to sea. For the first time we saw this vast armada in all its glory.

It was a glorious sunny June day, as clear as a bell. One could see for miles in all directions. There were not just hundreds of ships out there but thousands. It has been reported that on D-Day over 5,000 craft of all kinds were in use. Now that the build-up was under way there must have been many more.

LCTs spewed out tanks, carriers, jeeps, lorries, guns. DUKWs floated in direct from supply ships and sped off inland on their four wheels, taking urgently needed stores and ammunition. Columns of men were snaking their way from the water to the rendezvous points in the dunes. All the while warships of the Allied Navies fired salvoes over our heads on to targets inland.

For more than half an hour we observed the scene. We tried to pick out the ship which had brought us across but there were so many out there it was impossible to ascertain for sure as every ship and craft was on the move.

A Royal Engineers sapper was slowly making his way towards us as he swept the dunes with his mine detector. He came nearer, almost casual in his approach.

One or two of our chaps made to move away, but he held up his hand to stop them.

"Who told you to gather here? I've not swept that area yet — stay where you are and I'll sweep round you."

He moved round to the landward side of the group and moments later came the shrill note of detection.

"All right lads, stay where you are." He scooped the fine golden sand away with his hands to reveal an army clasp knife. He put the knife in his pocket and proceeded nonchalantly on his way along the dunes to our left. We all breathed a sigh of relief.

"As my old sar'nt-major used to say, never take anything for granted lads," said George knowingly.

When some two hundred men were assembled in the dunes the order came to proceed inland. We set off along a road which had been churned up by all the vehicular traffic during the past twelve days. Beyond the grass verges, barbed wire prevented access to the flat scrubland adjoining the road. Signs with the skull and cross bones and 'ACHTUNG MINEN' painted on them, denoted that they were all minefields.

"It's not taken the sappers long to use their sense of humour," said one of our party. In actual fact, the initial landing had taken the defenders so completely by surprise, that they had not had time to remove the warning signs put up to protect their own men. Subsequently, all the minefields along the beach-heads were advertised for all to see.

Notices proclaiming 'VERGES CLEAR' made progress along the roads just possible. Even as we walked on these tiny verges, huge snorting dragons, in the shape of American eight wheel trucks carrying ammunition, brushed our sleeves as we sweated in the hot June afternoon.

The incessant movement of vehicles and pedestrians caused a fine dust to arise to a height of some fifty feet or so which covered grass, hedges, trees, vehicles, and people with a reddish-brown film. The dust soon penetrated clothing, hair, mouth and nostrils. You could not lose direction, you just followed the billowing cloud of dust and you knew you were on the main road towards Bayeux.

After three or four miles of this torture we turned left off the road and took a small road leading to a sort of common. A signboard showed that it was an RHU (reinforcement holding unit). Here we were told to bivouac for the night. Groundsheets, anti-gas capes, rifles and slings were soon put to use and small bivvies were sprouting like the proverbial mushrooms in a meadow. We had our emergency rations with us and so decided to make a brew up.

Our little 'Tommy Cookers' were brought into use also for the first time. These were small pressed steel gadgets which opened up into three small legs about 2½ x 3 inches with a cut out in which was placed a small tablet of solid fuel, about the size of a candlewax nightlight, this was purported to be sufficient fuel to hot enough water to make a mashing of the powdered tea, sugar and milk in the emergency pack. The resultant brew was a tepid, off-white liquid, whose taste was not improved by the sterilized water we now had to use. The rock hard army biscuits were not made any more digestible, just because each packet bore a small label 'BEST WISHES FROM BREEZY BLACKPOOL.'

Just as twilight was descending, the sound of a plane could be heard.

"Don't worry lads, it's one of ours," someone said.

Next moment came the rat-a-tat-tat-tat-tat of machine-gun fire as a lonely Messerschmitt fighter strafed the site. Seconds later it made a second run across the field. Some people hit the deck, others fired rifles at the plane, others watched unbelievingly as it sped out of sight.

Away to our right came a call, "Stretcher bearers."

In an instant, first-aid personnel were dashing across to tend the wounded. The total tally was one killed two wounded. What had seemed an hour ago to be another exercise like the 'Louth Circuit' had now become a reality.

It was Sunday the eighteenth of June 1944. I had reported to Budbrook Barracks in Warwick on the seventeenth of June 1943, so this was the first day of my second year in the army. For me, like so many others, it would be a year I would never ever forget.

FOUR – FOLLOW THE CLOUD OF DUST

Monday dawned a lovely dewy morning. The sun rose in a clear blue sky as we awoke from our slumbers and the faint gunfire in the distance sounded a little unreal on this bright start to the new day. The events of the previous evening had been pushed to the backs of our minds as we awaited the orders which were bound to come within a few hours.

Meanwhile, breakfast called, just a mug of tea and Canadian rolled bacon which had been slightly warmed to make it almost edible, and the never-ending supply of army biscuits. Water-bottles were filled from the tanker by the gate. As George's sar'nt-major had always said, "Always keep your water-bottles topped up lads."

Water for washing was drawn from another tanker and biscuit tins were improvised as containers for our ablutions, each man in his turn skimming off the scum from the top of the ever darkening water before completing his wash and shave.

Mid morning saw us on the move once more. We joined the traffic on the dusty road towards Bayeux.

As we got further inland, the damage to property became worse and worse, showing how after the initial surprise landing, resistance from the defenders had become stronger. In some of the narrow lanes, walls had been smashed down by tanks to make way for the advance and these gaps had now become alternative routes for the personnel marching inland. Jeeps were also using these routes, so that the perpetual swirling dust soon had us recoated a gritty reddish-brown and eyes and throat became sore as vehicle after vehicle swept past the never-ending file of men as they plodded on in the hot sun.

Progress was slow, motorized traffic having the right of way. Fully laden trucks still sneaking up behind us snorted impatiently, willing us out of the way. In the opposite direction ambulances with their large red crosses on the sides, made their way back to the beaches along with the empty wagons.

Now to the front we could see the twin steeples of Bayeux Cathedral, small now, but as we drew nearer to this ancient town, the first to be liberated by the Allies, the steeples grew in size and suddenly a brief gap in the traffic gave us our first full view of this magnificent edifice. We were three-quarters of a mile away, but from that distance it looked undamaged.

As we got nearer, we could see that it was indeed in good order and I wondered whether the famous tapestry had survived the war, or had it been taken away to hang in Hitler's chancellery in Berlin? My father was quite knowledgeable on cathedrals of Britain and the continent and I knew he would be interested to know. Perhaps we may be near enough to visit the Cathedral and find out.

Shortly after passing through Bayeux, we turned off to the left and followed a small country road for about a mile and a half. The dust cloud had now reached a more acceptable level as the road wound its way between the apple orchards on either side. The ancient trunks of the trees were gnarled and silver grey, mottled with lichen, they seemed to be centuries old with meagre foliage but heavily laden nevertheless, with small rosy apples, small sour tasting cider apples.

The sign '33 RHU' announced our arrival at our destination. We were met at the gate by a corporal who told us to walk around the perimeter of the orchard and make our bivouacs either into the hedges or under one of the trees to avoid any possible detection from enemy aircraft. Remembering the previous night on the common, George and I opted for the hedges.

At about five o'clock in the evening, we were introduced to the 14-man food packs for the first time. George and I fetched the wooden cased pack from the camouflaged tent near the gate and soon organized twelve others to get a fire going in the hedge bottom. Seven tins of stewed steak were pierced with the spike of a clasp knife and heated on the fire. Potatoes and treacle pudding were warmed in the same manner, to be followed by everyone giving half of their water from the water-bottle for mashing the tea. Packets of biscuits were dished out and the container used as a mashing can. Seven boiled sweets and seven cigarettes were also issued to every man together with three sheets of khaki-coloured toilet paper. The two tins of bacon were held back for the morning breakfast.

Thrown together as we were, a hotchpotch of soldiers from all sorts of regiments, it was surprising how soon we sorted ourselves out into those who could cook, those who could be relied upon to get a fire going quickly and others who were very adept at scrounging wood for fuel. Pits also had to be dug for latrines and other waste disposals.

After the meal we were each issued with a buff postcard on which we wrote our name and number and RHU number. This was forwarded to our next of kin so that they could write to us via that address.

As darkness approached we had to 'stand to' for half an hour, also sentries had to be posted and rotas were quickly arranged within the fourteen man pack group. George and I took the first 'stag' and then settled down for a good night's sleep. At least, that's what we had hoped for. We hadn't accounted for the 'Normandy Mossies'.

We knew that the forces in Italy were continually harassed by the mosquitoes, but no one expected to encounter these pests in Northern France.

These huge insects started attacking us as soon as it was dark; fortunately they were not the malaria carrying type, but they did bite viciously and each bite hurt. Very soon we were covered in lumps resulting from those bites and we spent the night sweating, scratching and cursing in between snatches of sleep.

We had scarcely finished breakfast when it started to rain. Very soon it was simply lashing it down.

What a difference a day makes. Yesterday the hot sun had shone from a cloudless sky and we'd sweated in all our FSMO. Today we were soon wet through to the skin. Groundsheet-capes were all in use, but with the rain being lashed by a strong wind, the capes were blown about and we soaked up the wet. Also as the long grass became wetter, we were soon wet through from foot to thigh.

Throughout the day there were calls for various fatigue parties for unloading stores to enable a quick turnaround for the three-tonners. The fires also needed to be kept going. It looked as though we were in for a wet spell.

The elements raged for three more days and we became rather morose, there was no way of avoiding the deluge, and of course no way in which we could get dry. Some of the lads changed into dry clothes only for them to be soaked within an hour or so. George and I decided to stick it out in our sodden clothes until the break in the weather came.

But there is always humour in adversity. We were visited twice a day by the old farmer and his daughter as they brought their three cows into the orchard for grazing. Each morning they would walk into the field leading one at a time a large brown and white mottled cow. The old man would carry over his shoulder a large wooden mallet made from a good sized log with a part of a branch from a tree as a handle. He would then select a patch of grass not used for some time and hammer a large steel spike into the ground, the cow would then be tethered to this spike and the gentle beast would munch away all day producing the milk.

In the afternoon, the daughter would bring her milking stool into the orchard and the animals would be milked one by one and she would leave the field to a barrage of calls from all the lads.

To break the monotony of the day, we would pull out the stakes and swop the cows around, always putting one right up close to the hedge, so that the young mademoiselle had to come into contact with the lads. But, we reckoned that the old man must have told her all about soldiers, because she steadfastly refused to be drawn into conversation. Nor would the old man sell us any milk, he said our money was 'pas bon'.

When it did eventually stop raining, we decided to walk into Bayeux to have a look round. However, we were denied entry to the road leading to the cathedral as the Military Policeman would only allow vehicles to pass.

George and I then tried to find a back way into the centre of the town, but the roads were full of traffic and we kept being moved on, so we opted to partake of 'une petite promenade'.

As we walked, we noticed a number of small troughs by the wayside.

"Drinking fountains," said George, knowingly, "I suppose the water supply has been turned off."

"Probably the hot summer has dried up the springs," I ventured. It seemed a likely reason to me.

We continued our perambulations looking at the buildings and the architecture. There seemed very little damage to many of the houses.

A young French couple overtook us, the girl hanging on to the arm of the fellow as they chatted away happily.

"Bon jour, m'sieur," said George, trying out his French.

The young fellow never answered, probably too engrossed in his conversation.

"Ignorant bugger," said George, loudly.

The Frenchman stopped as he came to the next fountain. I expected a little bit of hassle as we approached. But no. He just turned his back on us and pee'd into what we had thought to be a drinking fountain. The girl was still hanging on to his other arm and still rattling away in French.

"Bloody hell, I've seen it all now," said my mate.

"So has she," I said, "and not for the first time either by the look of it."

The couple continued on their way and we followed behind chuckling away at the nonchalant way in which the young man had emptied his bladder.

"I'd get locked up for doing that in Queni," said George.

We continued our way back towards our orchard, casually walking hand in pocket, with the other hand holding the rifle sling in place on our shoulders.

A motorbike roared up towards us from a side road and we stepped back to allow the bike to turn on to the road. Brakes were slapped full on and a noise like an enraged bull rent the air.

"What do you think you are doing, you 'orrible men?"

Just in time, I saw the huge coat of arms on the sleeve of the rider as I answered, "Moving out of the way to let you pass, sir."

"You're not going anywhere, you 'orrible men, until you are properly dressed. Get that blouse buttoned up ... put your hat on straight ... and you don't walk about with your hands in your pockets," bellowed the loudest voice in the British Army.

We did up our battledress necks and adjusted our berets to his satifaction.

"What unit are you from?" he demanded.

"We're from 33 RHU," I answered.

"Reinforcements ... reinforcements ... God help the unit who is unfortunate enough to get you! Right, you 'orrible men, quick march — on your way."

We marched away conscious of his glare. Moments later the motor bike came alongside and we awaited the blasting on our eardrums.

"That's better, swing those arms," then the bike pulled away with the rider still sitting in an immaculate position of attention.

"You know who that was?" said George. "Bloody RSM Brittain of the Grenadier Guards — they always reckoned he was a bloody nutter."

We marched on keeping a wary eye open in case he should return before we reached the camp. However we never crossed paths again, but we passed the word around as soon as we got inside the gate.

As dusk approached, we were ordered to report to the tent by the gate, in full FSMO and ready to move to a forward dispersal unit. A small convoy of four Bedford three-tonners waited on the grass verge of the small road and we embussed in the gathering gloom.

Inside the truck, everything was pitch black and we stumbled and groped around until all had a spot of floor to sit down. Then we were off in to the night.

The route twisted and turned this way and that way until someone at the rear of the truck said we were on the main road from Bayeux to Caen. By now the sounds of the guns were much louder and we were getting quite near to the line of action.

After leaving the main road, we were twisting and turning again and then came intermittent stops as the driver asked the way, or the whereabouts of our destination. No one seemed sure.

One of the drivers came to the back of the truck.

"Sorry about this lads, we can't find any sign of the dispersal unit. We'll carry on and make our way back towards the main road again."

A few hundred yards further on we heard a voice challenge, "Halt! Who goes there?"

The driver spoke to the unseen voice and told him the facts, whereupon the voice replied, "I don't know where the bloody hell you've come from, but we're the forward unit on this sector — you must have come through Jerry's lines."

Someone pulled back the rear tarpaulin to check that we were what we'd said we were, and being satisfied, he instructed the driver to follow the sign of the unit back to the Command Post. Here we were returned on to the Bayeaux-Caen road and were redirected via country roads to our eventual destination where we debussed as dawn was breaking.

We entered another orchard and once more found a spot near the hedge where we put up our home-made bivouacs. Breakfast was issued from a tented cookhouse and we studied the lie of the land.

It seemed vaguely familiar. We walked on to the road out of curiosity and again it looked rather familiar, so we walked down the small hill and round the curve in the dusty road. We saw the sign '33 RHU'. We were about 400 yards away from the place we had left the night before, but on the opposite side of the road. Six hours of bumpy tortuous journey during which we could easily have become prisoners of war, for a distance of only four hundred yards. It was later in the day when we were told that the D U had only moved into the field on the previous afternoon and that the signboard hadn't been erected until dusk.

"C'est la guerre," as George's old sarn't-major said.

Our stay at the DU was only short-lived, for on the next day we moved on once more, this time to yet another orchard on the outskirts of a small village. This time we walked.

It was another fine sunny Sunday morning. Our ears had adjusted to the distant gunfire and we were able to enjoy a bit of fairly unspoilt countryside for a change. As the leading column came towards the first houses, we crossed a small clear brook. On the far side of the little bridge, the bend in the stream had formed a wide shallow pool and the gently flowing stream was most inviting. A quick decision was made and we were soon washing and shaving in the cold fresh water. Boots were removed and feet immersed in the new-found luxury. Half an hour later we were on our journey once more and arrived at our new stopping place about two o'clock in the afternoon.

"NAAFI up," someone called.

"Some hope," I said to George.

The next thing we knew, there was a NAAFI van in the field, with the familiar blue uniformed staff opening the shutter and preparing to open shop.

Everyone dropped what they were doing and ran to the fast forming queue. Goods were strictly rationed to a bar of chocolate, a bar of Lux soap, and a packet of chewing gum, per man, but writing materials were on sale along with other odd items. The two girls were the only ones we had seen since leaving Southampton just over a week ago. Was it really only a week ago? It seemed to have been ages to me.

As we stood around the van chatting up the two girls, a young Lieutenant came up and asked when we had last had a bath.

"About ten days ago," said one of the lads, "but we've just had a good wash in a stream by the roadside."

"Well, you should have a bath once a week," said the officer, "I'll try and get it fixed up."

Half an hour later, he was back at the gate and he beckoned us over.

"Bring your soap and towel — I've got it fixed up."

"Might as well get what's going," I said and rolled my towel under my arm. "Come on, George."

The baths unit was about another mile further along the road from the village. We did not know what to expect nor were we surprised at what we saw.

In the middle of a smallish field, a framework of metal tubes had been erected. A hosepipe snaked across the field to a small river from whence the water supply was pumped by means of a generator on an army truck. A heating unit was connected to the framework and hey presto! one unit, baths, soldiers for the use of.

The procedure for a shower was as follows:

One undressed in the field and stacked one's clothes neatly in a pile on the grass. With towel and soap at the alert, one entered the framework, where twelve shower heads hung from the overhead pipes. Two men stood under each shower and the command "water on", signalled the cascade of hot steaming water to descend on to the men below. Thirty seconds were allowed for this operation and then the water was cut off, whereupon one minute was allowed for soaping from top to toe. Water was then turned on again for a minute and a half to swill away the soap and dirt. Just three minutes, and twenty-four men had completed their shower. This was army efficiency at its highest level.

No time was allowed for drying within the shower unit, one had to dry oneself standing in the field by one's kit.

A clean shirt and pair of cellular drawers could be exchanged for the soiled ones at the three-tonner by the generator, also, occasionally, socks and towels.

Of course, this open-air bath parade was quite often a hilarious romp. Dozens of naked squaddies enjoying the chance of a break from routine and getting the chance to get a bit of sunshine to their bodies.

The girls from the village enjoyed their Sunday afternoon's outing too.

Madam stood at the five-barred gate, arms akimbo, as she gave a running commentary on the different batches as they lined up for their turn under the showers.

"Bravo," she would shout as she clapped her hands whenever a well-endowed young man revealed his true potential. At other times, she would crook her little finger and point to some individual. Peals of laughter would erupt from the assembled mesdemoiselles as they stood on the bars of the gate to obtain a better view.

"I'll soon send them packing," said a well built lad.

He walked towards the gate, chest out, shoulders back, fully expecting the females to run off. A few did, but madam stood her ground, arms still folded across her ample breasts as the man marched towards her. Then, with a sudden flourish, she opened the gate and beckoned the man through.

He stopped dead in his tracks, nonplussed, then turned on his heels and walked back shamefaced, to gather up his kit and quietly get dressed.

The lady was still there in her black dress, commentating on the passing show as we passed through the gate on the way back to our camp.

"Bon jour, messieurs, en bon chance," she bade us all.

Back at the camp, the good news was that the café in the village was opened, so after we had eaten dinner permission was granted to pay a visit, but we must report back for 'stand-to' at dusk.

The café in question was simply a one-roomed bar, quite spartan inside, with only two tables and about half a dozen chairs. We elbowed our way to the bar.

"What have they got?" enquired George.

"Red wine, crème de menthe and some stuff called calvados," said the chap in front.

"No beer?" queried George.

"No — just a queer concoction they call lemonade. I reckon it's just water with green dye in it, tastes bloody awful."

"I think I'll have a crème de menthe," decided my mate. "Same for you, Ken?"

"I fancy trying that calvados, see what it's like."

I didn't expect a tumblerful of calvados, but when I saw the small tot which madam had given me in exchange for about a day's pay, I motioned George to move outside. I wasn't going to spill any of the precious liquid.

We leaned against the wall of the café and I took my first sip. As the colourless spirit slid down my throat there followed in its wake a bush-fire which completely took my breath away. Gulping air down my gullet as quickly as possible, I coughed and swallowed.

"By God, George, that's got a right kick in it, it's not as innocent as it looks — ruddy fire-water if you ask me."

"I'd better try one of them then," he said as he drained his drink, and went inside. He reappeared a few minutes later with two more tots.

"I've been making enquiries about this stuff," he said as he handed me one of the glasses. "It is made from cider — they distil the vapour from the cider and it is particular to this region of Normandy which is called Calvados, that's why it's so pricey."

We made the second drink last for some time. We couldn't have too many of those; not only were they so potent but there were only seven days' pay in one week. Anyway, we could always come down again tomorrow night.

Any hope of a return visit the following night was soon dispelled. A notice on the board at the office tent brought news of yet another move on the morrow.

Transport would leave at 09.30 hours, all the names on the sheets were those of **Royal Welch Fusiliers** and **Welsh Regt**.

Harry was checking the list carefully. He looked very pale and drawn. The effervescent humour that he had shown on the train journeys in England had subsided day by day and now one could see that he was quite apprehensive about this latest move.

"I reckon this is it lads," he said quietly, "we must be on our way to join a battalion this time — Gawd knows where we'll all end up." He shook his head sadly and went on his way, head down and hands in pockets, looking very dejected.

We stood in a little knot, talking amongst ourselves as we awaited the transport. We were joined by the young Lieutenant as he checked cheerfully the personnel against the list on his board.

"What battalion are we joining, sir?" asked George casually.

"Oh we're not joining any battalion at the moment," came the reply.

"I thought we were on our way to one of the mobs in the 53rd Div?"

"The 53rd Div. hasn't arrived over here yet," said the officer, "as a matter of fact, we're a bit of an embarrassment. We are the reinforcements for the 53rd Welsh Div. and they have been delayed by the gales and storm in the Channel, so whether they hold us back until they arrive, or post us to another Div., that is anybody's guess."

The conjecture as to our future continued as we sat in the three-tonner and felt it grind its way along the busy Bayeux-Caen road. There seemed to be a lot more noise up at the front today and we were heading much nearer to the fray than any previous excursion we had undertaken. Our own big guns were now firing from behind us. As we looked out of the back flaps, we saw trees which had only recently borne their fruits, now shattered by shell blasts, and in the side roads on which we now travelled at mere walking pace, there were ominous holes with jagged edges. We debussed and walked into a field in which a number of Sherman tanks were positioned around the inner perimeter.

We quickly commenced to prepare a meal from our 14-man compo pack. As we collected wood to start a fire, one of the tank crew shouted across.

"Can't light a fire around here, pal. If the Jerries see a bit of smoke they'll soon put down a 'stonk' on us."

"How the 'ell do we cook the bloody stuff?"

"Borrow this if you like." He pointed to a blackened tin.

On examination we found it to be an old biscuit tin half filled with sandy soil.

"Just pour some petrol on it, let it soak in and then light the vapour — instant cooking."

He proffered a jerrycan of petrol and left us to it. The instructions were followed and in no time at all we had the tins of meat and veg warming up and a can on for tea. This method of cooking had been widely used in the desert by the 8th Army, and presumably had been passed on by the Desert Rats Division who were now part of the Liberating Army.

From the conversations with the tank crews, we learned that they had recently been in action in the Tilly-sur-Seulles sector and were in reserve for a few days. The continuous crump and crash of shells and mortars was confirmation of the tough battles being fought all along the front. We were encouraged to dig slit-trenches around the field in between the tanks as they harboured under their camouflage netting, the crews sleeping on the ground close to their vehicles. Everyone was under one hour's notice to move should the order come.

As one wag was heard to say, "It's either advance or retreat."

"Retreat? Retreat? The British Army never retreats, mind you, as my old sar'nt-major used to say, 'They've been known to make some bloody nifty strategic withdrawals.' "

George, as usual, had got his punch line in.

FIVE – WE MEET JOHN THE 'B'

As a member of the Boy Scouts, I had searched for years for the ever elusive perfect camping site. I did not expect to find it within a mile of the front line in the bocage countryside of Calvados.

A small crescent shaped clearing nestled at the edge of a small wood to the east of Tilly-sur-Seulles.

The mixed wood of elm, beech and oak gave shelter from the cold north-easterly winds of the winter, whilst the crescent was surrounded on three sides by thick hawthorn and elm tree suckers which grew in thick abundance.

Facing as it did, south-west, the lush grassy haven was a perfect sun-trap. A small babbling stream which we had crossed in the transport which had brought us to this delightful spot, could provide water, whilst there was fuel in abundance within the well established wood.

This was indeed an ideal camp site.

The Regimental Quartermaster-Sergeant of the 11th Bn. Royal Scots Fusiliers, evidently thought so too. He had installed his B Echelon (rear stores HQ) in this delightful sun-trap. So well concealed was this small clearing, that were it not for the necessary signboards announcing his presence, he could have remained here undetected for months.

A tall, angular Scot, the RQMS was a typical regular soldier of many years standing. We awaited the rasping voice which we expected to assault our ears. To our surprise, a soft Scottish brogue welcomed our arrival.

"Welcome to the Royal Scots Fusiliers, laddies, you are very welcome at the moment. We had a wee bit o' bother yesterday and we're a wee bit shorthanded. We'd better make sure ye're all kitted up properly before you pass on to your companies. Ye've nae got any shell dressings I see – better get one from that pile over there laddies."

He pointed to a heap of equipment on a slightly higher piece of ground, where, in my mind's eye, I would have pitched my tent.

"Christ! That's an encouraging start," commented George, as he sorted through a blood-stained collection of sterilized shell dressings, which had obviously been removed a short time ago from persons unknown, who had no further use for them.

We sorted out the best we could find and tied them to our shoulder epaulettes.

"I would suggest ye change ye're steel helmets for one o' these assault type on this pile — and made sure that ye have a camouflage netting on it too."

Yet another collection of hardware was laid out for us to sort through. Some had gashes in the helmets which were mostly stained with dried blood and other scars of recent battles.

"Now make sure ye've 50 rounds of .303 ammunition and that ye'r Bren magazines are full — then take two 36 grenades from yonder."

All this was done with a soft Scottish voice and in a most kindly manner. None of the 'take it or else' manner of distribution of the usual quartermaster's stores.

"Noo — ye'd better awa' over here tae the truck, for ye'r Caps T-o-S. Ye cannae wear yon berets in this regiment."

At the trucks, we handed in our khaki berets which had been issued at Bury St. Edmunds and received in return a larger khaki headdress and an enormous brass cap badge.

"It's the biggest cap badge in the British Army," said the RQMS, proudly.

"I've always wanted one of these floppy berets with a pom-pom on the top," said a lilting Welsh voice.

The Quartermaster drew a deep breath and stiffened. Pulling himself to his full height, he fairly bristled with indignation.

"What de ye mean, laddie?" he demanded. "It's no a floppy beret wi' a wee pom-pom on the top — it's the finest headdress in the whole British Army, aye, an' it's called a Tam-o'-Shanter — an' dinnae everrr forget it, laddie."

The unfortunate young man who had incurred the RQMS's wrath, sheepishly took the Cap T-o-S as it was thrust towards him, knowing that he should watch his step, should he ever cross swords with the aforesaid gentleman in the future.

A timely intervention by an orderly who announced that char was now ready, brought to an end the acrimony which had flared up so quickly between the two Celts.

Within minutes, we were being 'put in the picture', by the kindly Scot. He told us that on the previous day, the battalion had put in a dawn attack on the village of Fontenay-le-Pesnil coinciding with an attack by the enemy on the same objective. In the ensuing battle, we had lost almost three hundred men, killed, wounded or missing, in three hours. Our party of some thirty men, was the third such party to arrive this day, to replace the casualties suffered in that short time. Quite a sobering thought.

The hot sun of the afternoon had now mellowed into a pleasant summer's evening as we followed the guide to the Battalion Command Post.

We were met by the adjutant who quietly welcomed us and then proceeded to ask, "Any Bren-gunners amongst you chaps?"

We all shook our heads.

"We're all specialists," replied someone, "signallers, Don-R's, carrier drivers, truck drivers, cooks."

"Dammit, what the devil are they playing at back there? We need riflemen, and in particular, Bren-gunners. You are the second lot of specialists out of the three we have received today — sorry, but we can't send you back, you'll have to go to rifle platoons as riflemen."

He called to the 'D' Company runner.

"Take these chaps along to Major Rowell at 'D' Company."

As we left the Battalion HQ area, a familiar figure emerged from a slit trench.

"What the bloody 'ell are you doin' here Paddy?" I heard George say.

"Sure, I was after gettin' here dis mornin," said the genial Irishman, "I'll see you'se later, lads."

'D' Company office and Command Post was simply a hole in the ground, covered with a couple of old doors and branches from trees. This in turn was covered with a generous amount of soil from the excavations of the trench.

As we approached, a head popped out of the opening and a young, rather high-pitched voice called, "Anybody from Leicester among you lot?" I stepped towards the speaker.

"Yes, I'm from Leicester and my mate is from Queniborough."

"I'm from Hinckley," came the reply, "and the name's Nattrass, Nat for short. You'll be joining No. 17 Platoon. Sgt. Hill is in charge at the moment. Hang on a minute and I'll take you along to 17 Platoon."

'Nat' emerged from the dugout. He looked to be only about eighteen years old, about six feet tall and slightly built. On his head his steel helmet appeared to be about two sizes too small, it sort of perched on top of a young boyish face. We chatted quietly as we walked towards a signpost at some crossroads.

A body lay beside the track along which we walked. A German helmet and a gas mask canister had fallen from the field grey body as it came to rest, face up and open-mouthed. As I looked at the black face with the thick lips and the black hands, I thought to myself, so much for the master race, these blond Aryans, we had heard so much about. After all the propaganda, they were using coloured troops.

It was not until later that night that I was to know that the black skin and the swollen lips had been caused by an Allied flame-thrower.

At the crossroads, the road to the right led to Juvigny whilst straight across the sign pointed to Fontenay-le-Pesnil. We carried straight on.

Within yards of the crossroads we saw the village for the first time. It took some minutes for the view to fully sink in. Most of the houses were completely shattered and still smouldering from the fires which had gutted them.

In the fields leading to the village, gentle cows lay dead, bloated and stinking, with their legs sticking grotesquely into the air. All around them the fields were pock-marked with shell holes and mortar bomb blasts. Trees in the orchards were shattered, the ground littered with branches torn from their trunks as if by some giant in the land of Lilliput. Trunks had been snapped off, to leave splintered stumps. In the air, there was the smell of cordite fumes, of stinking rotten cattle flesh and the sickly-sweet smell of human dead.

No. 17 Platoon was situated in an orchard hard by the crossroads.

Nat passed us on to the Platoon Sgt. and bade us *au revoir*, saying that he'd call around later to see how we had settled in.

Sgt. Louis Hill was a bespectacled Yorkshireman from Leeds, probably about thirty years old and of average height and build. Quietly and efficiently he bisected the group of men who had come to reinforce his platoon.

"If there are any mates together, you'd better stay together. I've got four sections to make up, lads, so first two go with L/Cpl Cragg." He motioned to myself and my mate.

Lance-Corporal Cragg led us to the centre of the orchard.

"See that slit there? Better get cracking on it and get down about three feet. The poor bugger who started it got picked off by a 'pot-shot Pete' — so keep your eyes skinned for snipers. We've bagged three but there's still the odd one about. Don't worry about the bloody cow, it'll probably be useful as a firing point if there's a counter-attack."

I looked at George and blew out my cheeks at the pong.

"Sod this for a lark," said my mate, "but as we've got about a foot started we might as well get cracking."

By stand to, we had deepened the trench by about another foot and a half. The shale in the ground made progress very slow despite the professionalism of my mate with the pick, and my own deft handling of the shovel.

When Craggy came round at stand down, he was suitably impressed by our progress.

"You two certainly have got your finger out. You should get a bit of cover in that tonight. Get your mess tins — grub's up now."

Walking across to the jeep, we passed Sgt. Hill.

"Sorry I've not been across to see you lads," he said apologetically, "but I've just been organizing a burying party for four of my lads, we didn't want them lying around overnight again."

There was no bitterness in his voice as he spoke, just a little sadness at the loss of four friends. The compassion for their interment was shown in his eyes, mere words were superfluous.

"Get your M & V now, lads. Oh! the password is blackberry — keep well on the alert tonight, the position's still a bit dodgy."

The tin of Machonochies that we received each that night was not meat and veg, but a tin of oxtail — a tin of water and bones which tasted the same as the horrible stench from the dead cow which lay two feet away from our trench. Somehow I felt that it was not the most appetising meal I had ever tasted.

We were awoken from our fitful sleep by a voice hissing in our ears, 'stand to'. We looked through the semi-light. Early morning mist obscured the view of the village just a few hundred yards away. Beyond the far end of the orchard it was as if the whole world ended there. An eerie silence had descended along the front as though each side was awaiting a move from the opposition.

No gentle cows contentedly chewing the cud. They were all dead. No humans moving either. They waited, as we did, with bated breath as they peered into the white mist as it moved slowly layer by layer in the faint breeze.

As the sun rose, we saw over the top of the mist, the remains of the village church spire. In the small valley between us and the church, the rest of the village was still shrouded in mist.

The sun was now fully in the sky, but we had to stand to until all the mist had gone. It must have been about eight o'clock when we saw with relief, the jeep making its way towards us with a breakfast of bacon, tea and hard tack.

The high, cheerful voice of Nat was heard soon after breakfast, asking for the whereabouts of the two Leicester lads. We waved him over to our humble abode.

"Should have thought you could have found a better sleeping partner than that," he joked, nodding in the direction of the deceased cow.

"Might have been worse," replied my mate, "it could have been a piggery."

"Thought about you early on," said Nat, "it was like that when we put the attack in two days ago. 'B' Company were about here, on the start line waiting for the creeping barrage to start. Unfortunately it started about 50 yards behind them and crept up on them — ruddy slaughter.

"As dawn approached smoke shells were ordered to give cover, but the mist was already forming and then the Jerries also laid smoke down, so it was chaos in there. There were SS and our blokes firing from the same houses. One of our blokes, yelled to the chap at the other window to give him covering fire. The two men looked at each other and found that each was the enemy. Our bloke dived out of the front window and the Jerry left by the side window, both to be swallowed up in the enveloping mist and smoke."

Nat went on to tell us how the battle became more and more intense, a battalion of the 'Dukes' (Duke of Wellington's Regt.) had been severely mauled and had had to be withdrawn. We were at this moment in a holding defensive position.

Louis Hill came round shortly after Nat's departure and informed us that all the reinforcements would attend the RSM's parade at 10.00 hours.

We duly fell in and marched off along the road into Fontenay. There on what must have been the main street of the village, was assembled a motley crew of men. All around were the battered ruins of the houses of the once neat little Normandy farming village. Debris now covered the road, in some places almost blocking the whole of the road.

The RSM arrived in his jeep and in a short space of time had found a part of the roadway that was comparatively clear.

"Right laddies, fall in in three ranks — come on, come on," he barked, "I havena got all day .... Come on, come on — right dress — eyes front," he continued.

"You now belong to the 11th Battalion of the Royal Scots Fusiliers. A fine regiment. You may not agree with me now, but it's the finest regiment in the British Army."

"Bullshit," whispered George, out of the corner of his mouth.

"Your Commanding Officer is Lt.-Col. Montgomery-Cunningham. I am your Regimental Sergeant-Major — Regimental Sergeant-Major John MacCreadie, to be precise. Some people call me John the 'B' .... " he paused for effect as he then barked out, "and it doesn't mean John the Baptist, either."

He paused once more for this statement to sink in.

"Bloody nutcase, this bloke," hissed the voice by my side.

"Now," continued the RSM, "you've all come from different regiments, so you will all be used to different drill timings. This morning you'll all learn to do the RSF's drill time."

We then proceeded to slope arms, shoulder arms, port arms, and all the other drill movements as he barked out one, two, three; down, two, three; up, two, three.

After twenty minutes of this arms drill, we commenced the foot drill. We had marched up and down about three times when the mortaring which had been concentrated on the far end of the village suddenly started to be directed on our end. As the mortars fell among the debris, we heard John the 'B' shout, "Fall out."

He was too late. George and I had already anticipated the order, along with about half the assembled parade.

As we dived into a shop doorway George was heard to remark, "Sod this for a game of soldiers. Whose side is that silly bugger on?"

The stonking lasted for about twenty minutes and miraculously no one was injured. The order was then given for everyone to return to their company lines and take up their positions again. So ended our first encounter with the redoubtable John the 'B'.

For the remainder of the day, the sounds of battle were heard to the south of the village as ground was fiercely fought for, attack and counter-attack by both sides.

We potted another sniper and so were left in comparative peace, for the rest of the day.

Nightfall brought the news that we were to move to new positions along the road towards Juvigny. At precisely 23.00 hours, we left the slit trench, now three feet deep, and set off along the road from the crossroads towards Juvigny.

A couple of hundred yards along the road we passed four new graves. The cross at the head of each grave had been made from a 14-man compo box and on each cross there hung an assault type steel helmet.

For those four young men their war was over.

For George and I, the real war was just beginning.

Ken West, 'Paddy' Deegan, John 'Nat' Nattrass

SIX – "DIG IN .... WE'RE MOVING"

I followed the man in front as he walked carefully and as silently as possible in the pitch black of the night. The single file of men of No. 17 Platoon peered into the darkness as they picked their way around the perimeter of the corn field.

Someone stumbled and an oath floated along the hedgerow as a steel helmet clanged against a rifle on its way to the ground.

"SShh .... sshh," whispered L/Cpl Cragg.

"Can't see a thing Corp, it's so bloody dark."

"Usually is at one o'clock in the morning," replied the Lance-Jack sarcastically.

"How many more times are we going to walk round this soddin' field?" hissed the chap, as he searched for his battle bowler.

"We can't find the battalion marker. Rest here, I'll go and have another look," said L/Cpl Cragg.

After a quarter of an hour's delay, Cragg returned.

"It's about 150 yards back there. Polar Bear 60, turn right, and then it's across two more fields to Company HQ."

Circumnavigating those last two fields proved to be no mean feat and we were relieved to find the advance party installed in the corner of a third field.

We were directed along the right-hand hedge and as we passed the Command Post, Nat's head appeared briefly.

"Pass the word along Ken, the place is crawling with patrols – keep as quiet as you can," he whispered.

The transfer of positions was completed without incident and the departing section of 'Dukes' seemed eager to be on their way.

"What's the ground like, mate?" asked George quietly.

"Bloody awful, you can only dig about a foot a night," came the private's reply as he hastened away into the night.

"They haven't done much digging, this lot," said my mate as he felt around in the hedge bottom, "it's only about eighteen inches deep."

I started to prise away at the stony ground with my shovel. There was a metallic clang as the shovel met a stone. L/Cpl Cragg was on us in a flash.

"Keep that bloody shovel quiet," he hissed, "you can hear it a mile away."

"Only trying to dig in a bit deeper, Corp," I said.

"Well . . . just keep it quiet, Westy — it's all night stand to tonight."

We prodded and poked about with bayonets and loosened the shale; pieces of flat stone came loose as we worked away, one at a time, whilst the other kept 'stag'. The pieces varied from a few inches in length, to nine or ten inches long, and they were placed carefully on top of the other spoil. By dawn we were about four inches deeper. We resolved that during the day, the sparks would fly as we showed the others what a real slit trench should look like.

In the light of day we were able to take stock of our surroundings. The large field had as its boundary a double hedge, each slightly banked with earth and stones, which left a gulley a few feet wide in the middle.

It was in this gulley that our slit was situated.

These hedges, typical of the bocage country of this part of France, were interspersed with oak and elm trees which had most of their lower branches pruned off. The result left a tree which, from a distance, looked rather akin to a Brussels sprout plant devoid of its leaves. Someone suggested that they had all had a poodle cut, but in general they were called pom-pom trees.

All the fields in the near vicinity seemed to be of a similar pattern and the overall scene from our hedge-bottom home, was exceedingly pleasant, apart from the dozen or so dead cows near to the hedge which ran alongside the road. By now we had become to consider them as a part of the landscape.

A visit by the 2nd i/c Company altered our plans for the day. Shortly after breakfast the Captain's voice was heard.

"I want you two chaps to dig a slit on the other side of the hedge — that flank has been left too exposed."

"Couldn't we just chop a hole in the hedge and build a firing point?" I suggested, hopefully.

"No . . . no field of fire there, chaps," he said as he squatted down to take a look, "start digging straight away."

With much muttering we started digging out the new slit. As we dug, we could see the road below us, some 200 yards away as it twisted along through a lovely wooded valley, until it disappeared behind another wooded area towards the village of Juvigny.

Across the valley, the fields rose gently to a wooded ridge about three-quarters of a mile away. The various greens of the foliage of the hedges and pom-pom trees in this undamaged part of the British sector, stood out in the early morning sunlight. It was a beautiful sight, worthy of any landscape artist's brush. We both remarked how peaceful it all seemed.

After about an hour's steady digging, we noticed some people moving around in the top left hand field just below the wooded ridge.

"Ay up George," I said, "looks like some of our lads are setting up their mortars over there."

"You're right, Ken, they're mortars all right — give 'em some stick lads," he shouted.

We rested and watched them for a few minutes as they set up the mortars, one, two, three.

A puff of smoke came out of the barrel of the middle one followed a split second later by the other two.

Zeeuuup ... bang ... zeeuup ... bang ... zeeuup ... bang. Three mortar shells crunched to earth just beyond our Company HQ one hundred yards away to our rear.

"Christ," said George, "it's bloody Jerry."

We dived back into the hedge bottom. Hardly had we scrambled into the shallow trench when three more shells landed about half-way between Company HQ and us.

I looked down at my knees. They were dancing up and down like puppets on a string. Try as I might, I could not stop my knees from knocking together.

"Hey up George — look at these."

"I know, mine are the same."

I looked across at my mate and sure enough, his knees were jitter-bugging in time with my own.

"And we stood and watched them," I said.

"Well, they've got our range now," replied my mate. That statement coming as it did, from an old artillery man, didn't sound too reassuring to me. Our reverie was interrupted by the return of the Captain.

"Why aren't you digging that firing point?"

We explained about our presence in the field bringing on the mortaring.

"Nonsense, just a coincidence — carry on digging, they've got to be ready by tonight."

We decided, on our return to the field, to dig one at a time as we lay flat on the ground. It is difficult to dig like that, with one eye on the hole and the other on a mortar detachment three-quarters of a mile away across a valley. However, we carried on in this manner, turn and turn about for about another hour and a half, then I suppose we got a little over-confident.

George was on top of the hole, shovelling away the spoil when I spotted a puff of smoke.

"Down George," I yelled.

Three strides and a dive and we were inside the hedge again.

Crash .. crash .. crash .. crash .. crash .. crash ....

The hedgerow was now being straddled. The explosions were only yards away. Shrapnel hissed through the branches and leaves and twigs fell on to us.

The knees started to jitter-bug again. I was frightened, really frightened, for the first time in my life someone was trying to kill me. This war was getting unpleasantly personal. My heart pounded as I looked across at George.

"Them lousy buggers are trying to kill us," he said angrily, "but as my old sar'nt-major used to say, 'If your name ain't on one, you'll be all right.'"

"Our names might not be on them," I replied, "but they know our address now."

"Let's hope that the postman never calls," said George, as he lit a cigarette.

Meanwhile, the mortars dropped their range after each salvo until the shells were landing on the road, then all was quiet again. Freddie Norris, the young stretcher bearer poked his head into the hedge.

" 'ave you got your mugs, lads? I've got some char here — anybody hit?"

"No, we're all right, Freddie," we said, as our mugs were filled with the welcome hot tea, "how's everybody else?"

"Nothing so far," said Freddie, as he went on his way.

On the way back, he called as he passed, "Just got one bloke here with a bit in his arse, he'll be OK though."

"That's good, thanks for the char, mate."

"If the 2 i/c wants that slit digging now," said my mate, as he blew the ash of his fag-end, "he can dig the bugger himself."

We never went out into the field again that day, instead we picked away at our slit in the hedge bottom and lobbed the stones out on to the heap of spoil in the field.

After dusk, we dug like demons and by first light we had trench number two more than two feet six deep.

We then returned to our stately slit and slept like babies, feeling safe and sound under the cover of the hedge.

In the middle of the morning, the sound of aero engines pulsated the air. We awoke, not fully conscious of what was going on. Looking to the hedge to our right, we saw formation after formation of Allied bombers flying across the valley.

"Paras," said someone lower down.

"No, they're Halifaxes," said George, "they're bombers, not troop carriers."

"Nah, too many bombers, I bet they're Yankie paras." As we discussed the differing probabilities, we received our answer. Booom ... Booom ... Booom ... Booom.

They were bombers right enough and they were dropping their bombs only a few miles away beyond the wooded ridge.

We looked up. Still they came doggedly on, never varying formation despite the German ack-ack which filled the remainder of the sky with shell bursts. For three-quarters of an hour they came across the valley. They bombed with unswerved discipline, then turned gracefully and headed for home, still in immaculate formation.

We watched silently at first, then as we saw clouds of black smoke rising above the ridge, we cheered madly, for we knew instinctively that they had done this for us. What lay beyond the ridge, we knew not, but whatever it was must surely be in one hell of a mess by now.

Sadly, as we watched the formations head for home, two planes were shot down. We saw the parachutes floating down from the first one, but the second one received a direct hit and blew up. Suddenly the cheering stopped as we watched horrified, as the burning wreckage spiralled to the ground.

Beyond the ridge, huge columns of thick black smoke continued to rise. Someone who had been stationed near an RAF camp, said it looked like a petrol dump or tyre dump fire.

At dusk, Nat came round to see us and brought the official account of the day's happenings.

The nine o'clock news from London had reported that 250 Halifax bombers had carried out a low level attack on the area of Villiers Bocage and had wiped out a German Armoured Division poised to attack the British sector. Those RAF lads had saved our bacon.

As for the slit trench in the field, we never used it again.

During the night, a new intake of reinforcements brought the platoon up to its full strength of 36 men. As we were one short in our section, we took a lad in named Bill. Coming from Nottingham as he did, George and I welcomed this young eighteen-year-old and found him to be a most cheerful and humorous character.

In order to allow passage from one slit to another, we had cleared away the hedge bottoms and so we were able to find out more about the news from the rear. Young Bill told us that another Division had landed, the 53rd Welsh Div. had moved into the area that they had just left. Too late for us to join them now, I thought.

He also told us a little more about himself. As soon as he was eighteen, he had volunteered to join the Sherwood Foresters Regt., and on completion of his 16 weeks training had asked to be sent overseas in the hope of being sent to the Middle East where one of his relatives was serving with the Nottinghamshire Regt. He was posted all right, but only across the Channel. Now that he was with us, he was determined to make the most of it.

Our conversation was interrupted by Louis Hill as he did his morning rounds.

"Check your weapons, lads, we're going to dig in at the other side of that wood," he pointed to a small wood about three to four hundred yards away to our left. "We shall creep round on the left flank, through the wood and dig in here," indicating the position on his map. "We shall move off at 13.00 hours."

"Fair enough, Sarge," we answered, then turned to the task of checking rifles, ammo, grenades, and Bren magazines. Water-bottles were also topped up.

Promptly at the hour of one o'clock we were on our way. Over the road, along the left flank of the wood, the whole platoon in sections making its way steadily as it hugged the fringes of the wood. Turn right into the trees and then left in the centre and follow the path to the far side.

The leading section had just reached the edge of the trees and about to take up their new position when the now familiar, zeeuup, zeeuup, zeeuup of the mortars was heard. Within minutes, mortars, 88 mm guns, and field guns were pumping shells into the wood.

"Stay put . . . take cover," came the shout.

I was in the rear section and had just reached the point on the path where it forked to the left. A couple of yards along the path was a depression in the ground which no doubt had been deepened by the passage of workmen's cycles through the puddle which must have lain there during the winter months. I dived into this shallow groove and lay there, face down, making myself as small a target as possible. As I lay there, others were running about trying to find better cover.

"Get down, stay where you are," I could hear Craggy shouting, but it is hard to make yourself stay in the same spot as the shells and mortars crash into the trees, scattering shrapnel and branches over a wide area.

The cry for stretcher bearers came from a number of directions. The anti-personnel shells which exploded at tree-top height were taking their toll.

I was tempted to crawl to fresh ground, but despite the countless feet which made their impressions on my backside and legs as their owners ran over me, I stayed in that shallow depression.

For almost three hours the stonking continued, every minute of which I expected to feel the burning heat of metal in some part of my body. Debris from the smashed trees fell across my back and somehow, this gave me a feeling of security.

The stonking stopped abruptly. I continued to lay there, head ringing from the blasting, half expecting the hell to restart.

"Regroup on the road, lads," the reassuring voice of Hill called.

As I extricated myself from the debris, I saw for the first time the appalling carnage around me. More than half the wood had been reduced to splintered tree trunks. The ground was pitted with black shaggy scars. The whole air reeked with the smell of cordite and in amongst all this lay a few still bodies. We stopped at each one, checking hopefully for sign of life, as we made our way back to the road.

A line of men crouched at the roadside. I looked at the faces as I passed. A familiar figure sat on a log, fag in hand. He looked very dejected.

"What's the matter, mate?" I said.

"Christ Ken, they all told me you'd copped it — they said that you were laying at the fork, covered with a fallen tree — your mate's had it right enough, they said. I'm bloody glad to see you though, I know I was getting down on my fags, but I wasn't that hard up," he joked, referring to our mutual pact made in England.

It wasn't necessary to tell him how glad I was to see him sitting there.

When all the fit and wounded were back on the road we returned to our original positions. The wounded were quickly despatched to the RAP

(Regimental Aid Post) for first aid before being sent to the rear for further attention.

Louis Hill came along with the late meal and gave us the latest situation report. Out of the 36 men who had left at one o'clock, only 13 were left to hold the position at stand-to, and for the fifth night in succession it was oxtail.

"I'll be glad when they've buried these bleedin' cows," said George.

"Pity about that young 'un from Nottingham," I said sadly, "what was his name?"

"Only knew him as Bill," replied George, "never asked him his surname — only just eighteen an' all. Poor little bugger didn't look any more than sixteen." He took a last swig of his mug of tea. "That'll teach you never to volunteer for 'owt in this man's army."

When Louis Hill returned at stand down, there was a new face with him.

"I'd like you to meet our new Platoon Commander, Mr Wilson."

Standing beside him was a full Lieutenant in Canadian Army battle-dress and wearing the unmistakable smaller Tam-o'-Shanter of a Canadian Scottish Regiment. About the same height as Louis, he also had the same type of easy going disposition and speech.

George and I gave our names and in exchange received a firm handshake.

"I'll see you in the morning lads," came the mixed accent of the North American and Scotsman.

"Seems a decent sort o' bloke," said George, a statement with which I was in complete agreement.

Lt. Wilson was the replacement for someone we had never seen, a casualty in the battle of Fontenay, and so Sgt. Hill had been operating in the dual role of Platoon Commander and Platoon Sergeant since the demise of his officer.

There was no doubt about the relief that our Sergeant felt now that he had a 'Can loan' officer to take the brunt of the decisions from now on. I might explain here that the nickname 'Can loan' was given to the Canadian officers who had been transferred on loan to the British divisions to make up the deficiencies caused by an abnormal number of casualties amongst the junior officers in the first phase of the Normandy campaign. Our Lt. Wilson was to be the first of a number of such officers to join the RSF.

The two men were chatting amiably as they came round on their early morning inspection.

" 'Morning fellows," was the cheerful greeting, "how's things this morning?"

We reported that all was well and all had been quiet during our 'stag'. The Canadian looked into the hedge.

"That's a good looking slit you've got there, it's the deepest I've seen yet — did you do a bit of blasting?"

"Aye, and a fair bit of buggering too," said George. The officer gave out a hearty chuckle.

"I like the floral decorations too," he said, referring to the wild flowers that we'd picked that morning and pressed into the damp earth we had placed on various ledges around the sides of our slit.

"Well, we've got to make the best of it," was our reply.

A serious look had reappeared on Louis Hill's face when he next visited us with 'the Bank Manager'. Always ready, like the rest of the Tommies, to give a newcomer a nickname, the lads in our section had quickly decided that our Canadian cousin had been a Bank Manager in civvy street. He looked exactly the part.

"We're off at 14.00 hours on a standing patrol, here," he pointed to a wood to our right front this time. "Just beyond that clump of trees there's a farm, we'll go through the farm and take up a position on the far side of the wood."

George and I exchanged glances. We'd been in a wood before.

"I know we're a bit down on numbers, but I brought a few with me last night who are back from casualty and we're borrowing a section from 15 Platoon -- so that makes us about twenty-five in all," nodding to us as he left.

The trees along the roadside gave us excellent cover as we moved off in the direction of Juvigny, with Lt. Wilson and his batman in the lead, followed by Signaller Corporal Jackie Thompson and his rifleman escort, then Sgt. Hill and the leading section. I led our section along the opposite side of the road.

Turning left from the road, we made our way along the hedgerows towards the farmyard. Situated at the rear of the farmhouse and outbuildings, the yard was surrounded on the other three sides by a high stone wall about six or seven feet high. On the eastern side, entry was by a five-barred gate, whilst on the southern side, opposite to the house, there was an opening from which the gate had been removed. We paused to check the planned route.

"Along that hedge in front, then back-track along the wall to the side gate ... through the yard and out of the southern gate, then straight across the field to the wood — pretty straightforward," said Sgt. Louis Hill. "Recce patrols have reported no enemy in the wood."

In the farmyard we paused until all were in position, the Lieutenant looked round at us, pulled his Webley revolver from its holster and waved us forward.

He turned through the gate followed by the batman, three fusiliers and the signals Corporal. As I reached the end of the wall, Louis held his hand out to slow me down until the rest of the section caught up. He gave the signal and turned to go through the gate. At that moment the short sharp staccato sound of Spandaus were heard, the unmistakable brrrup, brrrup, brrrup, as the bullets were pumped out at a rate of over one thousand per minute, as they opened up on the leading section as it went into the field.

"Take cover, don't shoot," called Louis, as he signalled us to get behind the wall.

"What's happened over there — are you all right, sir?" he called over the wall. Back came the voice of Cpl. Jackie Thompson.

"This is Jackie Thompson. The officer and two fusiliers are dead, I'm in a hollow with two more fusiliers. I don't think they can see us."

Someone fired a shot and the Spandaus opened up again. When they ceased firing, Jackie Thompson called, "One Spandau, ten o'clock from the gate, at the end of the wood . . . another at twelve o'clock and another at two o'clock at the other end of the wood . . . . Give us covering fire on all three and we'll come over the wall, it's only about four foot on this side."

"It's about six feet this side," replied Louis.

"I'll risk a broken leg," shouted back Jackie.

Instructions were given to those along the yard wall to give rapid covering fire on the command of the signaller.

Picking a part of the wall a few inches lower than the rest, I fired five rounds rapid fire when Jackie gave the OK. Before I could reload, the rifle was bashed almost out of my hands. Jackie had cleared the wall in one gigantic leap, rifle, signal set and all, and landed almost on top of me. Quickly reloading, I let off two more rounds and then away went the rifle again as the two other fusiliers followed the Corporal.

A withering hail of bullets hit the wall on the far side as the two flankers in the wood fired magazine after magazine. In the centre, bullets zipped through the gateway and hammered into the farm buildings.

Our own Bren-guns fired back in the hope of putting a stop to this hail of lead. Our rear section reported that a further Spandau was firing now from the left flank of the wood and was preventing anyone from getting back to the hedge. We had been ambushed, caught in a simple trap. Tracer bullets were now being fired over the top of the wall into the loft of the barn which was filled with newly-mown hay. Within minutes the whole of the barn was ablaze. The roof of the house was also alight and within the confines of the yard, the heat was becoming unbearable. Straw and faggots of wood in the yard itself were now also smouldering. I looked at George.

"I think one of your old sar'nt-major's strategical withdrawals is called for."

The radio set crackled into life as messages were passed from Jackie to the Battalion HQ. At last the order came to withdraw before we were caught up further by mortars.

A number of lads who were attempting to smother the smouldering hay and faggots, shouted across that they had found a hole in the wall which led to a ditch.

"Get out lads, before they lay on a stonk," shouted the Sergeant. "Potter, get to the end of the wall and keep peppering away with the Bren until I give the OK."

The ditch, as we soon discovered, was actually a drain from the manure heap in the corner of the stock yard. Consequently, it was rather damp and smelly.

I followed the chap in front as he wriggled along on his arms and knees. The ditch disappeared under a rotting tree trunk which straddled the small spinney. Under the obstacle and I would be free to scramble out to the path which lay beyond. But this was not to be.

With head and shoulders through to the other side, I became stuck. The pick which I'd carried on my back was now stuck fast in the rotting wood. I couldn't move forward or backward.

"Come on mate, get a move on," George sounded rather agitated.

"I can't. I've got my pick stuck across my back."

"It's no time to start boasting," said George.

"I said, I've got my pick stuck — it's jammed under the log. You'll have to pull me out."

"I can't move either, the bloke behind me has got his bayonet half-way up my arse," came the plaintive voice behind me.

"Well ask him nicely and perhaps he'll make a gentle strategic withdrawal," I advised.

The heated exchange between George and the other man behind him is unprintable. Suffice to say that whilst two men pulled a leg apiece, my mate used his spade as a lever on the obstruction and I was dragged out and duly soundly cursed. By the time that George and I had extricated the pickaxe from my harness, the others were away down the ditch, crawling on all fours like dogs after a rabbit.

"Come on now, Potter," Louis called to the Bren-gunner, "they'll give us covering fire from the road now."

When everyone had assembled on the road, the Sergeant gave the order to return to our position as quickly as possible. "But don't run," came the adjoinder.

We didn't run, but Lloyd Johnson, our local Bronze Medallist in the Berlin Olympics 50 kilometre walk, would have finished a poor second. I cannot say for certain that the Road Walking Associating rules of maintaining unbroken contact with the ground at all times, was strictly adhered to either.

George was already in the slit trench when I arrived.

"Nice to be home again," he grinned from the cosy depths of the hedgerow. I stood there for a few moments, waiting for him to make way for me to drop into the trench. He looked me up and down once or twice and then said, "You're not coming in here mate, covered in cow muck and stinking like a sewage-works."

"The trouble with you, George me lad, you're too ruddy house proud," I said as I jumped in beside him. He held his nose in mock disgust.

As we stood there chuckling, we saw the smoke and flames rising from behind the clump of trees as the Jerries let fly with everything they'd got on the now empty farmyard.

"That's another bloody hole, we didn't have to dig," said my mate cheerfully.

In the evening as dusk descended, a party returned with our three dead comrades and reported that the whole farm and farmyard had been completely gutted. Nothing could have survived that inferno.

Nat called by with the latest news. During a short mortar attack on Battalion HQ, our Commanding Officer, 'Big Monty', had been killed outright, a mortar bomb exploding by the side of his carrier.

Better news was that we were to be relieved by the Durham Light Infantry in the early hours of 1st July, tomorrow.

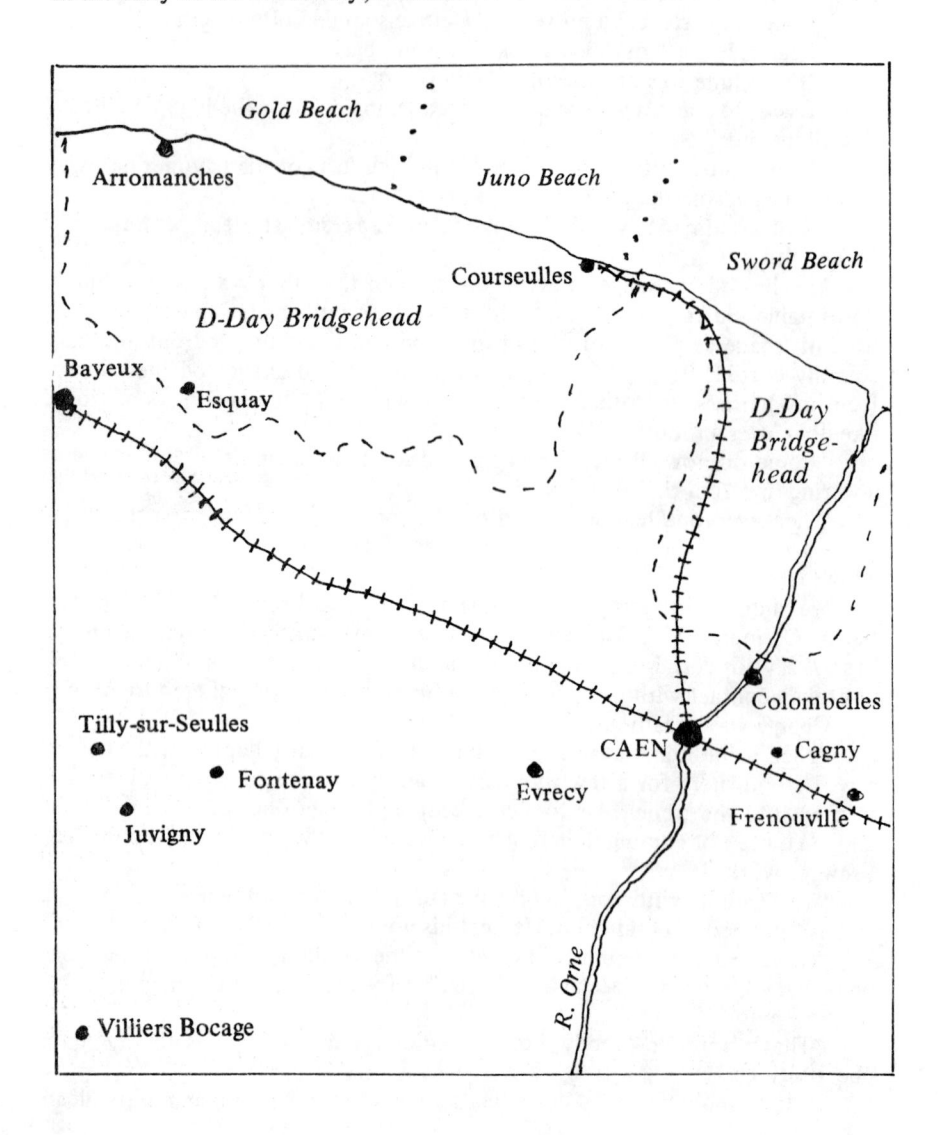

SEVEN – THE PHANTOM DAIRYMAN

As the name, 'Big Monty' might imply, Lt.-Col. Montgomery-Cunningham was an awesome figure. Well over six feet tall and built like a giant, he was a forceful and thrusting leader of the Battalion.

He had been in command from the day that the 11th Battalion RSF had been formed in the small county of Rutland back in 1941, and had been the inspiration behind the training of this new unit which was now, three years later, a fighting battalion in the Polar Bear Division.

Of course, some of the methods he had formulated to attain the present discipline and dedication to the job in hand, had not always met with the instant approval of the rank and file.

Tales of Big Monty were being retold to those of us who had recently become members of the battalion as we huddled under any sort of cover from the incessant rain on this Saturday morning the first day of July.

Back in the British Isles, Big Monty's constant companions were his huge thumb-stick and his ever faithful dog Bruce. Both had played a part in his disciplinary application.

We heard how the large black dog would lay at the feet of his master as he conducted the daily CO's orders. Many an unfortunate miscreant vowed that he had been sentenced by the dog and not by the CO, for on some occasions the CO would look at the dog and ask, "What shall we do with this laddie, eh Bruce?" then depending on how many times the dog wagged his tail, the fusilier would be given one day's confined to barracks per wag.

Bruce himself was not spared his master's wrath, for on the occasions when he cocked his leg against a signboard or happened to foul the pathway, he would be wheeled in on CO's orders and given terms of CB, and would be tethered to the leg of the table in the guardroom for the requisite number of days. Revenge was thereby meted out by sly prods and flicks of the toe-end of an army boot belonging to some fusilier who had at some time lost a few days of liberty, prolonged by the fact that he had at some time patted the Colonel's dog.

However, since the arrival of the Battalion on the twelfth of June on the invasion beaches, Big Monty had led them with courage and with complete disregard for his own safety. He had died as he set out to visit us at the wood. He was later awarded a posthumous DSO (Distinguished Service Order).

In the meantime, on this wet, soggy afternoon, we were complying with the orders of the other 'Monty'. General Montgomery, the deputy chief of the Allied Army had decreed that in order to combat the possibility of his troops becoming contaminated with lice, every man should have a bath at least once a fortnight and, if necessary, units would be replaced in the line in order to facilitate this order.

Wearing anti-gas capes and groundsheet capes to keep out the worst of the rain, we made our way along the side road towards the baths unit. On reaching the main road, we were halted abruptly by a military policeman and told to get off the roads, because urgent supplies were being given top priority.

We than began a tortuous journey around fields and hedges through waist high grass and nettles as we searched for the elusive baths unit. We persevered doggedly until after a couple of hours the familiar framework of the showers was sighted.

Everyone stripped off and because it was still raining heavily, anti-gas capes were worn to the showers.

For a few brief minutes we braved the elements as we showered, then, re-donning our capes we attempted to dry ourselves before re-dressing in our sodden battledress. As we retraced our steps back to the field from whence we had come, soaked to the skin and miserable, I heard the voice of George lamenting, "All this — just because some bloody clerk somewhere wants to tick our name off in his bath book."

The following day, Sunday, was a complete reversal of the previous day's weather. The hot July sun soon had our spirits rising and by mid morning the hedges and fences were festooned with all kinds of clothing and kit as it dried in the welcome sunshine. Bivouacs were dismantled and dried out and equipment was replaced wherever necessary.

One or two of the light casualties returned to the fold and a slight rearrangement of sections took place. Paddy Inglishby and his mate were reinstated with us, plus an old hand from Fontenay and a new lad from RHU.

The draw for the Bren-gun took place in the time honoured way of drawing a straw from the clenched fist of L/Cpl Cragg, the shortest straw getting the gun. The new lad from RHU was the recipient on this occasion.

Just as we were preparing to erect our bivouacs for the night, the order came to pack up; we were to return to the line that night.

The slit trenches looked vaguely familiar as we strained our eyes in the darkness, trying to locate our new position. The departing riflemen had told us briefly on changeover: "This is the Juvigny-Fontenay road," then they were gone.

When you are on stand to all night, dawn seems an awfully long time in arriving, although it was probably only about four to five hours at the most, the interminable mosquitoes making life most unpleasant and only kept to tolerable levels by the incessant smoking of cigarettes throughout the long hours.

As the faint streaks of light of the new day came into the sky, we gradually began to pick out the landmarks around us. We were in a soft sandy bank overlooking the road, with a good view in both directions.

Our eyes swept up to our right along the distant hedgerow. No wonder it looked familiar, we were in No. 15 Platoon's old slits, and about a hundred and fifty yards from our old hedgerow.

"Must have been a piece of cake digging in here," said George, ever mindful of our past labours. "Just think," he continued, "only five days ago you daren't put your head out, now everyone's walking about as casual as you like. They must have pushed them back over that ridge."

During the morning, little snippets of news filtered through. One piece of information was that our 'C' Company was not at all happy about their position and intended to 'clear their flanks' a little.

Within an hour the confirmation was forthcoming as a Bren-gun and a Spandau began to start an argument.

"Hey up," said my mate, "the kids have started arguing, then the old man will start. That'll bring in the neighbours and before we know what's happened the whole ruddy street will be involved." Rifle fire and more machine-guns become involved and shortly before noon the whole neighbourhood was going at it hammer and tongs, just as George had anticipated. Jimmy Cragg came back from Company HQ rather hurriedly.

"Pack up, lads, 'C' Company have had a bit of a bashing. They've been counter-attacked and we've got to go and reinforce them."

"I told you the whole bloody street would be at it," said George resignedly, as we gathered our kit together.

We had just reached 'C' Company lines when the mortaring started. Three shells for a start. We were caught on an incline with little or no cover. Only tree stumps had survived atop the hillock. Burnt cordite still lingered in the air from the morning's engagement. Ahead lay some slits. As I ran towards them I shouted, "Any room in there mate?" A Lance-Corporal with a shaved head answered as he turned his head.

"Bugger off, there's three in here now — find one of your own," he spat out, as he propped himself against the side of the trench.

Lousy bastard, I thought, as I dived under a tree trunk on top of the mound. Mortar shells crashed amongst the company positions, salvo after salvo. "Stretcher bearers, stretcher bearers," came the cry. I looked back towards the direction of the shouting. The Lance-Corporal's body was still propped up against the side of the trench, but there was no sign of the closely shaven head. A mass of bloody pulp was all that remained of the head and shoulders.

I was sorry that I had called him a lousy bastard. No one deserved that sort of fate. I also knew how possessive one feels about a hole in the ground which one has spent many hours digging.

Jimmy Cragg's call of, "Follow me lads," brought me to my senses. We charged, half crouching, over the incline into a series of half dug slits some two hundred yards on the other side where we took up firing positions in the hedge at the side of a small farm track which ran down to a stream fifty yards away to our right. Crunch .. crunch .. crunch ... The mortars were now going over our heads into the old 'C' Company trenches.

"Keep your eyes peeled down towards the stream," called the Lance-Corporal, "this is what the argument's been all about — and watch out for the snipers."

For the rest of the day we prodded away with our bayonets enlarging the slit as we kept constant vigil on the stream. At dusk, extra Bren-guns were delivered so that we had a Bren in each trench. Throughout the night we dug, the spoil was banked to form a firing position, and then grass and foliage was placed over it for camouflage.

The morrow brought forth yet another beautiful dawn, still, and strangely quiet, as both sides licked their wounds. Mist and smoke hung in the hollows of the field below us. Behind us lay the smashed trees and bushes of an orchard. Debris was scattered in all directions and the smell of cordite permeated the air in the stillness of early morning. It looked exactly like one of the artist's impressions of the First World War battlefields I recalled looking at in my father's *War Illustrated* volumes, 1914-18. I looked again towards the field. The mist was slowly lifting in the morning sun. About two o'clock right, 150 yards away, a couple of small farm buildings rose out of vapour as if placed there by some unseen stage hands. From the buildings, a low fence ran across our front to a low wall on the left. Beyond the fence, the ground rose as it formed the other side of this small valley. Fields bounded by hedges and the pom-pom trees and an occasional low stone wall completed the landscape.

"Look at that," I said quietly to George. "Normandy in all its splendour." George stood on tiptoe and looked over the parapet.

"Christ, look at that bloody cow," said my partner. I raised myself on to my toes and looked to where he was pointing. In a shallow dip in the middle of the field was a water trough and tethered near by was a large brown and white mottled cow. I couldn't believe my eyes. Only moments ago the mists had screened the animal and now it was standing there quite unconcerned as it chewed away.

"How the hell did she survive that lot yesterday?" I queried. "She must have been there for a day or two by the look of her udders — she's full of milk."

All day long we kept a close watch on the farm buildings, the stream and that brown and white cow as it mooched around within its tether, oblivious to the noises of war. During the afternoon, I noticed that the barrel of the Bren-gun was glistening in the sunlight.

"I'll put a bit of grass over that barrel to stop it shining." Carefully gathering a handful from behind a bush, I slowly raised myself up and stretched out my arm, covering the offending glint of steel. Crack! A shot whistled just over my head.

"Christ, it's pot-shot Pete," I said.

"The sod's got a bead on us right enough," said George.

We forgot about the cow and her ever filling udder for a time, as we searched in vain for the tell-tale puff of smoke from his rifle. Every time anyone moved that day, crack went a bullet, but we couldn't get a sniff of the sniper. Fortunately he was either too far away, or wasn't as good a shot as we'd at first thought.

'Betsy' the cow was now beginning to feel the effects of her bulging udder. She was bellowing agonizingly, pleadingly, for assistance. Day turned into night and she still called for help.

Around midnight, Jimmy Cragg came along the line of trenches with the rum ration and a hot mug of tea for each man.

"Have you heard that bloody cow?" he asked.

"Yea, we've just about had a belly full of it."

"I reckon if it goes on tomorrow we'll have to shoot it, put it out of its misery," said Jimmy.

"I'd have a go at milking it myself," said my mate, "but not with that ruddy pot-shot Pete about. They reckon that the Jerries have got night sights on their snipers' rifles."

"Shouldn't be surprised," said the L/Cpl as he departed.

Throughout the next day the poor beast laboured in pain until she could stand no more, and just lay there calling in agony. The pitiful cries continued into the night, becoming more mournful as the hours passed by. About an hour before dawn, I mentioned that I hadn't heard anything from Betsy for some time.

"Poor old girl's probably snuffed it," said my companion. "Christ, she won't half stink in this heat."

As we listened, we began to conjecture about her fate and felt quite sad that the gentle animal who had survived a battle fought across the field in which she stood, should have died a painfully lingering death through neglect.

The mists cleared slowly in the morning and we looked anxiously down the slope towards the water trough where we expected to see the horrible sight of a cow with its legs sticking grotesquely into the air.

The hollow, always the last to clear, took an agonizingly long time to clear this morning. Eventually it did and there before our astonished eyes stood Betsy, munching away contentedly at the grass, her udder completely empty. Someone, somehow, had crept up to her in the silence of the night and had milked her dry right under our noses.

"I've heard of hedgehogs suckling a cow's teat," said George, "but it would have taken a family of 'em a week to empty her." All day long we had a grandstand view of Betsy as she moved around on her tether, oblivious to the game of cat and mouse that we were playing with pot-shot Pete. We thought that he must be hidden in some trees behind the farm buildings, but due to the fact that we kept any movement to the minimum, his shots were few and far between.

Whenever either side shelled or mortared the opposition lines, our first reaction was to check to see how Betsy had fared. Throughout the stonkings, she continued her charmed life, contentedly chewing the cud. We wished her well and hoped that she would survive.

Towards evening she began to start bellowing again and continued through the night. We checked with Craggie, but he'd not heard who the phantom milker might be.

"Well at least she'll be quiet for a few more hours," he said hopefully.

"She's got a fair amount in her bag again," said George. Next morning, Betsy was dry again. I looked at George. "Don't look at me Ken, it's not me, nor any of us."

"Unless it's pot-shot Pete," I suggested.

"It's the sort of thing that cheeky bugger would do," added my digging-in companion, not without appreciation.

We never did know the outcome of Betsy's fate, for that night we were relieved by a unit of the South Wales Borderers.

"There's a Bren to each slit," I said as we handed over our positions. "Keep your eyes peeled down to the stream, there's a pot-shot Pete having a crack at anything that moves. We think he's in the trees behind the farm buildings — two o'clock right. Keep the Bren well covered, the sun gets at it in the afternoon."

"Aye, an there's a bloody cow out there that'll need milking tomorrow night," said George, his eyes twinkling. The Welshman gave us an old-fashioned look. George gave me a nudge as he nodded in the direction of Betsy, "We'll let them sort that one out, Kenny lad."

EIGHT – "HAVE YOU HEARD THE RUMOUR?"

Rumour is always rife amongst army personnel. There is always someone who knows somebody who knows someone who is a clerk in an office somewhere who knows just what is going on.

The true story is stretched, pulled and contorted, as it passes from mouth to mouth to such an extent that by the time it reaches the end of the line it is hardly worth the proverbial pinch of salt.

Rumour had it this time, that we were going out of the line to enable the 147 Brigade to be reorganized. The badly mauled battalion of the Duke of Wellingtons was to be disbanded and another new battalion was to be brought in to replace them.

Motor transport from the divisional pool awaited us as we reached the rear area, so we were very happy as we embussed and settled down for the journey which we hoped would take us for a short time away from the interminable noise of the front line.

We debussed shortly before dawn and made our way across country for a mile or so and took up a company area in a large field. Quickly settling in some partly dug slits, brewing cans were being primed for immediate use and fires were beginning to flicker around the perimeter of the field. Sgt. Louis Hill visited each fire and passed on the news that we must take care not to make too big a smoke.

"We're not quite sure yet what the situation is," was his parting remark. It didn't seem too optimistic to me. Confirmation was soon forthcoming. We were not in a rear area as we had thought, but found, much to our chagrin, that we had taken up a holding position in the line between Caen and Evrecy. So much for the rumours.

Although the surroundings were of the typical bocage country, the atmosphere was undoubtedly different. Huge amplifiers blared out recorded music by the hour. Glenn Miller and his orchestra entertained us with their entire repertoire from 'Moonlight Serenade' to 'Amor, Amor, Amor', and the 'Chattanooga Choo-choo'. The Old Girls Choir of America also weighed in with their charming homespun serenades. We had heard this sort of entertainment in the rear area around Bayeux, but now it was fast becoming part of the psychological warfare being waged by the Allies to keep up the morale of their troops, whilst at the same time, undermining those of the enemy.

Someone said that this was the way that the Yanks went to war.

'Little Monty' Montague from the Welsh Fusiliers, said that it was a decided improvement on the bagpipes. He was promptly subdued by a horde of gentlemen from the other side of Hadrian's Wall.

No sooner had we become acclimatized to the sweet music of Glenn Miller, than another type of psychology took over.

Formations of bombers came from the west, flying rather higher than those we had seen at Villiers Bocage, but in the same tight formations. We tried to count them as they passed overhead, but there were so many it was difficult to keep track of the numbers.

Very shortly we heard the explosions as the bombs landed on the ancient town of Caen. For more than an hour they came in a steady stream, Halifaxes, Lancasters, Wellingtons, ploughing on through the flak from the enemy batteries. Noise from the tremendous bombing reverberated through the air. The very ground we stood on shook beneath our feet as the really heavy blockbusters dropped into this linchpin of the German defences, more than eight miles away. For almost three hours the raid continued without respite and without any interference from enemy fighters. The raid by 250 Halifaxes had taken three-quarters of an hour, so by our rule of thumb reckoning, there must have been about one thousand planes taking part on this morning's raid. We had witnessed history in the making. Never before has so many planes deployed on a single mission in preparation for the capture of a town.

Very shortly a clerk in an office would set the words in motion for them to travel by the bush telegraph.

The American Forces Network (AFN), continued to broadcast its musical programmes and also news items throughout the rest of the afternoon and evening. The nine o'clock news confirmed what we had witnessed in the morning, that 1,000 bombers had bombed Caen and reconnaissance had shown that a greater part of the town was completely destroyed.

We awaited the reaction to this devastating blow.

The immediate follow up by the British 2nd Army was 'Monty's Moonlight'.

Searchlight batteries were called up to the front lines and their huge searchlights were switched on as darkness fell. The beams of light were shone in a horizontal direction so that the whole countryside was lit up almost as bright as day. Directed towards the enemy lines, they not only dazzled the infantry in their front line trenches, but also showed up any movement of their immediate rear. The glare from the brilliant beams prevented detection of our own forces who were able to move more freely in this artificial light.

There was also a change of mood over the airwaves. The music of Glenn Miller was replaced by sound recordings of armoured vehicles being moved around. We could hear the distinctive roar of Sherman tanks and other tracked vehicles whilst in the background was the noise of trucks on the move.

All night long this cacophony of sound went on, but like most battle sounds, one got accustomed to the new noise and sleep came in four hour snatches.

During the few days we spent in this delightful field we were also privileged to witness the antics of 'George' in his spotter plane.

Flying Auster aircraft, a light single-engined monoplane, which incidentally was produced at Rearsby, a village two miles from my mate George's home, the pilots were mostly over thirty years of age, middle-aged to us, and were acting as the eyes of the artillery and to a lesser extent, the infantry.

These small planes were highly manoeuvrable, and with the pilots very adept at hedge-hopping and twisting and turning between the pom-pom trees, they were a constant bane to the enemy as they ferreted out gun emplacements and armour. They were also very quick to pick out signs of forthcoming attacks or counter-attacks. The drone of their engines as they buzzed about like busy bees was one of the more welcome noises of the day. Passing at times only feet above our heads, we would look up and wave, happy in the knowledge that, "It's only 'George' doing a bit of spotting."

Knowing their capability of landing and taking off in the confines of only a medium sized field, it was no surprise to see one land one morning in our field.

The pilot calmly climbed from the cockpit, asked for Battalion HQ, delivered his message and was airborne again in a matter of minutes, having skilfully avoided the latrine on his take-off run.

Each night, listening patrols and 'snatch' patrols were out harassing the Germans.

The *modus operandi* of the former, was to worm one's way on stomach and elbows as near to the enemy trenches as possible without being detected, and to lie there for any given time to observe movement or noise. These observations would be pin-pointed on a map for intelligence. The 'snatch', as the word might imply, was to creep up on an enemy trench and snatch a prisoner to enable him to be interrogated and searched for information which might give details of regiments and divisions opposing us. Such was our involvement in holding the line at this time.

More rumours were now afoot this day. Firstly, that a new Commanding Officer had been appointed. Secondly, that we were to leave on the morrow for five days' rest, during which time we would welcome our new CO and receive further reinforcements. Thirdly, that the 49th Division would be transferred to the Canadian Army to assist General Crerar in the break-out from Caen, following its recent capture.

The first two were quite palatable but the third was a different kettle of fish. The Canadians were having a hell of a slog, ferocious fighters that they were, they were being pinned down by a determined foe. Advance on their front was being measured in yards per day, not miles. But of course it was only a rumour.

Pleasantly surprised by the accuracy of our inside information, we duly moved on the morrow. TCVs conveyed us to a rest area well away from the front line. We were mildly amused *en route* to see two RAOC men emerge from a field carrying a Sherman tank. When one considers that the weight of a Sherman is in excess of 35 tons, it did seem to be rather incongruous.

Closer inspection however, proved the tank to be a dummy made of rubber and plastic. They were being inflated by the RAOC chaps and carried to a side road where they were lined up in squadrons as if ready to move off. This also explained the reason for the vehicle recordings which had poured from the amplifiers each night.

The Germans were being bluffed into thinking that we had far more armour at our disposal than was in fact the case. Batteries of field guns were also to be seen in the orchards, their inflated gun barrels waving slightly in the breeze, but from the air they would seem to be genuine.

It was nice to be amongst the orchards once more. We washed and shaved beneath trees laden with apples shining bright red in the morning sunshine, a light breeze causing the tips of the old trees to sway gently to and fro. An old man clothed in sun-faded blue cotton drill dungarees and short smock, repaired so many times that they were more patches than original cloth, brought in his dairy cow on a long tattered tether.

We helped him knock in the stake with his home-made mallet and made our pathetic attempts to converse with him. The cardboard fag jammed into the corner of his mouth as he spoke, did very little to assist his pronunciation. We did however manage to glean a little information, with the aid of a certain amount of shrugging and gesticulating, that a café and bar existed in a small village a couple of kilometres away. The word calvados was mentioned and George's eyes lit up.

Our big packs suddenly appeared from nowhere. Fresh kit was now at hand. Boots were exchanged and cleaned as we smartened ourselves up.

The Tam-o'-Shanter was worn for the first time. I wasn't used to the large floppy brim which felt heavy and rather off balance, then I noticed that the original members of the Battalion had hats with stiff brims. The secret was wire.

A piece of wire about a metre in length was commandeered from the orchard fence and threaded inside the hat until it formed a perfect ring around the inside of the brim. The hat now felt much more comfortable, and with the lower edge pulled down over the right ear, the balance was perfect. I was now one of the jocks.

Major Rowell, our Company Commander, called for an inspection of personnel and arms in the afternoon. This gave him his first proper chance to meet some of his men for the purpose of getting to know them by name. A tall, young looking man, his manner was sharp and his questions incisive. He knew what he was doing and he would brook no laggards in his company, of that there was no doubt.

"Tomorrow, the RSM will hold a Battalion parade in the large orchard down the road. You will parade in best BD and Caps T-o-S with rifles unloaded. 'D' Company will be the smartest company on parade." Turning towards Sgt.-Major Cookson, he ended with "Dismiss the Company, Sergeant-Major."

Gradually we began to relax and as the day wore on paper and pen were put to use, letters long overdue were sent to my family. Because of the censorship restrictions there was very little army news we could include, so it was a matter of family chit-chat and rather vague descriptions of beautiful countryside, of orchards and apples and milkmaids and cows. War was never mentioned.

Although still only about two-thirds full strength, 'D' Company marched smartly into the large orchard at the prescribed time next morning. Wheeling to the left, we took up our appointed place as the Battalion formed up in review order.

"Battalion .... Battalion, SHUN," barked the RSM. He then introduced himself in his own inimitable style, mainly to impress the newer members lined up before him. " ... and they call me John the 'B'. An' it doesna' mean John the Baptist," he continued. "We're now going to drill and drill until you are good enough to meet your new Commanding Officer."

Standing stiff as a ramrod, his eyes swept the ranks. "Stand still there 'A' Company — you're waving about like a field of corn. Sgt. Duncan! That man behind you, take his name." The sergeant swung about. "That's him — that man next to Fusilier McKenna."

"Fusilier McKenna's away wounded, Sir," replied Sgt. Duncan.

"Well take the name of the man next to him," demanded John the 'B'.

The genial Sergeant winked at the unfortunate fusilier, "Sorry son, you heard what the man said, you'd better give me your name and last three — I'll do what I can."

For the next hour and a half we practised arms drill, foot drill, including quick and slow marching, the whole of this operation being carried out in this undulating orchard, roughly the size of a barrack parade square, but interspersed with apple trees which had to be sidestepped and avoided, as the RSM steered us around with great expertise. I give the man his due, he could certainly handle a parade.

"Will he never finish?" I asked George as we presented arms once more.

"It'll take a bloody stonking, the same as Fontenay," came the reply. "He's got the bit between his teeth."

All good things must come to an end sooner or later and now almost two hours later we saw a hand reach up to put an extra twist to the waxed ends of his moustache. John the 'B' was almost satisfied.

"You're beginning to get the hang o' it now, but I'll expect an improvement on this tomorrow morning."

With this riposte he ended the session and we marched back to our little orchard for a bit of peace and quiet.

The two kilometre walk into the nearby village proved to be very pleasant indeed. Narrow tree-lined roads with the banked hedges on both sides gave welcome shade in the hot July afternoon. In places the tops of the trees intermingled overhead and we heard birds whistling for the first time for many days.

The small village had come through relatively unscathed. The few houses looked empty as if awaiting their owners to return from the fields. The café was open and business was booming, with Tam-o'-Shanters well in evidence both inside and sitting at the old tables on the dirt path outside. Conversation was mainly confined to the latest 'whisper' about L/Cpl Mitchell, MM, who had gone missing from a patrol one night at Juvigny. It was an intriguing story.

Young Mitchell had arrived in France in 1940 with the 51st Division as a band-boy of sixteen. Following their surrender at St. Valery-en-Caux, he had escaped capture and had lived with a French family in Brittany for a time, working with the local resistance until he was eventually captured by the Germans and taken to a POW camp.

Either because of his age or some illness, he was repatriated to Britain where he was rewarded with his Military Medal. He then was posted to the 11th RSF and arrived in Normandy with them.

This was, be claimed, a contravention of the Geneva Convention which stated that a repatriated POW must not be returned to the theatre of operations in which he had been captured.

The army authorities claimed that this was not the same operation, but young Mitchell was adament that it was still the North-West European operation and believed that should he be taken prisoner again he could be shot. In the few days that we knew him, he certainly became very scared about being sent on night patrols, so much so, that he said he would not take part again should he be chosen. He was chosen and promptly vanished into the night.

The story now being circulated was that he had been picked up in the American sector as he attempted to reach his old friends in Brittany. He was now awaiting trial by court martial for desertion. (He was found guilty, stripped of his rank and the MM and sentenced to a detention centre. After the war, I was pleased to read in a national newspaper that his case had been taken to the House of Lords and consequently he had been completely vindicated. He gained a Royal pardon and his Military Medal was restored. A unique case.)

However, on this sunny afternoon, the young L/Cpl who was barely twenty years of age, was toasted with calvados and the subject was changed to conjecture on our part as to what sort of CO the new chap would turn out to be. All we knew was that he was an outsider.

Washed and shaved, brushed and polished, we formed up in the large orchard, this time with all officers on parade with their Companies.

The previous day's performance was repeated, but this time as we passed the saluting base, we saw a tall, slimly built man with a full moustache neatly twirled at the ends. The face was kindly and the eyes alert as they checked the men for whom he was now responsible and whose lives would be governed by the decisions he would have to make. He was introduced to us as Lt.-Col. D.A.D. Eykin and then, in a speech which followed, his message was clear that he expected nothing but the best from his Battalion and in return he would give nothing but his best for his men.

The order 'Stand at Ease' preceded the inspection of each company by our new Lt.-Colonel. He looked at every man and spoke to many as he walked between the ranks. His questions, though varied, were mainly concerned with the well-being of the fusiliers, both mentally and physically. Our first impressions were that here was a kindly and caring gentleman and an intelligent and efficient officer.

On that sunny summer's morning he was Lt.-Col. D.A.D. Eykin by his men and from that day onwards he was known affectionately as 'Dad' Eykin, the father of the 11th Battalion the Royal Scots Fusiliers.

The scene was changed somewhat for our next parade in the large orchard. In the place of the saluting base, an altar had been erected and the whole Battalion formed in a square around it. The service was conducted by our Church of Scotland padre Captain Wylie for all members of the Church of England, Church of Scotland, Odds and sods, as other denominations were irreverently called. Roman Catholics held their own service with their own chaplain.

There is something about an open air service which makes even the more unchristian of us appreciate this type of worship. Those who would very seldom attend any church service, seemed to be less restricted as they joined in the hymn singing.

Here, in a small corner of a foreign land, we sang together 'Praise my soul the King of Heaven' and the 23rd Psalm. The Colonel read the lesson, followed by a lusty response of 'Onward Christian Soldiers'.

We prayed for our dead comrades, for the wounded and for those posted as missing and for comfort for their relatives and friends. The service ended with a lone piper playing the lament, 'Fleurs o' the forest' and the blessing.

For the first time for almost three weeks, the singing had silenced the noise and battle. Not even a single plane was heard whining overhead and our own field guns were silent as if under orders not to disturb our simple act of worship.

In the afternoon we indulged in a baths parade in a nearby field. Once again it developed into an Anglo-French occasion, we supplied the mannequins on parade and the French girls were the captivated audience who applauded from the wings. A pleasant Sunday during which we had cleansed both the body and the soul.

Confirmation of the third rumour came the next day. We were to become a part of the 2nd Canadian Army and would leave the next day to take our place in the line, somewhere in the vicinity of Carpiquet.

The pretty bocage country was now behind us as the land flattened and the foliage gave way to fields of corn, golden ripe and all ready for harvesting. For the moment it must wait until the tide of war had passed.

In some fields, intrepid farmers had scythed the edges in the hope of starting this mammoth task, for civilian vehicles and horses were few and far between.

The River Orne, for which there had been bitter fighting in the early days, was crossed and we marched to the rolling plains around the town of Collombelles, once again the sound of artillery fire assailed our ears.

A quick order to disperse because of enemy shelling, found us amongst the golden wheat and lying on the soft warm soil. I rubbed ears of corn between my hands and blew away the husks, the grain tasted refreshingly ripe so I had 'seconds'.

Somewhat surprised, we were told to dig in for the night, there was a hold up further on and we must consolidate. The soft earth was the best terrain we had encountered so far and George and I soon had a good trench dug and our packs off our backs to make a makeshift pillow for our tired heads.

The spluttering of an aircraft engine brought us to our feet. An RAF Typhoon was in trouble as it returned from a rocket attack. Smoke poured from its fuselage as the pilot guided the plane away from traffic jams on the road and away from our tenches to make a perfect belly-landing some half a mile away.

Before the pilot could evacuate the 'tiffy' the surrounding cornfield began to burn. A spurt of flame and suddenly the dry ripe wheat was ablaze.

Two ambulances appeared as if from nowhere, charging towards the inferno, followed by an assortment of vehicles. Men were running through the waist high corn as the pilot was seen emerging from the cockpit. Braving the flames, he was half dragged through the burning corn to the awaiting ambulance.

Horror of horrors, as this scene was being enacted, the enemy put down a stonk on the area around the plane. Despite the shelling we were called to put out the fire in case it spread to our position. An hour's steady beating was needed to put out the flames and all was left blackened and scorched.

On returning to our slits, we were accosted by an irate farmer gesticulating wildly and ranting away at the top of his voice about the damage we had caused to his crops. Almost beside himself with rage, it took quite some time for us to quieten him sufficiently enough to try and talk to him in his native tongue.

George, always the man to use his limited command of the French language, tried to appease the little man, explaining that we hadn't started the fire and that it wasn't our decision to dig up his fields.

"C'est la guerre, monsieur," he ended.

The blue-overalled farmer continued to bemoan his loss. In over four years, he said, the Germans had never burned his fields. They had not dug holes and defiled his ground, nor had they driven tanks and lorries through his growing crops. We had come and in less than three weeks we had ruined his crops and killed his cows.

George, who had been most restrained during all this tirade suddenly lost his cool.

"You ungrateful little bugger, we've come to liberate your lot. If you're not satisfied, we'll all go home again and let the soddin' Jerries reoccupy your land — but I'll tell you this mate, I'll never come here again for my bleedin' holidays."

With that, he turned on his heel and dropped into the slit, utterly disgusted.

I had to have a quiet smile to myself, for George had never been abroad before. But he stuck to his principles. After the end of the war, he never returned to that country.

He was still upset as we marched off towards Cagny the next day. Everything was wrong that day. His boots hurt, the sun was too hot, he drank his water-bottle dry and smoked about twenty of my fags.

Things didn't get any better when, just after digging a decent slit, we were ordered to proceed along the fencing of the Caen to Liseux railway line. In the pitch dark, we stumbled over half dug slits, disturbing the occupants as they rested.

By the light of the match as George lit yet another fag, I noticed the shoulder flash of the men in the slits. The pithead emblem showed them to belong to the 59th Division and we were to take over from them forthwith.

The battered signpost on the outskirts of the village proclaimed that this was Frenouville, a long straggling village, and George still complained that his feet were sore.

NINE – KYBO

Each branch of the armed services has its own lists of priorities during the times of war. In the Army, these priorities are determined by the nature of the role played by the differing arms of that service. Most infantrymen would, I'm sure, agree that their overriding thoughts are for their own personal safety and comfort, allied to their particular participation as a combat unit. Their priorities would therefore be as follows:
    a. The care and maintenance of their rifles.
    b. The care of their feet.
    c. The state of their bowels.
— although, not always in that order.

The care of the rifle is of utmost importance being as it is, in many cases, the only weapon at their disposal for their own personal protection. The many hours spent in training an infantryman has instilled into him the fact that "your rifle is your best friend, laddie, and don't you forget it." Subsequently, it becomes second nature to clean, oil and treat with loving care your best friend.

From the very first time one places one's foot in an army boot, one is left in no doubt whatever that they are two incompatible bedfellows. The tender foot coming into contact with the hard new leather protests in the only way it knows and erupts with blisters and calluses, giving the unfortunate new recruit considerable pain and anguish, until he learns the ropes of how to protect his feet for the miles and miles he will cover without the aid of any vehicular assistance. One could always tell an 'old sweat', by the way he would rest his feet by lying on his back, with his 'dogs' propped up higher than his head, thereby taking all the weight and pressure off his feet. It was also well reported that one of the best conditioners could be found under the bed in most infantry barracks, although I have never used this method of treatment myself. An uncle of mine from the First World War, swore by this, and according to him there was no better cure for chilblains.

However, in Normandy we were able to wash and care for our feet fairly regularly.

A few eyebrows may be raised by the inclusion of the third priority. We do all take for granted the natural body functions of disposal of our waste products and it is usually only in times of stress and strain that we may have difficulty with our bowels. There we have the crux of the matter, for the infantryman is continually under stresses and strains of varying degrees, caused at times by long periods of inactivity in cramped conditions which can cause serious constipation. On the other hand, there are times of swift movement and violent action together with the fear of the uncertainty of what lies ahead in the next hedgerow or the next turn in the road. At times like this one either feels like vomitting, or your most urgent desire is to down slacks and empty your bowels with an explosion of wind and waste that is difficult to control.

In this battle for Normandy, one was either 'up front', 'in reserve', or 'moved to a rest area'. The rest area was usually in some orchard way behind the line of fire and one could relax from the rigours of constant alertness and enjoy the pleasures of showers, clean clothes and best of all, to be able to use the latriness provided, in a leisurely manner and taking full use of the toilet paper which the Army in its infinite wisdom, allocated 3 sheets per soldier per day in the 14-man food packs. We, for our part, decreed that these should be used in the folllowing manner.

a. For wiping up.
b. For rubbing down.
c. For polishing.

When an infantry unit, be it Company or Battalion, is in reserve, it is merely moved into a position just behind the front line and must be ready to move forward at a moment's notice, back into the line to cover whatever contingency may have arisen. The reserve position was usually under fire from mortars or field guns, so that although one was not on full alert, one had to be ready for any eventuality. One's thoughts were thankfulness for having survived the period 'up front' and a grim determination not to cop a 'Blighty' whilst in the reserve position.

With this in mind, the following story may illustrate the difference between 'rest area' and 'in reserve'.

We were allocated a field some 800 yards behind the front line in the vicinity of Evrecy. 'D' Company was on the right hand side of the field roughly square and completely surrounded with the typical Normandy hedges, with their double banks interspersed with tall trees whose trunks were devoid of branches and topped by a pom-pom of foliage making a perfect hiding place for snipers of both sides.

On the opposite side of the field was HQ Company, with its Command Post for the Colonel and staff, together with the redoubtable RSM, John the 'B'. Movement across the field was possible, but because of the sporadic mortar and shell fire one usually moved around the shelter of the hedge.

There were, however, a number of slit trenches in the field and for some unknown reason, it had been decided that the communal latrine should be dug in the centre of the field. Its construction was of the usual type in a reserve area.

A pit was dug approximately 6ft x 6ft x 6ft deep, then another slit trench was dug at the bottom approximately 5ft x 1½ft x 3ft deep. The method of usage was for one to watch for any previous user to leave and then cross to the pit before anyone else beat you to it. Somehow it seemed that whenever one wanted to use the latrine, the Jerries most inconsiderately decided to drop the odd shell or mortar in the vicinity. You therefore, would prepare for action by undoing your regulation braces, unbuttoning your trouser flies, and at the appropriate moment, dash across the open field holding your trousers up with the left hand and carrying your rifle in the right, finishing with a leap into the pit, where the natural function was carried out as quickly as possible, wipe, rub, polish and return in the same manner, adjusting your dress upon reaching your own slit trench.

The Colonel's batman, Fusilier Donaldson, saw his chance and streaked across the field. Just as he reached the perimeter of the pit, a mortar shell landed in the field behind him and with a gigantic leap which must have equalled the Olympic Games record set by Jesse Owens, he landed, whoosh, straight on top of someone else, pushing him full length, face down into the lower pit. Donaldson lay there heaving with the exertions of his dice with death, as below him came the muffled sounds of the unmistakable voice of the RSM.

"Will ye get off ma back man?"

"I'll no get off ye back."

"Ye'll get off ma back noo, ma man."

"I will no get off ye back, an get ma bloody head blown off by yon bloody Jerry."

"Is that ye Donaldson?"

"I'm no tellin ye wha it is, an I'm no movin awa'."

"Get off ma back man, I canna laie here covered in shyte."

"Ye can so," said Donaldson, then deciding on his course of action he pushed John the 'B''s head and shoulders firmly into the lower pit, giving himself the necessary leverage to leap out of the pit and come charging hell for leather for 'D' Company lines. Just before he reached the hedge, the face of the RSM rose above the parapet of the latrine pit, contorted with rage and covered with excrement and paper. He viewed the departing offender as he disappeared into our lines and then with a bellow like an enraged bull, forgot all caution and followed in pursuit.

"Somebody stop that man, I want his name and number." The bespattered RSM reached us. "Which way did he go?" We in our innocent way pointed to the left. Scarcely waiting to draw breath, the RSM charged off down the field, whilst Donaldson quietly made his way to the right, back to his own slit trench, where he waited for the RSM to arrive, protesting that he had never left that spot for the past half hour and denying all knowledge of the incident.

John the 'B' never found out the truth of who had descended on him, but to his eternal credit he often recounted the story to us during the long lonely months of the winter in Holland.

Some weeks later we had moved up into the salient north of Caen, once again being faced by the SS; we knew that this was about the time for a push out of the Caen area and it was with some foreboding that we took over the front line position on a pitch black night.

I remember saying to George, "I don't like this place George, I've got a feeling in my water, that we shall be lucky to get out of here." When morning eventually dawned, we found ourselves on the furthermost point of the village of Frenouville. Ahead lay the road to Paris and all round on three sides were the green bocage woods.

George summed it up succinctly as he said, "I feel as though there's just the two of us on Blackpool beach and we've been caught coming out of the sea 'starkers'. Ain't it bloody quiet?"

"Too bloody quiet," I replied.

The quiet interlude didn't last for long, for someone in a nearby slit got up and stretched himself. Crack, went the sound of a sniper's bullet just over us, fortunately missing everyone, and that's how it was for the next twelve days; no one could move without it brought a 'stonking' of shells or the crack of a sniper's rifle.

The only time we moved from the trench was at night, we filled the water-bottles from the supply containers brought up under cover of darkness, this was when we also had our hot meal. The meal usually consisted of one tin of stewed steak, or oxtail, one packet of biscuits 'hard tack', probably 1/7th tin of suet pudding and the usual 7 sweets, 1 bar dark chocolate and 7 cigs.

During the day we took it in turns to keep awake, and maintain a 24 hour vigil, but the continuous inactivity and the stodgy food caused us to become constipated. Having reached the 8th day, George decided that he would have a look round the houses that night. Night came and off he moved, quietly and stealthily, and after about an hour he came back.

"Look what I've got," he whispered. There in his hand was a bottle of cider. "I found it over there in an old barn." What he'd found was a bottle of the local cider which the farm workers made out of the inferior apples.

"Have a swig," he said. I took the bottle and took a light sip.

"It's like ruddy vinegar," I said, "you're welcome to the lot."

"Oh, I don't know," said George, whereupon he downed about half the bottle.

About 11 o'clock the next morning, George was rolling about in the trench, holding his stomach.

"Bloody hell, that cider must be working me," he said.

"Well, I thought it was a bit rough," I said.

"You'd better pass the tin," said George. "I can't last till tonight."

Now we had devised a plan of operation whilst in this very tightly held position. The slit trench was about 6ft x 2ft x 4ft-6 deep. In this position we could not dig too deep as it had to be a firing position. So what with the snipers and the stonking from the Jerry guns every time we moved, we saved the tins from our night's food and used them as containers whenever we had to pass water. We then stored them in little alcoves around the slit and then at night we threw the contents as far as we could in the direction of the Jerry lines. When one needed to pass a rear motion, this was a delicate operation where the tin was held under the backside and one had to aim blind, into the tin.

As neither of us had been for about 8 days, this operation had never arisen at Frenouville, but now George was going to alter all that.

After about 20 minutes of straining and grunting, George said, "It's no use, Ken, I've got a bit about half an inch long that won't come in or out."

I suggested that he pulled his slacks up again and thought that if he sat down, perhaps the weight of his body would put things right. The resulting language from George told me that he was in dire trouble.

"It's no good," said George, "I'll have to have another go." He thereupon dropped his slacks and turning his back to me, went through the same procedures as before, with the pain getting more severe all the time.

"Can you see anything blocking the passage, Ken?" I looked and saw this dark brown protrusion from his back passage.

After some thought I said, "I think the only way you'll have to move that George, is to prise it out."

"Well use your bayonet," replied George, "I'm desperate." Thinking that I may need my bayonet to open that night's tins, I said, "No, I'll use yours, George." Without a word, George unclipped his bayonet from his Mk 3 rifle and I took it from him. With the bayonet in one hand and a ragged topped stewed steak tin in the other, I started the delicate operation of unbunging George.

"Hold still," I said, then piece by piece over the next half an hour or so I worked steadily as each piece, rather like the dried brown peas that a school pal of mine fed to his pigeons, dropped into the tin, rattling like those same dried peas.

From time to time, I caught George with either the bayonet tip or the edge of the can, only for him to call anxiously, "Be careful with that bloody bayonet, you could ruin me for life." By the note of alarm in his voice I rather think he was more than a little concerned about his future role in the procreation of the human race, than in a slight nick in his bum from the lid of a can of M & V.

I reminded him of the tale about the fellow who nicked his bum on a rusty old can.

"Why, what happened to him?" said George.

"They reckon he died of arsenic poisoning," I replied.

"Don't make me laugh," said George, as he held his hands on the pit of his stomach. "It don't half hurt when I laugh."

In trying to suppress my laughter, I again brushed the lid of the tin against the bare buttock in front of me.

"For Christ's sake, watch it mate," said George, then rather wearily, "I'll have to have a rest for a bit."

We stopped periodically for George to rest from his straining. Then the cider would start to roll around again and once more he would be on the move.

For my part, being on the receiving end, I was rather apprehensive that after the blockage would come a veritable flood and so I had other tins at hand to cover that possibility. However, after about another hour we decided that it was safe for him to sit down again and hope that he could last until nightfall.

At last night came and George took full advantage of the enveloping gloom to finish off the good work which had been started by the illicit cider.

I heard him coming back some time later, humming to himself. I couldn't help smiling to myself as I recalled in my mind, a passage I had read as a boy, in Lord Baden-Powell's book *Scouting for Boys*.

'Whenever you are in camp or in any strange environment, it is essential that you keep yourself healthy and fit. Make sure that you are always able to keep your bowels open. This may not always be easy and sometimes it may be necessary to knead the stomach to persuade the bowel to discharge and so alleviate constipation. Whatever you do, do not over-strain yourself and take plenty of exercise. Remember the word KYBO – KEEP YOUR BOWELS OPEN.'

TEN – YOU NEVER HEAR THE ONE THAT GETS YOU

A group of four small cottages huddled together on the eastern edge of the village of Frenouville. These farm workers' homes, now unoccupied, would make a useful Platoon HQ for No. 17 Platoon.

Sappers from the Royal Engineers were called to check them for booby traps and once cleared, Sgt. Hill moved in.

The single storeyed building chosen, had just two rooms and a small kitchen with a modicum of furniture scattered around on the earth floor. A small lean-to at the side of the building would give shelter and cover to a jeep or carrier should the occasion warrant the use of such a vehicle.

One room was utilized as a kitchen and stores, leaving the one with a better view to be used as a strong point with two machine-guns strategically placed to cover the Paris road.

The main meal of the day was served out, section by section, after dusk and breakfast was issued during morning stand to just before dawn, during which time a quick wash and shave was also undertaken. We then retired to our slit for the remainder of the long hot day.

Wooden doors, fencing and other like objects were utilized to cover part of the slit to afford a little protection from the elements and shrapnel. After darkness had fallen we would pile on more soil, etc., one night we dragged a sack of stones across the top to hold down a piece of tattered old tarpaulin.

Now that we had been with the Fusiliers for about a month we started to receive mail from home. The wheels of the Army Postal Service, no doubt weighed down by the avalanches of delayed mail, was now grinding slowly into gear.

The first to arrive for me, was from Margaret, full of chat about her Land Army activities and news of friends. The second was from my father in which he told me to get into Bayeux and have a look at the Bayeux Tapestry for him.

George thought this to be highly amusing. He promptly crossed two fingers and held them up high above the parapet.

"Don't shoot, Jerry – Ken's just got to pop into Bayeux for a few minutes to check on some embroidery." He looked at me and said with mock severity. "You'll have to have a word with your old man, doesn't he know there's a war going on?"

In answer, I told him about my dad's interest in churches and how well read he was about the French cathedrals and chateaux.

"I don't suppose we'll see you for a few days when we get to Paris then," he joked, "you'll be looking around the Louvre for your dad."

The mention of Paris started a chain of thought about when we would eventually reach the capital. Taking into consideration the amount of time taken to reach Caen and the distance in kilometres from Caen to Paris, we reached the conclusion that it would take us another year and a half, give or take the odd diversion along the way.

It looked like being a long war at this rate of progress.

The constant one hundred per cent stand to throughout the night began to make us extra sensitive to any unusual sound. On one such a night, we heard the 'Moaning Minnies' being fired. These were German six-barrelled mortars which fired their shells one after the other, and they fell to earth screaming like a banshee. Being fired from one base, they all exploded within a radius of approximately ten yards of their target. Very unpleasant when one was on the receiving end.

This night, there were no screaming banshees, just a whine as a projectile was launched towards our position.

What could it be, this new projectile which did not explode on landing? Could it be gas warfare?

We sniffed, but in the mist of early morning we could not smell anything different. The yellow detector patch on the sleeves of our gas capes was checked for change in colour. All was in order.

"Perhaps the wind is carrying it in the opposite direction," I whispered to my mate.

"We'd better keep our eyes skinned in case they sneak up with a surprise attack at dawn."

The interminably long night dragged on, then, shortly before dawn was heard the sound of movement to our immediate front.

Peering into the misty half light, we searched the back garden of the house, looking for the perpetrator.

Rifles poised with safety catches off and fingers on triggers, we awaited with bated breath, as the sound came nearer. It was in amongst the cabbages now. Wild thoughts ran through my mind — a snatch patrol? A fighting patrol? Or was it the real thing, an all-out attack?

The tall grass about ten yards away began to move, then suddenly the grass parted to reveal a face with two long ears flopping over it. A ruddy great buck rabbit sat looking at us as it nibbled at the grass.

"I'll have to write to my dad and tell him we were very nearly taken prisoner by a Giant Flemmish rabbit," I said as I wiped the beads of perspiration away with the back of my hand. The dawn was never more welcome than when it arrived about an hour later. The mysterious projectiles were reported at stand down, but we never did find out just what they were.

"Probably their gunners firing nose-caps to clear the barrels," suggested

Louis.

"Sunday morning again," said George. "What would you like for dinner today — roast beef, baked spuds and Yorkshire pud, or would you rather care for lamb chops and mint sauce with green peas?" he added lightheartedly.

"Anything — as long as it isn't ruddy oxtail," I replied.

"I'll just sharpen the carving knife on the step whilst you make up your mind," said the lad from Queniborough.

"What's the date?"

"30th July," came the reply.

The sound of hearty laughter and someone singing the popular song 'Lili Marlene' interrupted our banter. We stood up to hear more clearly who was singing.

A delightful baritone voice wafted across the field and from the hedge beyond. Other voices joined in to swell the volume. Quite clearly they were German voices and they too were happy on this beautiful morning.

We had heard rumblings during the night and presumably a fresh opposition unit was occupying the lines slighty to our left flank. Like ourselves at Evrecy, they were mistakenly under the impression that they were in a safe area.

Our 25-pounder guns opened up and we saw the flashes as the shells burst amongst the hedges some 400 yards away. The singing stopped abruptly and was replaced by screams, spine-chilling screams and hysterical shouts which must have been calling for stretcher bearers.

"I didn't think his singing was as bad as that," said George laconically, as the brutality of war wiped out the magical moment.

We stood talking to the rest of the Section about the sequel of events, when, bang-whoosh, a shell from an 88mm landed very near to Paddy Inglishby's trench. Down we all ducked as two more came over bang — woosh, bang — woosh. After a pause we peered carefully out of the slit.

On either side of our slit were two blackened holes, each about three yards from the trench.

"Christ! look at this," said Groege, as he pointed to the roof.

The sack had been ripped open by a piece of shrapnel to reveal not stones as we had believed, but hand grenades. I stretched out a hand and checked one, a 36 Mills grenade already primed with a four second fuse. We looked again, there must have been more than thirty lying there on top of our roof. After much deliberation, we thought it safer to leave them there and keep under cover, than to emerge and bring about another shelling which could blow us all up.

We shouted to all the others not to move all day and we sat there and sweated it out until dusk, when we swiftly collected them all up and handed them in to Louis Hill.

"Just what we wanted Ken — take half a dozen with you and share the others out between the other slits." The look on his face told me that he'd got the same feeling in his water that I had.

"Mail for you Westy," said Craggy, throwing in a folded newspaper. The buff coloured austerity cover of the paper told me that it was the *John Bull* from my mother.

For the past few months, mother had been sending to me this popular periodical. Inside would be a single sheet of writing paper written in her own unmistakable handwriting, cheerfully written and asking caringly about the well-being of myself and my mates. In this letter, having heard about the storms and heavy rain in June, she hoped that we were drying out OK and not to forget that socks should be changed frequently.

On the top of the front page of the *John Bull* would be written postscripts as snippets of news came in prior to posting. These comments on the front cover, were of constant amusement to the lads as the paper was passed around.

"Just the sort of thing my mother would put on — if she could write," grinned Barnes the Bren-gunner.

The order to sally forth and dig new slits in the middle of the field was not very well received by anyone.

"We've got to get a listening post out there by tomorrow morning," explained the Platoon Sergeant. "Stay out there all day and return tomorrow night — there'll be wireless contact."

"Charming," said George, "out in the middle of no man's land, yelling our heads off, over an 18 set."

We crept out and dug as silently as possible with the Bren-gunner covering us all the time. By the end of darkness we were only eighteen inches down. An impossible situation. There was no alternative but to return to 17 Platoon and try again the next night.

Nat came across during the night and handed me a 38 set for the wireless contact. I was to open up at dawn and at two hourly intervals during the day to report on any enemy activity observed by us.

By morning light, we were about two feet six inches deep and it was possible for me to lie in the trench with the long aerial pointing in a horizontal position towards the company signallers. A message was passed that all was well. I laid there with the sun in the east to my right hand side.

My next recollection was to be rudely awakened by stones thrown by other members of the section trying to make contact. The sun was now on my left hand side. For a few minutes I was slightly disorientated, then I realized that I had been asleep for twelve hours. I called for them to stop throwing and that all was well. I checked the 38 set. The air waves were open, but I was in a dilemma, if I opened up they would want to know why I had not contacted them before.

I decided to keep mum and only open up if anything urgent came up.

Luckily nothing happened for the rest of the day.

As soon as it was dark, I knew that someone would be out to find out the cause for the lack of contact. Suddenly I remembered someone who had accidentally dropped his set on to a stone wall, rendering it u/s. I looked for a big stone and dropped the set. Minutes later, an irate Signals Corporal demanded to know the reason for lack of communication. I shrugged and handed him the set.

"It's u/s Corp," I said weakly. "Must have banged it on a stone."

"Well don't bang this one on a bloody stone, son," he said rather unkindly. "You'll need this at four o'clock in the morning — we're putting a stonk on Jerry at that time and we want a first hand report and commentary on the whole sheebang, report in every hour on the hour from now on."

"Best of luck Ken, I'll see you tomorrow night," said Nat as he hurried after the Corporal.

Barnes, the Bren-gunner came across for a word as I tried to deepen my solitary slit.

"Christ, you've not got much cover in there Westy, you would be better off with Monty and me — we're in clay over there, got a beauty of a trench over three feet deep. You'll be better off for transmitting and we can all see what's going on in comfort."

I looked at his trench and it was just as he'd described, just twenty yards away from the stone and shale which I had encountered. I never gave the trench at Juvigny a second thought as I jumped in at the western end beside little Monty.

We took turns on 'stag' and as it approached the crucial hour, I said in a mock Welsh voice, "I'm going to change my socks lads. I've had a letter from my mam, see, she said don't forget to change your socks, so I'm going to do what my mam says."

"Well, I'm going to see what's going on," said little Monty.

Switching on the wireless set, I placed it on the parapet to get the maximum reception. Slipping off my small pack, I took out the fresh socks and sat down on the pack and undid my bootlaces.

"Hold your noses lads," I called as I bent down to remove my boots.

My next recollection was of rising through a misty vapour, as strange harp-sounding chords penetrated my eardrums. So this is what it was like to be dead.

I heard my innermost voice saying "I wonder what my poor old mum will say when she hears the news .... but I must have been a good lad, because I'm going to heaven." Any moment now the angels would take me by the arm and lead me through the pearly gates.

But what was that unpleasant smell? The vaporous clouds became more pungent and my acceleration slowed to a stop. I felt panic for a split second. Had the devil got me after all? Faintly I heard a call.

"Are you all right, Westy? Get out o' there man."

There was the sudden realization that I was not dead, but something had happened to upset my equilibrium. My eyes focused on the swirling white smoke and I recognized the smell of the phosphorus. I was out of the hole in a jiffy.

The scene around the trench was unreal, the whole area glowing with white hot phosphorus. The soil around the parapet was covered with a white smoking layer, the 38 set was burning fiercely and everywhere the choking fumes from the burning liquid.

I looked down at my hands, they too were covered with glowing phosphorus and they began to smart like hell.

First-aid training had taught me that this stuff only burned when exposed to air, water would give relief but there was no water about, so I dug my hands deep into the cold soil of a nearby trench. As I did so, my helmet fell off; I turned to pick it up and replace it on my head but it was cove with the same glowing whiteness, and in the side I glimpsed a jagged rent, but my hands were burning again. The sleeves of my battledress were smouldering and there was a hammering in my head.

"I'd better get down to the RAP (Regimental Aid Post) and pass the word on to HQ," I said as I made my way across to the road, bootlaces dragging behind me.

Vaguely remembering the RAP sign as we had entered on the first night, I turned right and started walking along the middle of the road, my loosened boots clanging metallically on the granite sets. With my hands tucked under my armpits to prevent the air getting to them, I stumbled over debris as I passed damaged houses *en route*. Ever mindful of self-preservation I ran diagonally from side to side in the clear patches, praying that the clatter from my studded soles would not alert the Jerries who at times throughout the night, were wont to fire a heavy machine-gun on fixed lines along the village street. My luck was in and I reached the RAP safely.

No one stirred as I walked around the room. There was someone under the table, so I gave him a kick and asked sharply, "Who's in charge around here?"

The three pips on the shoulder of the body which stirred from under the table told me that I had kicked the MO himself. I had a feeling that he wouldn't be very pleased.

"I'm in charge," he replied, "who the devil are you?"

"Fusilier West, No. 17 Platoon."

"What do you think you're doing barging in here waking everyone up?"

"I've just come from the listening patrol. We've been hit by smoke bombs — everywhere is covered in phosphorus. All three in our trench have been hit, there may be many others . . . ."

"And are they all running about like you, without their steel helmets?" he demanded. "Go back and get your helmet."

"It's covered in the stuff," I said angrily. "If I wasn't wearing it, it would have been all over my head."

At this time, the RAP Sergeant saved the day for me.

"I'll attend to this chap, sir, you get your head down again." He picked up the Tilley lamp and led me to the next room where he bathed my hands and wrists.

"The Captain's had a pretty rough couple of nights," he said, explaining the MO's angry outburst.

"Where's all this blood come from, son, your top is covered in blood?"

He examined me and then found that it was coming from a gash in the side of my head. My hair was cut away and the wound dressed and then bandaged heavily.

Strips of cooling layers of bandage soaked in a solution were wrapped around my burning hands.

"Feel a bit better now son?" said the Sergeant kindly.

At that moment Barnes walked in, he was bleeding from his hands and he had a gash on his knee.

"They're bringing little Monty along on a stretcher," he said to me as he sat down to be attended to. This being done, the Sergeant woke the jeep driver.

"You'd better get these two back to base hospital straight away, there may be more along later."

We walked to the door just as the stretcher bearers arrived with Monty. The Sergeant took a quick look at him and said, "Leave him there for now, we'll tie these two on to the jeep and I'll see to their mate afterwards."

Barnes and I were placed on a stretcher apiece and the stretchers were then securely fastened on to the rack across the top of the jeep from front to rear. Before we set off, the Sergeant gave me a shot of morphine.

"That'll mebbe help you on the journey." I raised my hand in thanks.

The jeep sped off in the direction of Caen. Even with the blankets which were tucked well around us, it was a cold journey. My teeth chattered with the cold, but the cool air certainly soothed my hands somewhat.

"We've got to go straight through Caen," said the driver apologetically, "it'll be a bit bumpy so hang on."

Forewarned is supposed to be forearmed, but no one could have imagined the devastation which had been wrought on this fine old town. All roads were impassable, so two roads had been bulldozed at right angles across the rubble of streets and houses to enable some degree of access to and through the city centre. The jeep lurched from side to side as it negotiated the rough track and after a thorough shaking up we reached the comparatively smooth cobbled roads on the western outskirts. Where we went from there I know not, for I was past caring.

Base hospital was situated in a large field, where a number of large camouflaged marquees marked with red crosses on white backgrounds to denote their use, were pitched in neat and orderly fashion.

Removed from our rocky perch on top of the jeep, we were taken into a small marquee for documentation and to await the doctor for examination. An orderly brought in a most welcome cup of tea, and sat with us chatting about the events which had brought us to this hospital.

Barnsey did most of the talking, explaining how the mortar bomb had exploded about three feet away from the back of my head, just on the edge of the parapet.

"You were lucky, Westy, a good job you weren't holding the wireless set." He turned to the orderly and said, "We never heard it coming – no warning at all."

"Just like George's old sar'nt-major always said, you never hear the one that gets you," I said. Then in all innocence, I asked, "I wonder how little Monty is?"

Barnsey gave me a queer sideways glance. "You mean you don't know? He was killed outright."

"I thought he'd only got concussion. There wasn't a mark on him when we saw him on the stretcher," I said.

"I know, he must have been caught with the blast," he said quietly, "he never knew what got him."

The doctor arrived and quickly examined us both, spoke to the orderly and a VAD nurse cut off my torn and scorched battledress and put me on to a high metal stand, still lying on a canvas stretcher.

On looking round, I could see that I was the only occupant of this 60ft tent. Lying there all day with a large buff coloured label tied to my shirt collar, my only visitor was the male orderly who, in between my drowsy catnaps, brought further cups of tea.

When he asked if I was ready for the evening meal, I replied, "Yes – providing it isn't ruddy oxtail. They know what they can do with that!"

It turned out to be stewed steak and spuds, which was fed to me by a nice cheerful nurse, who cheekily remarked that she didn't mind feeding a big baby, but she wasn't going to change any nappies. Feeding finished, she looked at my label and said casually, "You're a lucky chap, won't be long before you see your wife again."

I must have looked puzzled as I asked what she meant by that.

"Your card is marked UK, so you'll be flying home tomorrow. You should have gone this afternoon, but there has been a hold up – no more planes today."

There had been a rumour that because of lack of space and supplies, anyone with wounds expected to take more than ten days to heal, would be flown back to the UK for treatment. I lay back and relaxed my head on the soft white pillow.

Sleep came very fitfully through the night. Heavy artillery in the vicinity, kept up a barrage from just after midnight and carried on well after dawn had broken.

"Tea in bed, M'Lord," called out the orderly as he breezed in about six o'clock.

"What's the weather like?" I asked, thinking about planes.

"Oh, it's a lovely morning, not a cloud in the sky — you'll be on your way soon after breakfast."

No sooner had I received my breakfast, forkful by forkful from the orderly, than I was carried out to a waiting ambulance, where I joined another lucky chap with a similar label dangling from his collar. After some minutes, we were taken out of the ambulance and carried across to another marquee as the ambulance sped away.

This time, no special personal service, as the large tent was filled with stretchers upon which were all ranks, with all sorts of bandages covering a multitude of wounds.

Someone stopped by my side and dropped a paper on my chest. A Sunday newspaper dated 6th August 1944. I racked my tired brain ... today was Sunday ... they were today's papers ... they could only have been brought in by plane. Oh, happy day.

A moaning individual with three pips on his shoulder, kept up a series of calls for the nurse, asking for all manner of silly, petty things for his comfort, until in sheer exasperation she blurted out, "Will you please stop making a nuisance of yourself, sir, I have others to attend to. After all you have only got a boil on your backside."

Everyone in the marquee roared with laughter and the red-faced Captain disappeared behind a copy of the *Sunday Pictorial*.

Shortly after midday a fleet of ambulances arrived and we were soon sorted out into flight numbers. I was to go on the first flight and so within minutes my stretcher was carefully placed in the ambulance along with three others and we were on our way to the airstrip.

The airstrip, consisting of wire mesh, similar to that used for reinforcing concrete, was laid out along a narrow strip bulldozed flat across a large meadow. A couple of American Dakota aircraft were on this tiny airfield, one waiting on the wire mesh and already being loaded up with stretchers. Most of us had received another shot of morphine to ease the pain during the flight and when all eighteen stretchers had been strapped on to the struts fitted to the inside bulkheads, another three chairs were brought in and screwed to the floor to enable three more walking cases to be flown home.

"Brace yourselves lads," called the RAF medical orderly, as the Dakota which only an hour or so before had brought in much needed supplies, started to taxi along the mesh on its take-off run. Bumpety-bumpety-bump-bump-bump, and then we were airborne. We turned in a wide circle and headed for the English Channel.

This was my first time in an aeroplane and I watched apprehensively as each wing waggled independently. It didn't look safe to me.

It didn't look safe to the chap sitting in one of the chairs either. He was making quite a commotion, calling out, "Me no like big flying bird —

me want get out."

At first we thought it was some comedian fooling around, but then as the orderly shouted to the navigator for help, we realized that this chap was a full blooded Canadian Indian, complete with tribal scars on his face, and he was terrified.

"Sit down, or I'll call the pilot," he commanded. We thought he was joking, until we saw the pilot emerge from the front of the aircraft.

"Never mind that silly bugger," said the bloke on the next stretcher to me, "get back into the driving seat, mate."

The pilot looked and winked as he said, reassuringly, "It's all right lads, I've put her on George, the automatic pilot." He walked up to the Canadian and looking him straight in the eyes said in mock seriousness, "Me pilot of heap big flying bird." He held out his arms to imitate a bird's wings. "If me no drive heap big flying bird, big flying bird crash in big heap."

The dark skinned Indian turned pale and sank back into the seat, wide mouthed, and with fear in his eyes. We never heard a whisper from him for the rest of the trip.

The pilot came out a little later to tell us that we were going to a higher ceiling to avoid incoming aircraft and would be crossing over the Cherbourg peninsula in the hope that we would also avoid contact with enemy planes.

We felt the plane soar higher and then through a side window I could see the Channel below, shimmering like a piece of crinkled silver paper in the afternoon sun. Turning as far as the retaining straps would allow, I watched as the coast of southern England came into view. Now the fields below us stood out with their distinctive colours like a patchwork quilt — differing green of meadows and crops interspersed with woods and copses, the golden yellows of cornfields, and the winding, thin, blue-grey ribbons of rivers and streams — and criss-crossing the whole fairytale picture were the brown, slate grey and black-coloured roads.

The fields became clearer and we could pick out houses and villages, then cattle and sheep grazing in the fields as we lost height almost imperceptibly.

"Prepare for landing," came the call over the intercom. We braced ourselves for the bump as we touched down. We were home again — I'd got my return ticket!

ELEVEN – BLEEDING HEROES

We landed at an RAF station near to Swindon in Wiltshire and were quickly taken from the aircraft and conveyed to the RAF hospital annexe. The Nissen huts were quite sparsely furnished, but everywhere smelled of cleanliness and disinfectants. There were no beds in the hut, but small brick pillars had been erected to support the stretchers and to bring them to a manageable height for the nursing staff. There was a little whisper that it was actually the mortuary which had been put to this new usage in order to cope with the ever mounting casualties being flown in. Perhaps this accounted for the austerity of the interior.

The warmth of greeting from the staff however, was very uplifting to us all. Cheerful WAAF nursing orderlies met each man as he was placed gently on to his appointed perch. Cigarettes were lit and passed to those who smoked, hot sweet tea in gleaming white pot mugs distributed to all.

The attention with which we were accorded would suggest that we were the first to have been received in this manner, but already more than 10,000 had been flown back from Normandy since the first airstrip was opened on D-Day plus 7.

It must have been a gruesome sight as the bandages were removed to reveal the various wounds on the tousle-headed exhausted men, unshaven after days of battle conditions. None of the nurses and orderlies batted an eyelid as they cut away dirty smelling clothes and commenced a tidying up operation of the new intake.

From my perch, about half-way down the line of stretchers on the right hand side, I watched with some amusement as a girl washed each patient, the large enamelled bowl being religously emptied after each wash and filled again with fresh hot water. She was washing hands and faces only.

For some reason or other, my bandages had not been removed and so, as the fellow next to me was dried, I said to the girl. "No need to change the water for me, love."

"Oh, you can't use someone else's water, it's not hygienic," was her reply as she hurried off to change the water.

"Now let's have those arms out of bed so that we can have a good wash," she said on her return.

I withdrew my arms from under the blanket to reveal that the bandages reached from above the elbows right down to the fingertips, nothing to wash there at all.

Letting out a merry peal of laughter, she held her hand in front of me, saying, "You were right, there wasn't much need to change the water, you've only left that much for me to wash," indicating with her finger her outstreched hand.

She soothingly dabbed the cotton wool swabs around my eyes and nose and mouth. Small though the surface area was, I found it to be very refreshing and found myself laughing at my thoughts as she went away to empty the fouled water.

She would have thrown her hands up in horror, if she had seen us just a few nights ago, a platoon of men washing and shaving in turn in an old biscuit tin using the same gallon and half of water, after skimming off the scum first.

Being a burns casualty I had been left until last for tidying up. A cute little brunette removed the grey blankets and eyed me up and down.

"Right young man, where shall we start?"

"Please yourself," I replied, "I'm all yours."

"I think we'll have these socks off for a start then. How long have you had them on?" she asked casually.

"About a fortnight," I said slowly, trying to recall.

"Good Lord! You should change socks every day," she said, carefully gripping the toe of one sock between her forefinger and thumb. She pulled the sock off to reveal a foot, thick with reddish brown grime and smelling to high heaven. Still holding the sock between finger and thumb, she carried it at arm's length to the waste container in the middle of the room. The action was repeated for the second sock.

Nose wrinkled in disgust at this scruffy individual who lay before her, she drew her scissors from her tunic pocket and looked at my cellular drawers, once white but now a yellowy reddish brown in colour.

"And how long have they been on?"

"Same as the socks," I replied.

A look of apprehension came into her eyes as she said, "I hesitate to think what I'm going to find under here."

Clipping away with her scissors, the cellular drawers were eventually removed, to reveal muddy rivulets in the creases of my groin. She shook her head as a blanket was pulled across my nether regions.

"You really are a filthy little boy," she said scoldingly. "I'll get one of the RAF orderlies to give you a good wash all over." And as she snipped away at my shirt and vest with the scissors, she said with a twinkle in her eyes, "You'd put my girls off their tea with that smell."

I felt so much better after the RAF lad had cleansed my dirty and smelly body. Dressed now in hospital pyjamas, I was ready for sleep. Acriflavin had been applied to my burns and nice clean soft bandages protected them from the weight of the coarse blankets. I lay with my arms at my sides and relaxed.

A hand shook my shoulder slightly. I awoke instantly. Surely it wasn't time for my 'stag' yet? . . . I'd only just come off . . . . I looked around me wondering where I was.

Beside me stood a smiling blonde, tall and adequately proportioned.

"Would you like a peach?" she asked kindly. I nodded.

A peach the size of a grapefruit was placed on my chest. The delicious smell from this delectable fruit as it sat on a saucer only inches from my nose, caused me to drool with expectation. I tried to raise myself on to my elbows, but my body wouldn't respond, the reaction was beginning to set in. I tried to lick my lips but my tongue wouldn't obey, so I lay there drooling into my bandages.

The blonde returned some minutes later, pausing at the bottom of the stretcher. She asked me whether I wanted the peach or not. I nodded in assent.

"Well, come along then, get up and start eating it."

"I can't . . . I can't get up," I heard this slurred voice say.

"Now come along," said the blonde, "you mustn't give in. Here, let me help you up."

She slid back the blankets to reveal the bandaged arms.

"Oh you poor boy . . . . Shall I feed it to you?"

Sitting on the side of the stretcher, she nestled my head between her soft breasts and fed that delicious peach to me, spoon by spoon, like a mother feeding her baby. In between the mouthfuls of the soft fruit, I asked from whence they had come.

"Some of the RAF lads have just flown in from North Africa and they have brought back fruit for those in hospital."

"That's very nice of them," I said.

"Just a small reward for our bleeding heroes," said my bosom friend. Then, when only the stone was left on the saucer, she mopped up the drool and juice from around my mouth and gently lowered me back on to my pillow, cheekily giving me a kiss on the nose as she said, "Now you can go back into your sweet little dreams."

The little RAF orderly returned shortly afterwards to see if anyone had letters to post. It was his day off really, he said, but because of the crash yesterday he thought that they might be short-handed, so he was doing an extra duty.

When asked about the crash, he replied, "That Dakota that crashed on the runway yesterday — you know, when all the nineteen Yanks were killed."

So that's why our flight had been cancelled last night! The sudden movement of my stretcher brought me to my senses.

"All right mate, we're just moving you all off to a Military hospital — taking you to the railway station now."

The two RAF lads sounded very reassuring as we were carried out to the waiting ambulances. Nurses and orderlies waved and called to us as we passed by. My little blonde nurse came across to me, stroked my hair and winked.

"You should be able to get your bit of sleep soon."

At the railway station, those dear, dear ladies of the WVS were quietly, almost surreptitiously, moving amongst the men on the platform. Kneeling beside each stretcher in turn, they were taking particulars of each man's next of kin. The home address of each man was written on an official buff coloured card marked OHMS, and on the reverse side, a list of prepared sentences about wounds, etc, were crossed out where inapplicable and the card was then signed by the soldier.

A dear old dowager parked herself on her camp stool by my side, placed her pince-nez firmly in place and asked in such a polite manner which sentences would I wish her to delete. She was kindness herself, as she bent down to hear my slurred answers to her questionnaire and was visibly moved when she helped me to sign my name at the bottom of the card.

This touch of human pity had the reverse effect on my wife later when she received the card. Knowing that the signature was not my handwriting, she promptly came to the assumption that my right arm had been shot off.

These stout ladies in their county tweeds, must have given hours and hours of service throughout that summer, with always a cheerful word to the tired men on the stretchers. Perhaps not always quite in touch with the reality of war, but all of them so delightfully English.

"Oh you are a lucky boy," said the lady in the trilby hat as she glanced at the address on my card. "This train, like the last one, is going to the General Hospital in Leicester. You will be near to home and your wife will be able to see you in a few days. Bye-bye my dear and good luck."

With that encouraging news, I was taken into the hospital train and stored on to a rack in one of the carriages and strapped in. Very soon the clickety-click of the moving train as it journeyed through the night, lulled me to sleep.

Once again the movement of my stretcher aroused me from my slumbers. Civilians were moving around in the carriage. The train was stopped, so I knew that we had reached our destination. I listened for the flat tones of the Leicester accent, awaiting the usual greeting of "Hello me old duck," so peculiar to the district.

When I heard the Welsh voice asking kindly about our journey, I thought it was just a case of an evacuated Welshman working at the London Road sidings in Leicester. More Welsh voices were heard as we were wheeled on trolleys along the platform. The station too, looked a little different.

"Where are we?" I asked at the first opportunity.

"You're in Swansea, boyo," said the dark haired porter cheerfully. "Don't look so disappointed, mon."

"But . . . we're supposed to be going to Leicester," I said.

"Well, they must have put the engine on the wrong way round, musn't they?" he joked, in that lovely lilting dialect of the south Wales valleys. "We'll look after you just as well at Morriston hospital as they would have done at Leicester." He was right of course, but I was about one hundred and eighty miles away from my wife Margaret, instead of the four or five as expected. I could have wept.

Strong hands guided the trolley along the passages of Morriston EMS Hospital towards No. 12 ward. I joined the rest of the patients at about 10 o'clock in the morning of Monday 7th August, and was placed in bed No. 22 of the 36 bed ward. Ah — bed at last. I could not remember just when the last time was that I had been in a real bed, but this was heaven. Hospital beds are not renowned for their comfort but compared to a trench dug into the shale of a Normandy field, it felt like a feather bed fit for a princess. I wouldn't complain even if there was a pea in the bed. A princess might, but not me. Beds were made to sleep in and I went into a sleep which lasted for two whole days.

An irate ward Sister was slapping my face to arouse me from my long sleep.

"Fusilier West! You are malingering! No one needs two days' sleep. You have had nothing to eat or drink for that time and the Doctor wants to examine you thoroughly — so stay awake."

"What time is it?" I asked the chap in the next bed.

"Six o'clock," came the reply.

"Six o'clock at night?" And then before he could answer, "What day is it?"

"It's six o'clock on Thursday morning, an' you'd better stay awake. The old Doc was mad as hell yesterday — said he'd put you on a charge today if you were still asleep."

I thanked him and dozed off again.

More shakings on the shoulder revealed a young soldier standing by my bed.

"Sure, yees got to keep yees eyes open," said the Irish voice urgently. "De ole quack's only one bed away an' if yees goes to sleep agin, sure yee'l be for the firing' squad." The Irish laddie stayed with me and kept up a steady chatter until the Doctor arrived.

"So — we've decided to wake up at last have we West?" said the Doctor sarcastically. "Now perhaps we can see what is the matter with you."

He examined the burn wounds, one or two of which were deep and showing the bone. Medical mumbo-jumbo was exchanged with the ward Sister and he moved on to the next bed. The ward Sister paused at the foot of my bed and checked the chart.

"Have you had your bowels opened since you came in here?" she barked out belligerently.

"No Sister," was my reply.

"How long is it since you did?" came the bark again.

"Dunno Sister — must be about two weeks now."

"What?" she snapped. "Two weeks? .... Sir," to the Doctor. The Doctor turned to face the unbelieving Sister.

"Sir, this man has not opened his bowels for two weeks."

"Is this true?" asked the medical officer.

"Yes sir. We were twelve days in the line, where it was not possible to move around, and we all got a little constipated."

He prodded my stomach with his fingertips. There was very little give under his pressure.

"You've got about a half hundredweight of concrete in there by the feel of it my lad. Urgent enema, Sister."

The old dragon gave me a withering look which left me in no doubt that I was not her star patient of the day.

Mid morning, a fresh faced young nurse checked the chart at the bottom of the bed.

"You the soap injection?" she asked laughingly.

"If you say so," was my reply.

Screens were pulled around my bed and stands and pipes and other apparatus, together with a number of containers were lined up in preparation.

"Had one of these before?" asked the nurse.

I shook my head in reply. "Well then, I don't know who's going to be more embarrassed, you or me," said the girl blushing slightly. She looked slightly younger than myself and obviously knew that we would shortly have to be in close intimate contact. Removing my pyjama pants, she turned me onto my side and inserted the rubber tube. "Raise your hand when you think you have got enough liquid inside you," she said understandingly.

I felt the hot liquid moving around and felt as though I was beginning to swell up. I held up my hand.

"You've not had more than half a pint yet," she laughed, "you'll need two pints at least."

Two pints? The mind boggled — I'd burst with all that amount. However the hot liquid kept flowing steadily until the lady was satisfied that enough had been injected to do the job. Meanwhile, my stomach rumbled and gurgled as I lay in waiting.

"Sounds like Joe Loss's orchestra playing a rhumba," said the Welsh nurse cheekily.

"Don't make me laugh, please — it hurts when I laugh. Ooh ... pass the bedpan, love," I pleaded, as wind began to break and the torment started.

I thought instantly of George and his similar predicament in the slit trench at Frenouville and was thankful that whatever happened this morning, a Lee Enfield Mk 3 bayonet would be surplus to requirement.

With musical and water accompaniment, three bedpans were duly filled in the next thirty to forty minutes. The screen had now become superfluous.

Everyone in the ward knew what was going on behind them, not only because of the wind ensemble, but the smell which by now permeated every corner of the ward. For the remainder of my time in ward 12 I was known as 'Stinker' West.

Meanwhile, for Nurse Jones and myself, there was no time for any more false modesty. The dear girl cleaned up the mess to myself and the bed without a murmur. Later, when she brought me a most welcome cup of tea, she asked me how I felt.

"Rather weak," I replied, then added, "I don't know what it's like to have a baby, but give or take an inch or two, it can't be much different to what I've just been through."

Now that I had caught up on my sleep and my disposal unit was working properly again, I was able to sit up and observe the activities taking place in the ward.

The little Irish laddie who had helped me to stay awake was known to all and sundry as 'Pat'. He was a member of the 6th Airborne and had been shot through the upper arm. This wound had left a hole large enough for a pencil to pass through. It was also possible to whistle through 'Pat's hole'. A competition was taking place to see who could play the most notes through the wound in his arm. In the lead was a gunner from the Royal Artillery, minus a leg, who had managed five notes.

The genial eighteen-year-old Pat, was also in charge of the bottles. Twice a day, we were required to give a sample of urine for examination and young Pat, being a walking case, did the necessary fetching and carrying. With his Irish sense of fair play, he always ensured that there was always a return from every man, even if it meant topping up an empty bottle from one with a more generous supply.

This mine of information gave me a run down on all the patients in the ward. There were, he said, twenty-nine men who had lost one or two limbs. All making good progress, except young Jock in the top bed and he was in a bad way. This nineteen-year-old Scot was a former soccer youth international and had lost both legs below the knee. He lived in a twilight world, between consciousness and coma. In his conscious moments, he was playing football again, shouting and screaming at his team mates.

Throughout all this, his parents sat by his bedside for days and nights, leaving it only to come to talk to others in the ward, giving reassurance to those in pain.

The spirit of the rest of the ward was one of almost carefree abandon. It was difficult to realize that these young men would be maimed for life. Perhaps the full truth had not yet sunk in, or perhaps we had all been geared to living from day to day and the hard fact that we were in hospital and alive, was all that mattered. They were certainly some of the most happy and cheerful people I ever met in the forces.

We were never allowed to become lonely or morose. Every hour of the day some calamity would occur, only for it to be turned into a hilarious riot by some comedian or other.

The highlight of the day was the remedial exercises class. At three o'clock each afternoon, a large, buxom wench of a WAAF PT Sergeant would enter the ward dressed in regulation PT jumper and shorts. The ward would be divided into leg cases and arm cases and the two sections would be detailed to undergo various redmedial muscle flexations to aid worn and torn limbs.

The leg cases provided the best fun of the day. They lay on their backs on top of their beds and solemnly moved their limbs in unison with the WAAF Sgt. who demonstrated from a space on the floor. Some bright spark would complain that he couldn't see the exercise properly and would ask her to get up onto the table to demonstrate more clearly. Every day she fell for this and would agree to the request, much to the delight of all the lads as they watched her athletic legs rise and fall in time with the music, whilst at the same time showing a glimpse of white knicker.

The session usually ended with an impromptu ventriloquist act by a lad who used the stump of a leg just below his knee, rather like a clenched fist would be moved by the wrist. He had a face drawn on his bandages and would carry on a hilarious repartee with this shattered limb.

For two more days I rose early and walked about the ward, helping Pat with his chores and then there was a clear out of all walking cases to make way for another intake of bed cases.

We were taken in a fleet of ambulances to a convalescent home on the other side of Swansea.

A large red bricked house stood in its own grounds about two hundred yards from the Swansea to Mumbles road. The grounds were, like most of their kind at that stage of the war, overgrown and unkempt through lack of gardeners' attention. The call to non-essential workers for more urgent war work had taken its toll.

The lady owner of Llwynderw, unable to run her large house without her usual staff, had retired to the lodge by the main gates and had offered her house for use by the military authorities.

All groundfloor rooms had been transformed into dormitories and filled with single metal army type beds. I was shown to the front room to the left of the front entrance.

The double bay windowed room held about eight beds, all neatly made up, with a steel locker between each bed. I took the bed in front of the main window and put what kit I had into the locker.

We were called to meet the Matron, a large pleasant lady of about forty, who welcomed us and read out the rules of the home. In her rich contralto voice she stressed that in no way were we to upset the owner of the property by behaving in an unruly or ungentlemanly manner. The son and heir had been serving with the Welsh Guards in the Italian campaign and was posted as missing believed killed. The Matron's concern for the lady's distress was quite understandable.

Our rehabilitation programme was centred around the garden. Paths and former flower beds were weeded and hoed. Those with arm or trunk defects would wield the hoe or rake, whilst those with leg defects would push wheelbarrows or cut the grass on the old croquet lawn with lawn mowers. Likewise, the tennis court was raked, watered and rolled each day prior to its use for play during the remainder of the day. I spent many happy hours rolling the red shale in the mornings and then playing numerous games with the PTI Sergeant or one of the nurses in the afternoons, struggling with the racket in both hands, unable to control it single-handed.

The old stables at the rear of the house had now been fitted out as a gymnasium. Nothing grand, just the usual wall racks, climbing ropes, etc., but there were basket ball stands, volley ball nets, table tennis tables and the floor marked out with a badminton court. Our Sergeant physical training instructor encouraged us to use these facilities to the full and was a great help, but a cruel streak in his nature was revealed by the long sessions of hard work with the medicine ball. Notwithstanding this, he was a good ally in our running battles with the officious Nursing Sister.

I first crossed swords with this dark haired spitfire on the occasion of my second visit to her for dressing treatment.

Looking at my hands she said icily, "At last, someone who wasn't running away."

I asked what she meant by this remark and was somewhat taken aback by the answer she gave.

"Almost everyone here has been wounded in the back. Head, shoulders, buttocks or the legs, but always in the back. Doesn't anyone ever face the enemy or do they all turn and run? No wonder we are not making much progress...."

I cut her short.

"You want to be careful what you are saying Sister. You don't go walking around when the mortars are flying about, when you are ordered to take cover, you take cover."

"Just like the rest of them aren't you?" she carried on. "Cowering under cover when you should be fighting."

I was getting annoyed with this silly woman.

"If that's what you think, why don't you go up to Swindon and get on the next Dakota going to Normandy? You might find out what war is all about then, instead of sheltering here in Wales behind your nurse's skirt."

The dark haired Sister turned on me like a viper as she spat out, "You insubordinate young man. I shall put you on a Matron's report — you will apologize."

"I'm sorry Sister, but I will not apologize. I think it is you who should apologize to those men out there," nodding in the direction of the garden.

The spitfire snorted and filled in a report to the Matron. Looking at my unbandaged hands she continued in her wrath.

"Who dressed these hands? You have been getting the wrong treatment, you should have been on acriflavin. Didn't you tell them, or didn't you want them to heal up?"

I decided to ignore the snide remark and left as soon as my treatment was finished.

On my return to the gym, I reported what had happened to the PTI who told me not to worry, as the Sister was going on leave that night and he would see that the report would never reach the Matron.

I had only been at Llwynderw for a day, when I was visited by a Mr Williams, a schoolmaster friend of Margaret's parents. He was on vacation with relatives in Chepstow and had offered to visit me on their behalf to find out more details of my incapacities.

I couldn't understand at first why he kept looking at my right hand so intently, but after a few probing questions, we both realized that my wife's fears about my bad handwriting were not substantiated and that apart from a badly slurred speech and a few burns, I would soon be back to normal. The visit of this kindly Welshman brought solace to me from my family for which I was sincerely thankful.

Kindness is the only word which describes the way in which the people of South Wales treated us during our stay in the principality. Everyone from schoolchildren to local dignitaries and mayors, went out of their way to make our rehabilitation as easy and as happy as possible. Our first encounter with the generous hospitality of these wonderful people was on the sands at Mumbles Point.

This local beauty spot was just a quarter of an hour's ride away from Blackpill on the Mumbles railway which ran from Swansea, along the wide sweep of Swansea bay, to almost the lifeboat station at Mumbles Point.

Miners and their families would make this trip at the weekends, to enjoy the fresh air and the chance to swim in the lovely bays which were within easy reach of everyone.

In our hospital blue trousers and jackets, white shirts and red ties, we were instantly recognized by the families as they cavorted about on the sands. With embarrassing repetition we were asked to join "Ma and Da" for tea. Ice-creams were pushed into our hands by children, saying, "My Da has sent this for you and says will you join us for a pot of tea. We're over there, see."

In all politeness, we would walk over to the parents and try to explain that we had already had tea and cakes three times, whereupon a packet of cigarettes would be pushed into our blue jacket pockets as compensation.

Everyone wanted to talk to these heroes in hospital blue. We talked of our families, of their families, of our home towns and about their towns and villages in the Rhondda Valley of which they spoke with great pride in those lovely undulating tones of the South Wales valleys.

One evening I sat with Glyn, a young Welsh tank crew man from the Welsh Guards, talking to an old miner who had a son serving with a Tank regiment in Normandy. He fired question after question to us, eager to find out what sort of conditions his son would be undergoing on the other side of the Channel. His questions were answered with candour, but couched in such a manner to allay any suspicion that his son was in any great danger.

Walking back along the sands towards the railway, I said to Glyn, "I think we just about convinced him that it isn't too dangerous over there and that we are only here because we've met with an unfortunate accident."

"No point in telling him what it's really like to be brewed up in a tank," said the tall slim tank gunner.

During the four weeks that I was in the convalescent home, our hosts on a number of occasions were the South Wales Bus Company. Each week their employees subscribed to a forces fund which financed the many trips which we were fortunate enough to enjoy.

The first memorable trip was on the first Wednesday of my stay and our destination was the holiday resort of Porthcawl where the pleasure park of Coney Island was quickly taken over by the lads in blue. Armed with a handful of free tickets, the 'Big Dipper' was loaded with men with arms and legs encased in plaster casts, arms in slings and everyone shouting and cheering as the train sped uphill and downhill along the track. A couple of trips on this and thence on to the 'Dodgem cars', where astonished civilians watched as men with no arms worked the pedals whilst men sans a leg steered the car around the circuit with lights flashing from the overhead contacts. Everywhere there was a great spirit of camaraderie as we indulged in our boyhood enthusiasm of all the fun of the fair. Stallholders joined in the fun too and we were given many free goes on the various stalls. By tea-time, I think everyone had a prize of some sort to take back to Blackpill as a souvenir.

The tea, also supplied by the bus employees, was quite a spread for those wartime days and it was a very happy band of soldiers who climbed into bed that night, not a little more bruised than when they had left earlier in the afternoon.

Our next outing was of quite a different nature. On this occasion the bus headed up the valley from Swansea towards the mining villages which snuggled tightly below the gaunt black coal tips which rose mountainously above them.

We were met at our destination by a small reception committee of which the local Minister was the head. Quickly we were whisked off to different houses to meet the inhabitants who vied with one another for the honour of entertaining us for an hour.

The Minister, a youngish man in his early thirties, then rounded up the able legged ones in our party for a walk around his parish. At one point, atop one of the higher tips, he pointed out the landmarks to us, giving a most enlightening insight into the ways and life of the valley communities.

On our descent we removed our jackets because of the heat, but the Minister kept his coat on for a long time before the heat overcame his modesty. When he removed his coat, we saw the reason for his reluctance. The white cuffs which showed below his coat sleeves, became detached, and left him with a short-sleeved shirt, the rest of the sleeve being used to make up false cuffs to enhance his sartorial elegance.

"Clothes rationing doesn't allow for too many new shirts," he explained apologetically. He declined the offer of one of our comedians to cut off his army shirt cuffs, who said that he always rolled his sleeves up anyway.

We returned to the houses for individual teas with bread and home-made jams, scones and cakes before assembling in the local chapel for the early evening's entertainment.

A platform with its serried steps, rather like the one we used to erect in our own Methodist church for the Sunday-school anniversary, had been erected at one end of the building and was soon filled by the local choir. We joined the rest of the villagers on the benches and chairs in the body of the hall.

From the first chord played on the piano, the massed choir sang at us, rather than to us for the next hour and a half. The augmented choir sang so lustily that I'm sure that they must have literally raised the roof of that old building. The singing was superbly conducted by the choirmaster who presented a most enjoyable repertoire of national songs. Sadly we had to leave these warm hearted people as soon as the concert was over, but another treat was yet in store for us.

On our return journey the bus pulled into a pub yard. Our friend, the Minister, had been pulling a few strings and had persuaded the regulars to forgo their usual pint of beer to enable mine host to offer each one of us a glass of beer.

"I'm sorry boys, we can only manage a half-pint apiece, but you are most welcome to that," said the Minister.

We replied that it was most generous of the locals to let us have their allocation and that we would be most honoured to accept.

Sitting in the garden at the rear of the pub beneath a rowan tree and watching the bees working away in the late summer sunshine, the war seemed a million miles away. The happy laughter coming from the wooden tables dotted around this small paddock echoed slightly across the valley as the air became still.

Morgan, who came from a village just in the next valley, had been joined by some of his old school mates and they began to sing, as it seems all Welshmen can, at any time of the day.

On this still evening they sang softly a number of Welsh ballads with great feeling and in beautiful harmony, with the words seemingly more poignant in their national tongue. For more than an hour we sat entranced as we listened to those young men as they celebrated the return of their prodigal son. All too soon it was time to say our goodbyes to our new found friends, for we had to be back at the home by 10.30 p.m.

On the way back, I mulled over the wonderful hospitality from these mining folk and couldn't help reflecting on that evening in Hull on D-Day when we couldn't even get a drink at any price. That was just eleven weeks ago today . . . only eleven weeks? It seemed half a lifetime ago.

For the first time I really thought about my old mate George and wondered how he was coping on his own. I closed my eyes as the bus rumbled along and could picture more clearly that cheeky face with the fag in the corner of the mouth and the 'battle bowler' on one side, summing it all up in the words of his 'old sar'nt-major':

"Arr, Ken lad, tonight you're a bleedin' hero. Eleven weeks ago you and me were just a bleedin' nuisance."

The third week's outing with the bus company was a circular tour of the Gower Peninsula, beautifully unspoilt and a haven for wildlife, an ornithological delight. I have always loved the outdoors and to hear the curlews on the wing is a memory that I treasure still.

I saw for the first time, the beautiful coastline of the Gower. From the long stretches of sandy beaches of Llanrhidian in the north to the delightfully differings bays of Rhossili, Port-Eynon and Oxwich in the south and west. Caswell Bay we had already discovered from the vantage point on Pwll-du-Head. Our afternoon excursion was completed by a visit to Oystermouth castle and the adjacent Roman site.

We also benefited from the kindness of other organizations. A most delightful Sunday was spent with the owners of a number of private chalets above the Langlands Bay.

Glyn and I were the guests of a French lady and her escort who entertained us in the manner royal. Glyn, and John, the hostess's friend, had an enjoyable hour swimming in the calm sea, whilst Yvette and I talked of France and in particular of Normandy.

On return from their swim, the two men dressed and then we found to our surprise that John was a Captain in the Royal Artillery, but rank was of no consequence as we enjoyed the respite in the glorious August sunshine. Sitting on the veranda, we sampled the delights of Yvette's strawberries and her scrumptious home-made cakes.

On Saturday 19th of August we were the honoured guests of the Glamorgan County Cricket Club when they played a representative team from the National Fire Services at the famous St. Helen's ground in Swansea. We were presented to the players by the captain of Glamorgan, J. C. Clay, and I met two of my schoolday heroes in Wilfred Wooller the dual international and Cyril Smart their famous wicket keeper.

As the match progressed, we sat in the members' pavilion overlooking not only the cricket and Rugby union ground, but also the Mumbles railway which ran along the shore side of the main road. In the background, naval vessels and other ships made their way across Swansea Bay towards the docks to our left.

Not to be outdone, the proprietors of the Swansea Empire Theatre invited us to the Wednesday matinée of their current show 'Hit the Sky', starring the well-known comedian George Doonan, together with Freddy Frinton and partner, Sylvia Kellaway, and Doreen Dawne. This outing on the 30th of the month was the last one that I was destined to attend. My wounds were now healing very quickly and I was extremely pleased to hear that if the progress continued, I would soon be on my way home for a spot of sick leave.

The month of September commenced with the good news that my leave had been confirmed, so it would be goodbye to all those great guys who had shared the laughter and the tribulations of our early rehabilitation.

On the fifth of the month, Glyn and I would be off on leave and thence to our respective depots, whilst a number of others would be continuing their rehabilitation at Trentham in Staffordshire. Amongst them would be our Polish friend Jan, a dour character with a badly scarred chest and shoulders. After escaping from his native land, Jan had made his way through the low countries to Britain and had joined the Polish Division. Along with many others, he had been wounded by erratic bombing by the Americans when the Polish Div. had been mistaken for the enemy to the south of Caen.

Bill, the paratrooper Sergeant with the broken back who, despite the Coney Island dodgems and the Big Dipper, had made miraculous recovery, would, he said, be keeping an eye on Frank the rifleman from the North Staffs Regt who had been the scourge of the nursing staff at Llwynderw. The genial lad from the potteries had been caught by a piece of shrapnel which had almost severed his penis from the underside. With delicate stitching and fortified with bromide, he would reach the point of almost having the stitches removed and then by his amorous advances to a member of the fair sex, he would get over-excited and ping would go his stitches again, much to the consternation of the nurses.

Frank, seemingly nonplussed by the repetition of events, always laughingly informed all and sundry, that he was unique in that he was probably the only private soldier in Normandy who had received the distinction of almost getting his DSO.

A small farewell drink was made possible by the friendly landlord of the local hostelry. Despite the fact that only two half-pints of beer were permissible, we were in good voice as befitted our stay in the land of song.

We parted, never to meet again.

TWELVE – THE CHARM O' THE CHANTER

It was with regret that I handed in my hospital blues in exchange for the regulation khaki battledress. Not only was the royal blue suit the best fitting one ever issued to me in the army but the soft cotton white shirt with the collar attached was by far the most comfortable shirt to be worn by other ranks in the Second World War.

Suitably dressed in my new BD, I proceeded on leave to Leicester where I spent a most happy seven days before journeying north by rail via Derby and Northallerton to the city of Edinburgh. The long slow journey was only slightly relieved from Berwick-on-Tweed onwards, by two of our American comrades in arms who insisted that another lad and myself should join the two USAAF fighter pilots in their first class compartment to consolidate the Anglo-American alliance by emptying a bottle of malt whisky between us.

Emerging from Waverley station RTO on to the famous Princes Street, I boarded a tram which would, I was assured, deposit me at the Redford Barracks. The rickety old tram lurched its way along the wide street as it passed the Sir Walter Scott monument and the Castle high on the hill overlooking the old city itself.

On arrival at the barracks, I reported to the guardroom. The time now must have been getting on for midnight, but I was greeted quite cheerfully by the guard commander and shown where to get my bed and blankets for the night.

"Blankets and bedding, please," I said to the Colour-Sergeant.

Promptly, three planks ten inches wide by one inch thick by six feet long were laid on to the counter of the stores, to be followed by two wedge shaped blocks of wood and three grey woollen army blankets.

I must have looked at this array of kit with some disbelief.

"What's the matter laddie, do ye no ken how tae mak' up an army bed?" said the CQMS enquiringly.

"Don't I get a hammer and nails?" I asked jokingly.

"If ye put one block at the head and the other at the foot, then place the planks between them, ye'll sleep like a wee bairn," he said with a knowing wink.

I carried the planks to the barrack room and did as suggested and returned for the blankets and the rest of my kit. Folding the first blanket into three as a base and wrapping the other two around me, I found the bed to be surprisingly comfortable and with my big pack as a pillow, soon slipped off into a welcome sleep.

Reveille was announced at 6.30 a.m. by the Orderly Sergeant banging on the table with a pickaxe handle. Not yet used to this type of military alarm clock, I awoke with a start, to find to my horror that a most important part of my person had become trapped between the ten inch planking as I turned on my side. My mind flashed back to Frank. A cool head was needed at this moment. One quick movement in the wrong direction and I could be maimed for life.

Realizing that an equal distribution of weight on the planks would act like a guillotine, I decided that all my weight must be placed on the centre plank. This being done, I was then able to withdraw myself from my predicament, at the same time resolving always to go to bed in future with my cellular drawers worn back to front.

In the dining-room at breakfast time came another jar to my recent life-style. The Orderly-Sergeant stood inside the doorway calling to all who passed, "Real porridge tae the right .... sassenachs tae the left," intimating that those who went to the right would receive the salty flavoured Scots oats, whilst those to the left would receive the sweetened porridge. I went to the right.

During the course of the day, I was issued with the remainder of the kit necessary to bring me up to FSMO and issued with a rifle, not so much for the defence of our fair isles, but for the purpose of partaking in the foot and arms drill parades twice daily.

These drill parades were exceptionally lax, compared with those of John the 'B' in Normandy, but we had the fun of witnessing the drilling of the officers. On these parades, the drill-sergeants would shout and yawp terrible oaths as the officers made mistakes, then at the end of the session would have to ask permission from the senior officer on parade for 'permission to dismiss'.

Due to the large increase of personnel passing through the barracks, extra sleeping quarters were needed and so I found myself shunted into a bell tent on the edge of the sports field. No effort was being spared to harden us off. In the army you were either unfit or you were fit, there being no in between period of readjustment. There was, however a place in the training itinerary for ABCA (Army Bureau of Current Affairs) through which we were kept informed of what was going on in other parts of the world.

The ABCA sessions at Redford Barracks were conducted by a Sergeant who had recently returned from the Italian campaign and so he thought that we should get to know a little more about Italian Opera. The sessions usually ended with him leading the singing of 'Santa Lucia' and the forces' favourite at that time, 'Mama' in the Italian language.

There was a sense of urgency in the air quite early on Saturday morning of the 16th September. Lists of names were pinned to the notice-board requiring those personnel to report for prisoner of war escort duty at 10.00 hrs. Amongst the many names I spotted my own and, wondering what it was all about, duly reported at the appointed time.

We were to escort over a thousand German prisoners from the POW camp at Crieff to Greenock on the River Clyde and would be away for about three days.

Leaving 'Ould Reekie' (Edinburgh) by train, we headed north towards the lovely hills of Perthshire, purple now with the heather in flower in the early autumn sunshine and looking every bit as colourful as the picture postcards in my father's photo album. We left the train at Crieff and embussed on the TCVs for the short journey to nearby Comrie.

Even as we approached the POW camp, one could feel the atmosphere, it was electric. One had the feeling of sitting on a tinder box. The guards were very apprehensive and extremely cautious. In the dining hall, the CO of the camp explained the situation to us.

Within the camp was a large number of young SS and vociferous Nazis who had virtually taken over the running of the discipline within the German ranks. Kangaroo courts had been held and a number of victims had been found hanging in the ablutions block, apparent suicides. There were also fears of a mass break-out. This was to be nipped in the bud by shipping the majority of those in the camp over to Canada. On the Sunday morning we were to escort them to Crieff station and thence by rail via Glasgow to the port of Greenock. We were to be issued with ten rounds of ammunition as a precaution, but no one was to open fire unless the order was given by the officer i/c party.

As we dispersed to our huts, we could hear the uproar from within the barbed wire compound as the deep baying voices sang out their songs of hate. During the night we were on fifty per cent alert.

The singing and noise continued as the POWs assembled inside the compound on the next morning. The order came for us to load rifles and fix bayonets and then the gates were opened and the Germans marched through in fours in perfect step as they sang the 'Horst Wessel'. These trucculent Nazis, most of whom could only be in their teens, reminded me of the fanatical young snipers in Normandy who had strapped themselves to the pom-pom trees in a desperate attempt to stop our advance.

Marching along the country roads, the sound of their singing echoed amongst the surrounding hills. Some of the songs were indeed quite harmoniously sung, but always the fanatics amongst them would revert to the hate songs against England.

Once aboard the train, the doors were locked and we were ordered four to a carriage, two at each end of the central corridor. Instructions were also given that we must not talk to the prisoners.

During the journey we were continually taunted and cursed by the occupants, both in German and in fluent English. The singing had by now subsided, it seemed that they sang better when they were standing up or marching about. Sitting in the LMS coaches seemed to cramp their style. One of them, sitting by the doorway, carried on a one-way conversation with me for practically the whole of the journey. He was about my age and said that he came from Mannheim and kept repeating his address, saying that when we got to his town, could we inform his parents that he had been well treated and hoped to return, but he was quite apprehensive about surviving the war with this band of desperados.

Not wishing to be a soft touch, I let it go in one ear and out of the other, but I often wished in later years that I had remembered the address.

The journey took us through the appalling slums of Glasgow, something which was quickly seized upon by one of the SS.

"Your RAF bomb our beautiful cities and yet you allow these miserable apartments to exist. When we have won the war we shall blow up these places and rebuild new apartments in their place."

No one answered him.

At the docks, more soldiers were assembled to escort the prisoners on to ferries which would transfer them on to the *Nieuw Amsterdam* moored in midstream.

Our ferry edged towards the side of this huge ship, at that time the sixth largest liner in the world. From the water level the top deck of the Dutch liner seemed to be hundreds of feet above us. Sailors from above, tipped their garbage and slops on to the despised men below, abuse was also hurled in both German and Dutch. Unfortunately, we also collected some of the thrown matter, but those up above did not let a small thing like that deter them.

On the dockside, we were ushered into a warehouse which had quickly been transformed into a temporary transit camp. There we were able to have a shower and change of clothing where necessary.

After a most welcome meal, we were allowed out into Greenock, where we joined the local inhabitants as they celebrated the switching on of the lights for the first time since the war had begun. One of the most popular wartime songs was, 'When the lights go on again, all over the world' and went on to list the sort of things we would do on that day. Well here we were in Scotland witnessing that very occasion.

The whole town went mad. Blackouts were now a thing of the past as all available lights were switched on. We danced along the streets arm in arm with the girls and their mums as we sang all the Scottish songs, danced jigs and flung the Highland Fling as far as we could fling it. Everyone was happy and although it was past midnight when we got to the transit camp, no one cared. After all, the lights go on again all over the world only once in one's lifetime.

One of the so called joys of serving in His Majesty's Forces was the element of surprise which lurked around the corner and which popped up at the most unexpected times.

None of these returning from Greenock were prepared for the notice on company orders announcing the names of a draft for the 1st Battalion the Liverpool Scottish, stationed at Banbridge in County Down, Northern Ireland.

I could hardly believe it, but there it was: 14638023 Fusilier West K.J. ...I was on my way again, less than twelve hours after returning to Edinburgh. No more ABCA sessions on the sports field. It was 'arriverderci Santa Lucia'.

The quayside at Stranraer was lashed by high winds and heavy showers of rain, hardly the best of conditions in which to start a sea journey to Larne. Most of the older ports of the British Isles are filled with grey stone buildings with slate roofs, quite quaint and pleasant to the holiday-maker in the height of summer, but utterly dismal and depressing when lashed by half a gale on a wartime autumn day. Stranraer was very little different from any other port in this respect.

The relatively calm passage as we made our way north out of Loch Ryan, lulled us into a false sense of security. It was not until we had turned the headland that we met the full force of the fury of the northern part of the Irish Sea.

All decks were placed out of bounds and the hundreds of servicemen packed together in the confined spaces below decks were soon victims of sea-sickness. So bad were the conditions that about half of the crew and about ninety per cent of the passengers were laid low. Those of us who were not affected by the storm were quickly allotted specific duties to perform in case of emergency.

Crewmen said that it was the worst crossing they had ever experienced and I can well understand that, as the ferry was tossed around all night as if it were no more than a small fishing smack.

It was a rather subdued party of men who reached the pretty little town of Banbridge as it nestled astride the babbling river Bann.

The hutted camp on the outskirts of the town was now the home of the hitherto unknown battalion of the Liverpool Scottish. A pre-war Territorial unit, they had been on duty in Gibraltar for the duration of the war so far and had only recently returned to the UK to act as a training battalion. Like most old 'Terriers' they were a happy crowd and very easy to get along with.

The first two weeks were spent recapping on weapons and field craft, both of which gave rise to a number of hilarious situations.

Instruction was being given on the PIAT, an anti-tank weapon used by the infantry and quite evidently, never fired in anger by the Sergeant-instructor.

"When using this weapon, you first of all dig a pit," he said, repeating verbally from the training manual.

"You don't have time to dig a pit, Sarge," said one of our lads.

"You certainly can't fire this weapon without bracing yourself against the side of a pit," replied the Sergeant, emphatically.

"Nonsense," I said, "you fire them from whatever cover you can find — they reckon some of the paras and the commandos fire them from the hip."

"OK wise guy, let's see how you Fusiliers can fire this one, just lying on the ground." He pointed to the silhouette of a small tank made from old boiler-plate at a distance of about fifty yards, suspended from an angle-iron frame by wires.

Placing the butt between my feet, I pulled on the barrel as hard as I could and felt the mechanism click into place as I twisted the barrel in a clockwise direction. A difficult operation this for someone of my size. One either successfully cocked the Piat, or came periously near to getting a hernia in the process.

The practice shot was placed in the weapon and I lay on the wet ground. The sloping ground was in my favour, so I fired quickly at the target. I felt something akin to the kick of a mule on my right shoulder and was promptly propelled rearwards for some ten yards along the sodden turf of the Mountains of Mourne. A huge cheer went up. I had hit the target and to the delight of all the lads, it was lying flat on the ground. I was not only delighted, I was flabbergasted — and my right shoulder was sore for a week. Fortunately, I was not called upon again to attempt any other feats of skill, perhaps as well, for my luck might not be in next time.

Meanwhile, the war in Europe was still going on. Latest reports gave the news that northern France and most of Belgium had now been liberated and a grand scale airborne operation was in progress in Holland at a place called Arnhem. Bridges were to be captured in a daring advance, but around Arnhem things had become rather bogged down. We listened each night to the radio for the latest news from war correspondant Stanley Maxted who was with the airborne forces. The main bridge at Arnham had been captured and we celebrated in the forces canteen in Banbridge.

Then came the news that it was all over. The main forces of the British 2nd Army could not link up with the paras, they were stopped just six miles south of the bridge. The brave airborne men had to withdraw, leaving behind some three-quarters of their complement of 10,000 men as casualties. It looked as though the carefree gallop through the low countries had come to an abrupt stop and now winter was on its way.

For the last four weeks of my stay with the Liverpool Scottish, I recommenced my old job as signaller. This meant that I was billeted with the HQ Company, and the only bed space available was with the band section, namely the pipers and the trainee pipers.

I have always been an ardent admirer of the bagpipes, whether played as a solo instrument or as a complete marching band. The resonant tones of the drones give a wonderful depth of harmony to the mood of the music played on the chanter, as the nimble fingers change from the solemn laments to the strathspeys and jigs which set the feet a-tapping.

To become a proficient piper takes months of patient practice and dedication and I must admit that the continuous and repetitive scales as those teenagers practised their dexterity on the chanters at every conceivable opportunity, taxed one's patience to the full. I tried my hand on one or two occasions, but I'm afraid my efforts were not a howling success. However I did come to recognize many of the tunes, not least of all the march we used at the CO's parade every Saturday. The tune we knew then as 'The Liverpool Sands', became very well known many years later, as the theme tune to the television programme 'Z' Cars.

Our hardening up process gathered momentum with regular route marches in full kit and usually in pouring rain, in fact out of almost six weeks in County Down, only on two days did it not rain. Looking towards where the Mountains of Mourne stood shrouded by thick clouds and heavy drizzle, the usual greeting at breakfast time was, "Another fine soft morning up in the mountains."

The route marches seldom passed without incident. Passing by the potato fields, one was kept on one's toes by the hail of missiles thrown at us by the women workers. Sods of earth, stones rotten potatoes and a continuous stream of obscene abuse came over the hedges. We would return to our billets slightly wiser young men, to be entertained until lights out, by the charm of the chanters. Although my love of bagpipes hasn't diminished, I have been put off snake charmers for life.

'Night Ops' are usually light-hearted manoeuvres carried out after dark. Their object is serious enough, but so many things can and do go wrong, as objects and landmarks develop a new dimension after sunset.

One of our last 'night ops' was to have been based on finding our way round a circular route using stars and a compass for guidance. Inclement weather ruled out the former, so we reverted to map and compass. Two teams set out in opposite directions, with instructions to avoid contact or detection by the other team and the first team back to base would be judged to be the winners.

We were about a mile from our base by road when we thought we should try a short cut across the fields. Quickly crossing a few fields, we could see our camp just three fields away. A barbed wire fence stopped us in our tracks. After a quick look, I decided it would be quite an easy task to jump over the low fence and the ditch beyond.

Taking a good run, I cleared the fence and the ditch easily only to find myself sinking to my knees in a bog. My first thoughts were of panic as I tried to pull each leg free, only to find myself sinking slightly. My second thought was to stop wriggling about and not to panic.

"Don't jump," I shouted, "I'm stuck in a bog — fasten your rifle slings together and throw me a line."

This was done and I fastened my own sling around my waist and called for them to pull. Slowly I was extricated and splashed back through the ditch and over the barbed wire. There was nothing to do but to retrace our steps and we returned to base a very poor second.

In order not to disturb too many people unnecessarily, we were to use a hut near to the ablutions and to sleep in our kit. When we entered the hut, I was quickly kicked out. The smell from the slime and rotting vegetation in the bog was terrible and as I was pretty well covered from head to foot with the stuff, there was only one thing to do. I stripped completely and one of the lads emptied bucket after bucket of freezing cold water over me in order to sluice away the evil smelling slime. Even so, I was banished to the furthest bed. No one wanted to know the stinking little Scots Fusilier.

There was very little entertainment locally, but we did attend a show in the town one night. Top of the bill was Jack Doyle and his beautiful wife Movita.

Doyle, a former Irish Guardsman, had also been a notable boxer and had fought for the British heavyweight title. Well built and extremely good looking, he had retired from the boxing ring and was now an entertainer. His soft tenor voice, coupled with good looks and well-known Irish blarney, had made him into quite a personality and by his act that night in Banbridge, he thoroughly enjoyed his popularity.

He could charm the birds from the trees with his blarney and to see the ladies, young and old alike clamouring for tickets as he raffled off a signed pound note at one shilling (5p) per ticket, one wondered just how gullible people could be. He made an easy ten pounds from his one pound stake.

His act was quite enjoyable, but the eyes of most of the squaddies were centred on his beautiful film star wife Movita, a real South American dark haired beauty.

On the 27th of October, we said goodbye to the damp emerald isles. No more locking up our rifles when not in use, no more aggro from the fields and no more bogs to fall into.

Physically hardened in body, wounds healed over, though still a little sore, we returned home for fourteen days' embarkation leave. Then for me, it would be back to rejoin the Fusiliers, wherever they may be.

THIRTEEN – 'ROSIE'

The London train pulled slowly away from number three platform of Leicester station. Amongst the people standing on the platform was my wife Margaret, her shoulder length blonde hair showing up clearly in contrast to the WLA greatcoat.

Leaning out of the carriage window, I waved to her until as a small speck, but still waving in return, she disappeared as the train jerked its way round the bend in the line.

There had not been any tears in our goodbye. Separations had become a way of life to army personnel and their loved ones. Each knew that this could be the last goodbye, but it was never mentioned. For all young lovers, hope springs eternally.

My embarkation leave expired at 23.00 hours on the ninth of November at Victoria Station, London. Military police were there to see that it did. Redcaps marshalled the motley crowd of men into various pens formed by metal barriers. From there we were detailed to special trains awaiting at other platforms. We dozed until the train moved out in the early hours of Friday morning.

We arrived at the town of Newhaven at about eight in the morning and were promptly taken by TCVs to a former girls' school on the outskirts of Seaford.

The old building with its oak panelled halls and staircases was full of character; with its creaking stairs and brass knobbed doors, it remained one of a perfect setting for a St. Trinians film. But now the gym-slipped girls, with their jolly hockey sticks, were replaced by soldiers with their studded boots which echoed throughout the old building.

After roll call on Saturday morning, we found time to walk along the sea front. Almost every one of the pre-war guest houses and hotels along the front were damaged by mines which had drifted in on gale force winds and had exploded on the sea wall, thereby causing damage by blast.

When we assembled on the former hockey pitch on Sunday morning for roll call, we were informed that we would be embarking that night at Newhaven and would be landing somewhere in France the following morning.

"You will not be told at which port you will arrive in case the ship is sunk. We don't want any survivors telling a Jerry U-boat captain which ports we are using," said the duty officer.

An hour later we attended the morning service in the main hall and I think we all expected the hymn 'Eternal father, strong to save' to be sung in order to ensure our safe passage across the English Channel. However it was 'Onward Christian Soldiers' and 'Praise my soul' which echoed around the panelled hall.

Sunday dinner was a rather prolonged meal. We were savouring our last meal in this warm, homely old house.

To while away the time in the afternoon, a game of football was arranged and soon a full blooded match was taking place on the hockey pitch. I teamed up with a young Scots laddie from Edinburgh. Jimmy 'Bing' Crosbie was on his way to rejoin the KOSB (Kings Own Scottish Border Regt) in the famous 50th Div. This slightly built lad with a pigeon-toed walk, was quite a good inside forward and we blended well together on the left wing. We quickly developed a good rapport and became good mates.

All too soon, we were on the TCVs as they whined along the coastal road to the port of Newhaven. The ship was tied up at the far end of the groyne leading from the harbour. As we commenced our walk along this three-quarter mile long breakwater, sirens sounded the air raid alert. Within minutes the ack-ack guns were firing at the solitary raider as he made his run inland some way down the coast from us. Feeling rather exposed on the narrow walkway, it was with some relief that we boarded the ship.

I settled down for my second crossing of the Channel.

It was later that evening that we eased our way slowly into the port of Dieppe, too dark to see much of the damage wrought by the Canadian Army's raid of almost two years before. We disembarked on to the quayside under the shadow of the cliffs, with the old fishermen's church high on the cliff top, standing out in black silhouette against the patch of clear sky.

Crossing the swing-bridge leading to the inner harbour, we made our way along the dockside to waiting TCVs.

Once aboard, we moved off in a convoy towards the transit camp. After a bumpy, jolting and very uncomfortable ride of some two and a half hours, we entered a town and the vehicles pulled to a stop.

"We're in Amiens," said the Sergrant in charge of the convoy, "better get out and stretch your legs whilst I find out where the transit camp is."

I looked out of the back flap to find that we were in a cobbled square in front of a cathedral. I took one look at the odd shaped front with the tall spire at the right hand corner.

"This isn't Amiens, Sarge, it's Rouen," I said.

"No it's not, sunny boy, it's Amiens," retorted the NCO.

"In that case, what's Rouen cathedral doing in the middle of Amiens?" I said sarcastically.

"Don't be smart sonny boy, do you think I can't read a ruddy map?"

"Better check with the Town Major's office over there, Sarge," I said, as we relieved ourselves against the rear wheels of the lorry. It was cold as we stood there amidst the appalling damage scattered around the square. Masonry and debris had been bulldozed away to enable some sort of passage along the roads. One half of the cathedral appeared to have been bombed into rubble.

Only a few days before, I had been looking at postcards of this once beautiful church during my last visit to my parents' home. Dad must be told of this in my next letter to them.

The Sergeant and the driver returned from the Town Major's.

"How the bloody hell did you recognize this place as Rouen, in the black-out at two in the morning?" he asked. "You must have been here before, in 1940."

"Nae, Sarge, his faither's got a wee photie o' yon cathedral in his postcard album," said young Bing.

The distance from Dieppe to Amiens is about 65 miles and the distance from Rouen to Amiens is perhaps, slightly more, so it didn't need a mathematical genius to work out that we still had about another four hours' travel to endure, that is if the Sergeant didn't take any more wrong turns.

Despite the patched paved roads, I slept most of the way, lulled to sleep by the drumming of the lorry's tyres on the bricked roads as we made our way north-east from Rouen. I was awakened by a shout from the Sergeant.

"Ask that bloke from Thomas Cook's to come and check whether this IS Amiens or not."

I could sense by the tone in his voice that he knew where he was, so I shouted back, "I'll take your word for it this time, Sarge."

"Only a few more miles now lads and we'll be at the transit camp in time for breakfast," said the NCO cheerily.

The transit camp was in a small town by the name of Corbie, although untouched by the present campaign, it still bore the scars of the 1940 blitzkrieg by the Germans.

We were billeted in a school, where the classrooms had been transformed into dormitories by simply bringing in ex German Army wooden two tier bunks. Very spartan, but much better than the tents in which some of the others were billeted. The dining hall was just a marquee, the path to which was simply wooden duck-boards laid on top of the squelchy mud.

At the end of our breakfast meal, the scraps of bacon rind and left-overs of porridge were scraped into pig-bins. Around each bin hovered five or six French children. As our scraps were deposited into the bins, eager young hands would be plunged into the swill. Scraps of food would then be put into any container they could find in order to augment their almost non-existent rations.

This was the first time that any of us had witnessed hunger on this scale and to see children fighting like wild animals for scraps of food was most sobering. Bing and I made sure from then that all our scraps would go direct to the kids, but I don't think we enjoyed a meal at any time that we were there, not with those half starved faces watching us eat.

Our three day sojourn in this small French town did have its compensations. Bypassed by the retreating Boche and well to the rear by now, life had returned to something like normal. Three-piece bands, comprising drummer, accordionist, with either saxophone or violin to augment them, played in the cafés around the town centre.

A hall, something like the size of an English village hall, had been commandeered for use by the YMCA as a canteen. To make the forces feel at home, posters from different towns in the UK were hung in the entrance. One, with a knitting machine on it, proclaimed that Leicester was the most prosperous city in Europe in 1938. I warmed to the place straight away.

Bing and I spent a few happy hours in there, partaking of the odd 'char and wad' from time to time as we listened to the trio playing the now familiar tunes of 'J'attendre', 'La vie en Rose' and 'the Bridges of Paris'. There was also a small room set aside for those wishing to write letters or to sit and read. In a letter to my dad, I mentioned that I'd passed through Rouen and knew that I would be taken to task for not going for a look round the cathedral. Somehow my father never could quite appreciate the way of life in the army.

The next move in a northerly direction was preceded by returning south to Amiens railway station. Here we boarded a train and encountered a mode of transport well known to the men of the First World War, namely the large goods wagons of the French SNCF. These large wooden wagons, as the notice stencilled on the sides stated, were used to transport 8 Chevaux or 40 Hommes. Entry and exit was by the large sliding door on either side. Ventilation meant leaving the sliding door ajar, though in inclement weather the door needed to be shut, otherwise one third of the floor area would be drenched by the rainwater from the curved roof as it was blown in by the movement of the train. If you were one of the 40 hommes at that end of the wagon, you could have a most uncomfortable journey.

Calls of nature were attended to either by facing, or turning one's back on the passing landscape depending on your special requirement. In the latter case, friendly hands would hold your arms to enable the function to be carried out, preferably on the leeward side.

I suppose it was only fitting that we should use these old first war wagons as we followed the path taken by the fathers of many of us, through Arras, Bethune, Armentierres, Lille, Roubaix and all the other old Flanders townships on our way to the old Belgian town of Ghent.

Sitting in the dining hall of this new transit camp, I looked round and saw an old familiar face at the next table. It was Sid Hesketh, an old mate of Paddy's from the Royal Irish Fusiliers who had been one of the gang of reinforcements to join the RSF with me.

"Hoora doin', me old Hesky," I called.

"Sure it is you yourself, so it is," came the reply.

"On your way back too?" I asked.

"No, I'm on the staff here. I got hit in the leg and I'm waiting for down grading — it's a bit too rough up there for us old men over thirty," he chuckled.

"Seen any of the other lads?" I enquired. Then before he could answer, "What have they been up to since I've been away?"

Mess tins and mugs were pushed to one side as Hesky described how on the day following me 'copping a Blighty', the Battalion had put in an attack which had precipitated the breakout from the Caen pocket which carried them on towards the River Seine. There followed a 36-hour battle for the port of Le Havre. After the Canadians had liberated the town of Dieppe to a tumultuous reception, the RSF retired to a chateau at Luneray for a three day rest.

From there, orders were to 'advance to contact' as the 2nd Canadian Army swept through northern France and Belgium where contact was made at Dendermonde briefly and thence to Turnhout, north of Antwerp, where the regrouped Germans began to give more stern opposition. The RSF had taken part in the capture of Roosendaal and then moved across to the Venlo sector and now was somewhere in the Nijmegen area.

This was the first news I had heard of the Battalion since the beginning of August and as I was returning to my unit under the 'Monty plan', I was thirsty for a bit of news.

General Montgomery had found during the desert campaign that if men who had been in hospital were returned to their own units, wherever they may be, it was far better for the men and also very good for the morale of the unit to have people they knew returning to them, rather than unknown reinforcements, as had been the normal procedure during the 1914-18 war and for the early part of this war. I suppose this is why 'Monty' was so popular with the lower ranks. He took a common sense attitude to men's well-being which had been rather lacking with some of the former 'brass hats'.

Walks along the network of old canals was about the only excitement to come our way whilst we were in this old inland port. There seemed to be a lot of troop movements, with convoys of vehicles continually passing through the town centre. We were not surprised therefore to find ourselves on the move within 48 hours.

"Although we are fully paid up members of the King George VI travelling club, we never seem to be informed of the destination of our next excursion," said Bing as we set off next morning once more in the ever faithful TCVs.

"When you pays your money for a mystery tour, it spoils the whole day if you know where you're going," I replied. "Sit back and enjoy the scenery."

The miles of flat uninteresting Belgian landscape rolled away as far as the eye could see. Old men and women stoically husbanded their narrow strips of smallholdings, their faded blue dungarees giving them a rather forlorn look on this damp November morning. No horses or motorized tractors to help them of course, they had all been taken by the retreating Germans. Just a few pigs and cows and an odd gaggle of geese were the only livestock to be seen. Hardly a scene for any poetic masterpiece.

What a contrast as we drove into Brussels.

The Belgian capital was alive with people, walking, cycling, or pulling little four-wheeled carts. Everyone seemed to be going somewhere urgently. All had time though to return our waves and to occasionally answer our greetings in English.

Along the tree lined boulevards, some civilian cars and vans were to be seen amongst the preponderance of military vehicles. There were some trams operating, but on most of the boulevards the central reservations were piled high with weeks of accumulated garbage, caused by the breakdown in refuse collection when the local transport had been commandeered by the Germans in their desperate bid to evacuate the city, prior to its capture by the vanguard of the British Army.

Cats, dogs and rats could be seen foraging for scraps amidst the decomposing household waste. Roses may have been blooming in Picardy, but their fragrance didn't extend as far as Brussels.

In the city centre, we saw to our amazement, that the shops were full of merchandise — clothing, beautiful lace and wines, and in the greengrocers, fruit was stacked in high profusion, something we had not seen back home since before the war.

One of our party, wishing to get a better look at the shops, leaned out of the side of the vehicle and promptly had his elbow bashed by a passing truck. The elbow was well and truly smashed. Immediate first aid was rendered and a detour made to deposit him at the nearest Regimental Aid Post. Despite the intense pain, he was quite philosophic about it.

"That's me shooting arm gone for a Burton," was his only comment.

Any thoughts of a stay in this, the brightest capital in Europe took a tumble as we headed north-east to Louvain, or Leuven, depending on whether you were a Walloon or not.

We had noticed that quite suddenly, all villages and towns were spelled in two ways, French or Flemish, also that other signs and notices were of a similar nature. Rightly or wrongly, we plumped for Louvain.

King Albert Barracks was to become our new home for a few days. The barracks, named after the much loved King of the Belgians who had led his army so gallantly in the bloody battles of Flanders a quarter of a century ago, was relatively modern, compared with some of the barracks in England.

A wide ornamental staircase rose majestically from the main entrance to our block on the first floor. From that landing two flights of stairs led to the top floor, where two marble columns stood astride the staircase. As we looked up, we saw to our merriment, that these columns and the archway above had been transformed by some unknown German artist, into a pair of legs and the lower part of a woman's body. Repulsive perhaps to some it was, nevertheless, a remarkable piece of artistic painting in living colours.

"This room is confined to barracks tonight for duty as fire picket," the Orderly Sergeant informed us brusquely.

"Blimey Sarge, we ain't bin 'ere a bleedin' 'our yet," said a cockney character indignantly.

"Never mind son," said the NCO, "I'll make it worth your while — just trust me," he added with a knowing wink.

"Give us a break Sarge," said someone else.

"No, you'll do fire picket tonight lads — you'd only be down the town trying to get in to see Rosie and probably getting picked up by the Redcaps for your trouble."

The gentleman was adamant, so we settled down to writing and reading in between patrolling the barracks.

Next morning the Sergeant came into the room smiling broadly.

"Morning lads. Sorry about last night, but I've got a bit of good news for you. All those on picket duty last night get one of these free tickets to see Geraldo and his orchestra tonight at the forces theatre in the town."

We crowded round him as we had our names ticked off his list. This was to be a show well worth going to see.

Geraldo and his orchestra were one of the top bands at that time and like many more of the top line entertainers, were touring the BLA areas to give live shows for the forces.

Immediately after dinner, Bing and I made our first excursion into Louvain. As we looked around the shops, I suddenly remembered it was November the 18th, my twenty-second birthday. This called for a celebration drink, so we sorted out a nice little café with a tuneful trio and sat back to enjoy a pleasant hour or so.

I treated myself to a kilo of those large delicious black grapes which were on show at all the fruit shops. Bing chose the green variety. Carefully these were carried in the brown paper bags to the theatre.

Sitting in the stalls, immediately behind the officers, we enjoyed an excellent show provided by this premier orchestra, ably supported by other highly professional acts. The grapes too, were of the highest quality. All in all, a most enjoyable birthday under the circumstances. Far better than my twenty-first birthday which I had spent confined to barracks in the Marquess of Zetland's stables on the Yorkshire moors.

Sunday evening saw us searching furtively for a certain café, the name of which I have long forgotten. At long last the name which had been passed from mouth to mouth, appeared above the door. I noticed that on the windows was a black diagonal cross within a black circle, notifying to all that this café was 'out of bounds' to all ranks.

We entered the blacked out doorway and saw about two dozen soldiers, some British, some Canadian, sitting at eight or nine wooden tables.

Behind the bar stood two women dressed in black and they both looked to be about forty-five to fifty years old. A young blonde girl in her late teens came down the stairs in the corner of the café, followed by a Canadian soldier.

We walked over to the table next but one to the stairs and joined another youngster who was wearing an infantry badge in his cap. Two beers were ordered and we sat down to await developments.

About a quarter of an hour later, at a table across the room, two Canadians placed some coins on the table and one called out, "Exhibition, Rosie — exhibition!"

One of the women, built like an all-in wrestler, walked to the door, took a quick look into the street and came to the table.

"OK Tommy — exhibish."

A torch was produced and immediately everyone else left their seats and charged across the café floor. Pandemonium followed as those on the outside fought for a closer look at whatever was going on. We were taken completely by surprise and were left well behind.

The rugger scrum eventually subsided and we saw Rosie scoop the coins from the table into her hand and after counting them, drop them into her leather purse. She then resumed serving beers as though nothing had happened.

We sauntered across to the Canadians and asked casually, "What was that all about, mate?"

The Canadian, still chuckling, replied, "Just place fifteen one franc coins on the edge of the table and you'll soon find out."

I looked at Bing. Fifteen francs — at twenty to the pound, that was almost a week's money for me.

Bing thought for a minute and then said he would go round the other English lads to try to get a combined collection. This he did. The fifteen coins, about the size of an English shilling (5p) were placed on the table and Rosie was called.

The same procedure was followed as before, the quick check up the street and a call for a torch from the Canadian. Rosie approached the table, lifted her skirt and then someone jumped on to my back. My head was pressed sideways on to the table top and that was all that I saw of the performance. As I rubbed my sore ear later, I heard one of our cousins from across the Atlantic say, "She's a dirty old bitch — I'll teach her a lesson."

Meanwhile, the café had returned to normality. Drinks were served and the young blonde ascended the stairs followed by a chap from the Artillery.

Albert, the young north country lad sitting at our table then gave us a graphic account of what had happened.

The coins were placed on the table and arranged in various patterns and were then picked up by Rosie with various parts of her anatomy not usually used for the collection of coins of the realm. Her *finale* and *pièce de résistance* entailed the coins to be stacked one on top of another and then unbuttoning her bodice, out would plop two enormous breasts. Placing her hands behind her back, she was able, by muscle control alone, to pick up the coins between her breasts. She would then challenge anyone to extract more than two coins, using only the forefinger and the thumb in the process. No one had yet succeeded that night.

There was still a lot of laughter from the Canadian and it was soon time for another call for Rosie. She approached the table lifted her skirt and then — an ear-piercing scream rent the air.

Pummelling those around her, she called them everything she could think of in her native tongue. Pausing only to scoop the coins into her purse, she returned to the bar, shouting to all, "Exhibish finis! Tommies — feelthy pigs."

The reason for all this uproar was the coin which had been hotting up on the anthracite stove in the corner and had been surreptitiously included in the fifteen by the fellow with the torch. Obviously it was not only Rosie's pride that had been hurt.

Sitting with Albert as we finished our drinks, we noticed that whenever anyone ordered drinks and paid for them with a note, no one ever asked for the loose change. There was no telling which coins had been where.

Meanwhile, Albert had become incensed with the idea of accompanying the blonde upstairs. At last he went to the counter and paid his money. The look on his face showed that he was in his seventh heaven. I don't think he felt the steps beneath his feet, he was walking on air.

Within a couple of minutes he was back at the top of the stairs again and looking decidedly worse for wear. As he rejoined us at the table, he explained that as the girl entered the room she had slipped off her frock. The sight of her supple naked body before him, caused his pent-up emotions to explode. No longer able to fulfil his evening's ambition, he had no alternative but to rejoin us in the café and sat there dejectedly and almost in tears.

Madam came to the table and handed him an IOU.

We excused ourselves and made our way back to the barracks in the black-out, still chuckling at the evening's happenings. We were still laughing as we climbed the ornamental staircase. At the top, Bing kicked one of the pillars of the archway.

"What did you do that for?" I asked.

"After what I've seen tonight, there's no telling where the Belgian gels keep their money — and I'm about spent out now."

A couple of days later we were two of the 40 hommes inside a goods wagon as the troop train made its circuitous way from Louvain to the old cavalry garrison town of Burg Leopold. Although the distance was less than that from Ghent to Louvain, we were shunted back and forth all night long. Not only was it a bitterly cold night, but one of the sliding doors wouldn't close properly so it became a very uncomfortable and tedious journey.

Burg Leopold, we were told, was the last staging post before the front line. From here we would be sorted out into divisional groups and we would then have to await their transport to take us to our respective battalions.

With the uncertainty of the future, Bing and I made sure that we took advantage of whatever was available in the way of entertainment. There was a good canteen in the barracks and another in the town, so despite the weather becoming colder, we kept busy and warm for most of the time.

After a day or so, I sensed that Bing was not his usual bouncy self. He hedged away from my questions about this for a time, but then in a quieter moment he told me that he'd been having a dream. It was the same dream each night in which his older brother was meeting him at the door and beckoning to take him with him.

I told him not to worry. It was probably only wishful thinking. He just wanted his older brother to look after him.

"It's not like that Ken," he said. "You see, my brother has been killed in the war and I think he's calling for me to join him."

I felt a cold shudder run down my spine. The look on his face told me that he was quite serious. Inadequately, I tried to dispel his fears, but to no avail. There was nothing I could do or say to change his mind, so we let the discussion peter out. The dreams were never mentioned again.

When the 49 Div. names were posted on the notice-board, we went out and spent our last francs on a farewell drink. As we shook hands, I could see the look on his face that he knew that we would never meet again. I was sorry to have to leave him behind, he had been a very cheerful companion until the last few days, but even then, he had tried to come to terms with the cloud of foreboding which hung over him. I wondered what the future would have in store for this young man who was not yet twenty years old.

FOURTEEN – REUNITED WITH THE FUSILIERS

The greater part of November had been spent travelling to and fro across Belgium from one transit camp to another. It seemed to me that half the troops of the 21st Army Group were playing a gigantic game of musical chairs.

The camps themselves had been anything from a field of tents through to a range of billets in large houses, schools and warehouses, in addition to the Belgian Army barracks of one sort or another.

The old cavalry barracks at Burg Leopold had offered only spartan comforts. The horses may have been moved some time before, probably when the German Army had evacuated the town, but the smell had lingered on. It was with some relief therefore, that I received the news that a 15cwt truck from 147 Brigade would be leaving at 11.00 hrs. to convey personnel from that brigade back to their respective units.

At the appointed time, some half a dozen assorted men dropped their kit into the back of the truck and took up a position on that same kit, endeavouring to get into some sort of comfortable travelling position. We drove off into the murky drizzle, not knowing where our final destination might be. There were rumours that the 49th Div. had taken up the battle where the 1st Airborne Div. had left off. It looked to me as though we were in for a rather sticky winter.

During that wet dreary afternoon, we were jostled about in the back of the covered truck as we were driven along cycle tracks and the rough shoulders of the roads, giving the right of way to the armoured convoys and squadrons of tanks on the move, all going northwards. From the back of the truck we could not pick out any known landmarks and it was not until we reached Grave that we saw the red Maple Leaf signs informing us that we were on the main Canadian supply route taking us into Nijmegen.

Our first sight of the once beautiful university town of Nijmegen, was quite a contrast to the rather austere towns to which we had become accustomed in Belgium. Here in the southern area of Nijmegen were well built, pleasantly situated detached houses within their own grounds. Every house seemed to be festooned with signboards and insignia of every conceivable unit in the British and Canadian armies.

The 15cwt slowed down to a halt at the corner of a tree-lined street and we tumbled out, one by one. The driver pointed his thumb over his shoulder.

"I should drop your kit here lads. Apparently all the 'B' Echelons are around this area. The 'Dukes' are down here on the right and I think the 'Jocks' are just over there by the crossroads."

"Any idea where ours is?" queried the two 'Leicesters'.

"Not a bloody clue," replied the driver.

Throwing my big pack on to my shoulders, I walked over to the crossroads and on to the footpath leading to the large red bricked house, unblemished by the action which had followed the airborne landings some weeks previous. The neat little box hedges were still intact. All the bushes in the garden were dark green, giving a most friendly and welcoming atmosphere to the unknown visitor.

The white Polar Bear on a black background with the number 61 'B' Ech underneath, announced that I had reached the rear area of Battalion HQ where reinforcements, stores and equipment were held, stored or forwarded to the appropriate company. Here at last, was my immediate destination.

Along the drive at the right hand side of the house, I found the side entrance to be the one in general use. Jerrycans stacked four high along the outside wall, led to the garage at the rear, outside which stood a water carrier all ready and primed to take out the water rations to the various companies up at the front, where the unforgettable sounds of battle could now clearly be heard.

As my hand opened the door at the side of the house, a Scottish voice bellowed out, "Don't ye evair knock when ye entair a bloody room?"

I looked round the door and saw the thin face with the narrow eyes, ferret like in their intensity. There was only once face like that — the Pipe Major!

"Sorry Pipe Major, Fusilier West reporting back after being wounded."

"Have ye brought ye'r U.X.P.D.R.?"

"No Pipey, the transit camp wouldn't issue any rations."

"They must have a ration store as high as Ben Nevis back there, no one evair turns up with their unexpired portion. Well, we havnae got any for ye, ye might get a mug o' char off the cook."

"Where's the cookhouse?" I asked.

"Roon the back, doon in the garage," replied the Pipe Major. "Ye can leave ye kit doon there," he said, pointing to the floor under the table.

My presence at the cookhouse was greeted with equal enthusiasm by the cook, but after a game of wait and see, I eventually got a mug of hot liquid which slightly resembled tea, but nothing to eat, not even a packet of hardtack.

Shortly after I had gone back into the house, a truck pulled up outside. Seconds afterwards the sound of a kick on the door echoed through the room. The door flew open and into the room came a small chap with a Lance-Corporal's stripe on his arm.

"If you've got any post for anybody tonight Pipey, you can take it yerself. It's bloody chaos up there. Nobody knows what the hell's happening. They reckon 'C' Company is cut off and the CO is dashing about like a blue-arsed fly trying to sort it all out. The Guards Div. have got a tank on every bloody corner and crossroad from the roundabout to Bemmel."

"Well, somebody's got to go up after dark and this bloke has tae report tae Battalion HQ," replied the Pipe Major.

"You can bloody well walk mate," said the L/Cpl to me, "I'm not moving until I know what's what." With that he walked out, slamming the door behind him.

I couldn't help thinking to myself what a nice quiet house this had appeared to be just an hour or two ago.

For the next few hours the signaller at 'B' Ech. kept up a constant vigil by the telephone and No. 18 wireless set, he also checked with 147 Brigade HQ over the 39 set for further news of the day's events. The only news of our battalion was much the same as the concise report brought back by the L/Cpl. The only real contact with anyone was with the company in reserve just on the east bank of the river Waal on the bridge approaches.

The decision was made to take the ration truck up as far as that company and try to contact Battalion HQ from there. By the time the 15cwt truck had left the drive of the red bricked house, the sound of the battle had subsided a little, but the steady crump, crump crump of HE shells to the north, left me in no doubt that there was still some disagreement over a large part of the front line immediately to our front. We made our way through the blackened streets, passing the large concert hall the Concertgebouw, renamed by the forces as the Wintergardens on our right, as we rounded the shrub planted roundabout and on to the magnificent Waal bridge. Here we were stopped by the MPs for a document check.

"Ration truck for the 11th Royal Scots Fusiliers," said the driver as he showed the necessary papers.

"You should find them somewhere around Bemmel," said the policeman helpfully as he waved us on and over the bridge.

I looked out of the back of the truck. The huge archway of the bridge loomed overhead, Here and there was a jagged tear in the metal work where a shell had exploded and there were traces of cannon fire along the former cycle paths on each side. The roadway seemed to be hundreds of yards long in the dark.

We found the reserve company fairly easily and off-loaded the supplies before going into the office.

"Any news of Battalion HQ?" asked the driver hopefully.

"Only that they are somewhere in Bemmel," was the reply.

"OK, we'd better try and find them. So long."

We departed into the night again, eyes searching for the green 61 sign of the Polar Bear.

Sporadic machine-gun fire could be heard from a number of directions – the staccato beat of the German Spandau answered by the slower steadier Bren-gun. Intermittently came the rhythmic sound of the water-cooled Vickers. Very few single shots rang out, signifying that the hand to hand fighting had subsided for the time being. The machine-gun crews were holding on to the day's gains, or preventing any further chances of advance under cover of darkness.

Although we asked many times, we never got anywhere near to Battalion HQ. The roads were busy with ambulance jeeps which seemed to be carrying a number of 'Dukes'. As we stopped alongside one of the jeeps, enquiries revealed that a German attack in strength had been aimed to penetrate between the RSF at Bemmel and the Duke of Wellingtons at Haalderen and in the ensuing scrap the 'Dukes' had been cut off for a time, hence the need for the defensive screen of tanks and armoured vehicles we had witnessed during our evening's perambulations. There was no longer any sense in attempting to locate the RSF HQ, so we made our way back to the Waal bridge and thence to 'B' Echelon where we arrived around the hour of midnight. I was thankful to kip down next to the driver in one of the downstairs rooms.

I was surprised on wakening next morning to find that we had been allowed to sleep until 7.30 a.m. Pipey didn't seem at all interested to hear of our 'Cook's tour of the island' as my friend the driver called it. Breakfast was the only thing on his mind, so it was mugs and digging irons at the ready as we walked down to the garage to collect the morning's offerings.

"Bacon AND two slices of bread," announced the cook. Now this was a real treat. The army bakeries had only recently started sending white bread to the front line units for breakfast. Prior to this, army biscuits had been the only fare to start the day, to be washed down by the ever present mug of tea.

After breakfast, the ablutions were our next priority. The biscuit tin taken from a 14-man food pack was produced. This tin was duly half filled with water and one by one we washed in the same water, each man carefully taking off the scum left by the previous user, with a swift scooping action by the right hand, depositing the said scum out of the window in one continuous sweeping motion.

It was about eleven o'clock when a jeep pulled up outside the gates of the house. I went to the window. As I looked out I could see the unmistakable figure of the RSM, John the 'B' – or to give him his full title Warrant Officer first class, John MacCreadie, Regimental Sergeant-Major of the 11th Battalion the Royal Scots Fusiliers.

John the 'B' was not a tall man, something like 5ft. 10 ins., in height, medium build with a round face, the focal points being the red nose denoting a lover of a wee dram o' whisky and the waxed Kitchener type of moustache on his upper lip. On his head he wore the soft round officer type Tom-o'-Shanter, set so square that it was often said that it was screwed on with a British Standard Fine thread.

He strode into the room.

"Have ye got the day's rum ration, Pipe Major? The lads'll be needing it the day."

Pipey disappeared into another room, reappearing with a full bottle of rum. Placing the bottle on the table, he turned to the RSM and asked, "Will ye sign for it the noo, sir?"

The RSM duly signed the authorization book and swung round ready to depart.

"We've a laddie here who's to report tae Battalion HQ — can ye take him along, sir?" enquired the Pipe Major.

"Where are ye from, laddie?" challenged the RSM.

"I've come from No. 17 transit camp at Burg Leopold," was my reply.

"Ah, another reinforcement. Well ye're joining a fine regiment, we've a very high standard in this Battalion . . . . "

I cut him short as I explained, "I'm rejoining the Battalion sir, returning from England. I got a Blighty at Frenouville."

"Sorry laddie, I didn't know you were one of our lads — but ye're no one o' the original Battalion." His manner had changed.

"No sir, I joined you at Fontenay le Pesnil."

He stuck out his right hand and as I returned the grip, he said, "Good man, good man — what's ye name then?"

"Fusilier West, signal platoon," was my reply and I observed a quick mental check in his eyes as he looked me up and down. I could see that he couldn't place me in that role, but he let it pass.

"Welcome back tae the Battalion West, ye'd better come along o' me. Put ye kit in my jeep — I'll no be long." He walked off in the general direction of the cookhouse. I said cheerio to the driver of the previous night and climbed into the jeep.

We swung on to the main road from the roundabout and the whole scene before us was completely changed from the previous evening. The dark shadowy streets were now bathed in a watery sunshine, the tree-lined roads strewn with mud and leaves constantly being chewed up by the wheels of every conceivable vehicle in use by an army on the move. The whirring of the tracked vehicles assailed the ears. Half-tracks, Bren carriers and here and there a tank moving up added to the noise and fumes which filled the air all the way to the long approach to the great Waal bridge. In the side streets the build up of transport filled every available space.

"Ye're now coming on tae the famous Nijmegen bridge," said the RSM. "It was captured by the Guards Armoured Division after a terrific battle."

"Yes, we came over it last night," I interposed.

"Ye couldna been over it last night laddie — no one's allowed over after dark."

I knew that we had indeed crossed it in both directions in the hours of darkness. I also knew that it was useless to press the point this morning. The

RSM carried on with his narrative.

"It's a fine piece of bridge building, the longest single span bridge in Europe — and built by a Scottish firm in 1937. It'll take more than yon Jerries to knock out this bridge."

His Scottish chest filled visibly with national pride.

"Down here in Lent, this is the Command Post of the Guards Division," he continued, waving his hand to the sentry at the gate of the house near to the damaged church. Near by stood a burned-out tank, as if planted there by some giant hand in a child's war game.

The roadsides all the way from the bridge were festooned by signal cables of every hue and looped from hedge to hedge, tree to tree, in fact use was made of any type of anchorage that would keep the lines off the ground and wherever necessary, high enough for trucks and tanks to pass underneath without incurring the wrath of indignant signals personnel, who strived night and day to keep open the lines of communication.

"Ye'll no doubt see many changes, West." His rasping voice stopped my train of thought. "We've lost a lot of good men — let's see, who'd be the Signals Sergeant back in Frenouville? Aye that would be Sergeant Ward."

"Yes," I replied, "and there was Corporal Thompson too."

"Aye Corporal Thompson is still here and Sergeant Ward is still the Signals Sergeant."

He carried on with many names of some good lads who had dropped by the wayside. A lot of them were the original members of the Battalion who I didn't know personally, but I made appropriate noises in tune with the pitch of his voice as the RSM waxed on eloquently, bringing me up to date with all sorts of stories and anecdotes.

"Aye, a lot of changes." He sighed. "But we've made a name for ourselves too. The Battalion made a big contribution to the capture of Le Havre." He swung round in his seat. "Man ye should ha' seen our lads that day, they were tremendous." He faced the front again.

"After Antwerp, we took Dendermonde and Turnhout, them up to Roosendaal after that it was across to Venray, plugging the gaps as the Jerries tried to cut the corridor up to Nijmegen."

The penny dropped for me. Now I could understand the continuous shuffling about back and forth across Belgium. 49th Division was part of the Canadian Army and the front was so fluid that Brigades were taken away from the Division from time to time, to help strengthen an attack, or to help consolidate a position. Back in the build-up areas, they must have been doing their nuts trying to reunite people with their units.

Damage, both to property and to the countryside in general, was now beginning to resemble that which I had known in Normandy. Knocked out guns, an anti-tank here, a light field piece there, a burnt out carrier with a couple of crosses near by, looked fairly new to me. The orchards on either side of the road, now shed of their fruit and leaves, had also taken a bashing from the defensive fire plans of the two opposing armies. The smell of cordite was in the air, but everywhere sounded fairly quiet as we approached the crossroads of the two country roads. The names read Bemmel-Nijmegen one way, the other read Bemmel-Ressen. I was to get to know these places very well in the next few months.

"We are coming up to Bemmel." The voice of John the 'B' brought me back to concentration once more.

"We had one hell of a scrap all day yesterday," he went on, "There were bloody Jerries everywhere. They got as far as Battalion HQ before we could stop them. 'C' Company were bypassed, but held out with flying colours, but it was nightfall before we could sort out just who was who. There were cases where some of our lads and the SS were actually firing out of the same house. In one instance they were in the same room before they realized the fact. They were so surprised that they dived off in different directions one through the door and the other through the window."

This I thought was John the 'B' at his best. However it did confirm that much of what we had heard the previous night was true. There HAD been one hell of a scrap.

The road now was littered with the very recent debris from all sorts of shelling, mortar and anti-tank fire. Broken limbs from the trees in the orchards on the left were scattered all over the apples which lay in the grass below. Large yellow cooking apples, bright red eaters, stood out on the lush green carpet. The arrival of the airborne troops had preceded the harvesting and now the fruit lay dying and rotting on the ground, as the continuation of the liberation of Holland went on.

The jeep rolled up at the fifth house on the right. The RSM turned and said, "This is Signals HQ, West."

As he spoke, I saw the tall figure of the Commanding Officer coming out of the house. He saw the RSM and called.

"Mr MacCreadie, a word with you please."

The RSM jumped out of the jeep. "Sah," he rasped as he slammed his right foot to the ground. His body quivered as he threw a Guards Brigade salue to the Colonel. They spoke for a minute or two as I got out of the jeep, disengaging my kit from the other items on the back seat.

Suddenly I felt like a young boy who had returned to school after a long illness. Pleased to be back, but in some way rather apprehensive as to what the future had in store for me.

From the time I had left my wife on the station at Leicester I had been 'on my way back'. Now I was back. My stomach rolled a little as I stood by the little bridge which crossed the ditch in front of the typically Dutch house with its green shutters now rather askew. I crossed the small bridge, rifle on one shoulder, small pack on the other. The CO looked at me enquiringly. RSM MacCreadie sensed that this was an opportune moment to give a good impression.

"Fusilier West, sir — one of the old members of the Battalion rejoining us after being wounded."

"Welcome back to the Battalion, West," he said as he shook hands warmly. "Where did you leave us?"

"Back at Frenouville," was my reply.

"Frenouville eh? That's where the advance began. You can see we've kept up the momentum whilst you've been away — all the way to Nijmegen. We had a spot of bother yesterday, but I think we've sorted it out now. I hope that you will settle down all right with us again, you'll find it a bit strange at first, living in houses, but it's much better than the slit-trench life of Normandy. Good luck, West."

As he strode off, he turned to say, "Sergeant Ward isn't there at the moment, but I'm sure you will see someone you know. Tell Sergeant Ward I'll call later this afternoon, I'll see you then."

"I'll take him in sir," said the RSM, ever the man to make the most of an opportunity. The Colonel returned our salutes.

As he went on his way, the RSM said in a confidential manner, "A fine man Colonel Eykin, he'll be back tae have a wee word wi' ye'. He's a man who keeps his word." With that we walked into the Signals HQ.

"Ah, Sergeant Goldie, I've a new signaller for ye."

The jovial faced Sergeant nodded to me and gave a welcome in a Highland dialect so broad, that I could hardly understand a word, but I did catch the words "Wha de ye ken?"

"Is Paddy Deegan or Nattrass about?" This was a shot in the dark on my part, but it bore fruit.

"Aye, Paddy is still here, he's out on a line the noo. Nattrass is still at 'D' Company. Ye'd better stay here, Paddy will be back in a wee while." These pieces of information came from three signallers unknown to me.

Someone mentioned a mug of tea and the RSM rubbed his hands in expectation. I did better than that, I unclipped my mug from my small pack and placed it on the table.

The discussion turned to news from the home front and what was happening at the rear and 'behind the line' in general. I related how I'd been kicking my heels in Belgium for a few weeks, but that there had been highlights such as the Geraldo concert in Louvain and the various film shows I had seen in strange out of the way places. I then went on to tell of the rumours that abound in the transit camps and Army Group offices, some optimistic and others despairingly pessimistic.

"I heard at the last Transit camp that the 50 Div. was being broken up," I said.

"That's hardly likely," retorted the RSM, "they are one o' the finest Divisions of the British Army. They've mebbe been withdrawn for regrouping, ready for the final push into Germany."

"They are starting a 3-day leave scheme to Brussels any time now," was my next offering. "Brussels really is unbelievable — all lit up, with plenty to buy in the shops, especially fruit and lots of souvenirs to send home."

"Yes, I've heard about that from 'Tilly'," said one of the signallers. The RSM also concurred that this was within the realms of possibility.

"They are also going to start a 7-day Blighty leave in the New Year, starting with those who landed on D-Day." This was a little gem which I had heard from a very reliable source. However, this was just a bit too much for John the 'B' to swallow. He rounded on me.

"Now look here West, that's just an idle rumour and ye'd be well advised to no spread rumours like that around."

"But I know this to be true, I've seen it in writing."

"It canna be true laddie, or the Commanding Officer or myself would have heard about it — officially." With that he put his empty mug on the table and went on his way.

Everyone now wanted to know more about this Blighty leave and we talked for some time about the pros and cons until Paddy came back. On being told that an old mate of his was back, he came into the room wondering who it might be. He saw me at the table.

"The great O'West. Hooradooin? I t'ought I'd never set eyes on you agin — you know when to come back y' old divil. Sure 'twas a bloody shambles las night."

He turned to the others and said in mock seriousness, "It'll be all right now lads, things will soon quieten down now the great O'West's back — he doesn't like it too noisy."

We slapped each other on the back. Now I knew I was amongst friends again.

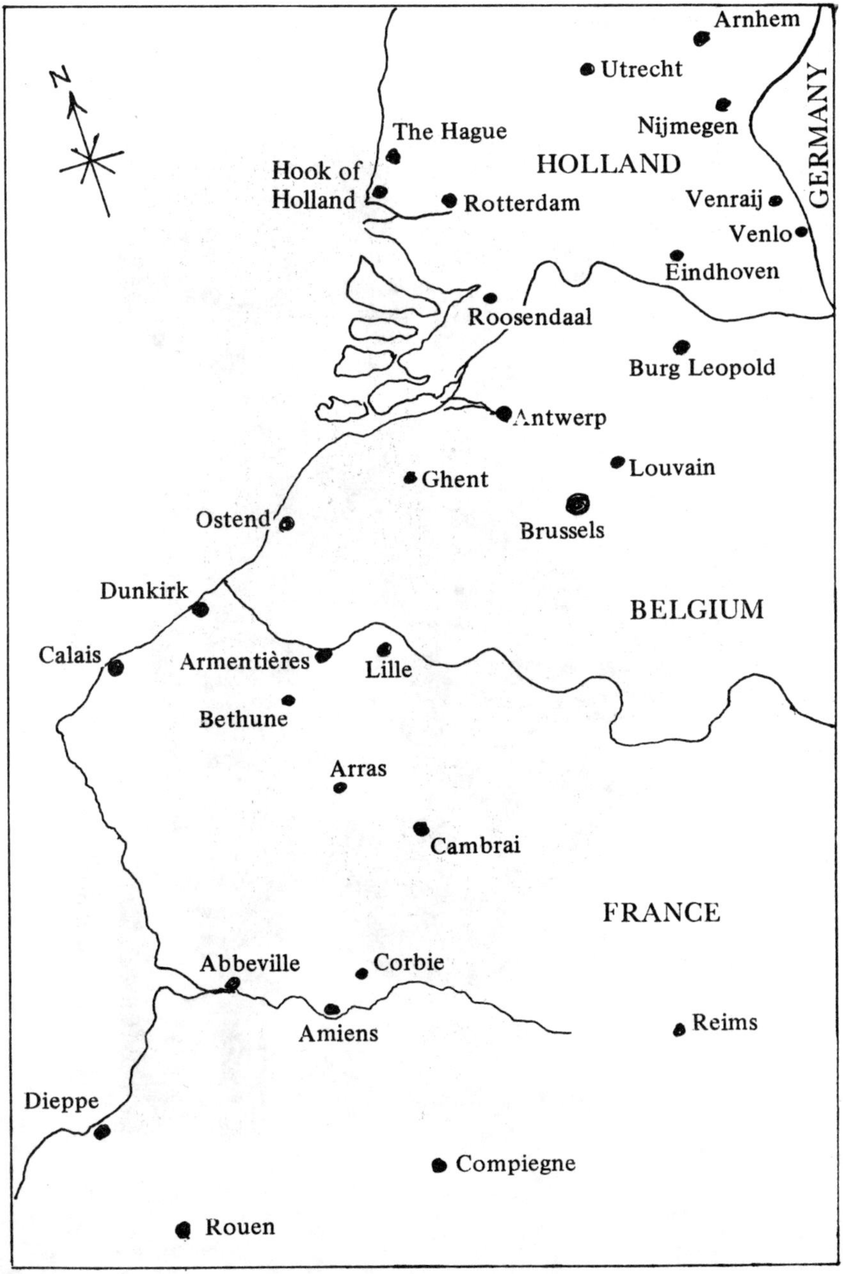
N
Arnhem
Utrecht
Nijmegen
The Hague
HOLLAND
GERMANY
Hook of
Holland
Rotterdam
Venraij
Venlo
Eindhoven
Roosendaal
Burg Leopold
Antwerp
Louvain
Ghent
Ostend
Brussels
Dunkirk
BELGIUM
Calais
Armentières
Lille
Bethune
Arras
Cambrai
FRANCE
Abbeville
Corbie
Amiens
Reims
Dieppe
Compiegne
Rouen

The Waal Bridge, Nijmegen, looking towards 'the Island' and Arnhem

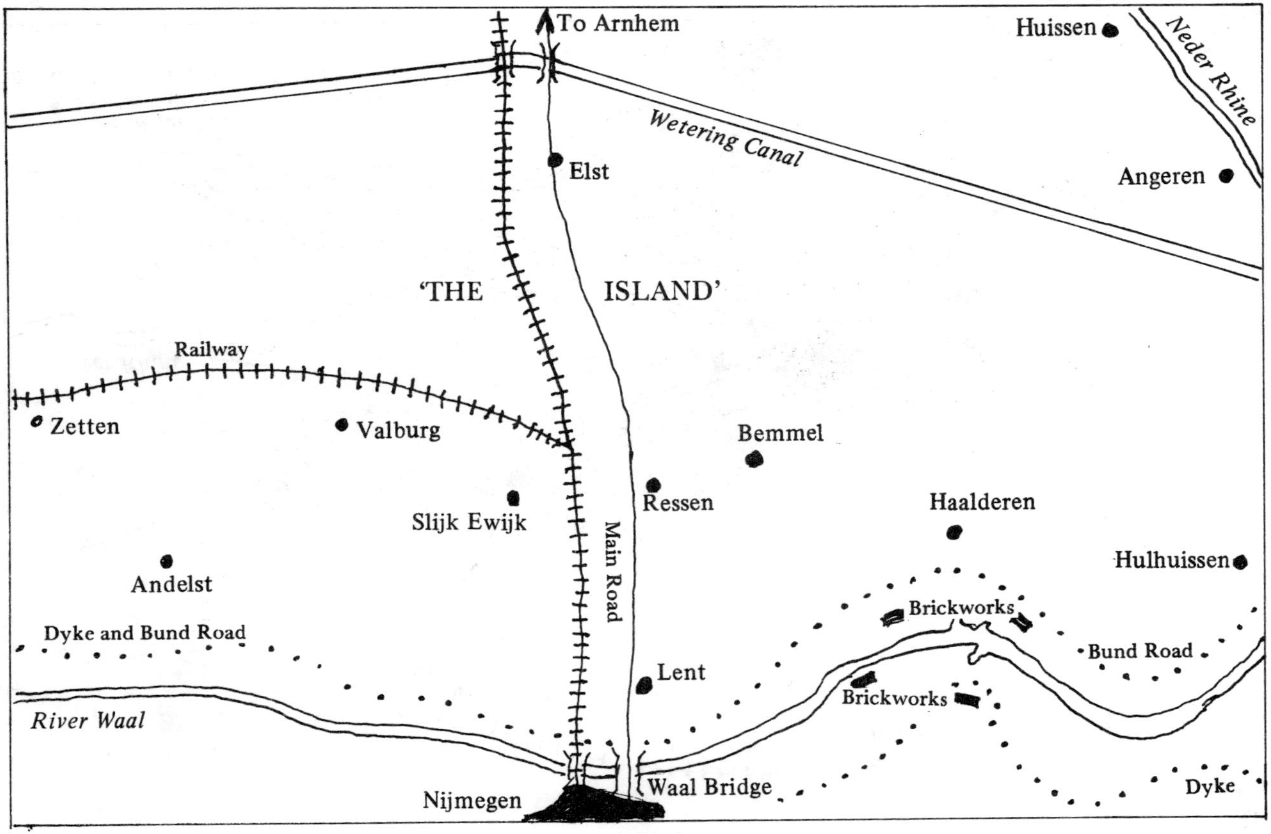
To Arnhem
Huissen
Neder Rhine
Wetering Canal
Elst
Angeren
'THE ISLAND'
Railway
Zetten
Valburg
Bemmel
Ressen
Slijk Ewijk
Haalderen
Hulhuissen
Main Road
Andelst
Brickworks
Dyke and Bund Road
Bund Road
Lent
Brickworks
River Waal
Waal Bridge
Nijmegen
Dyke

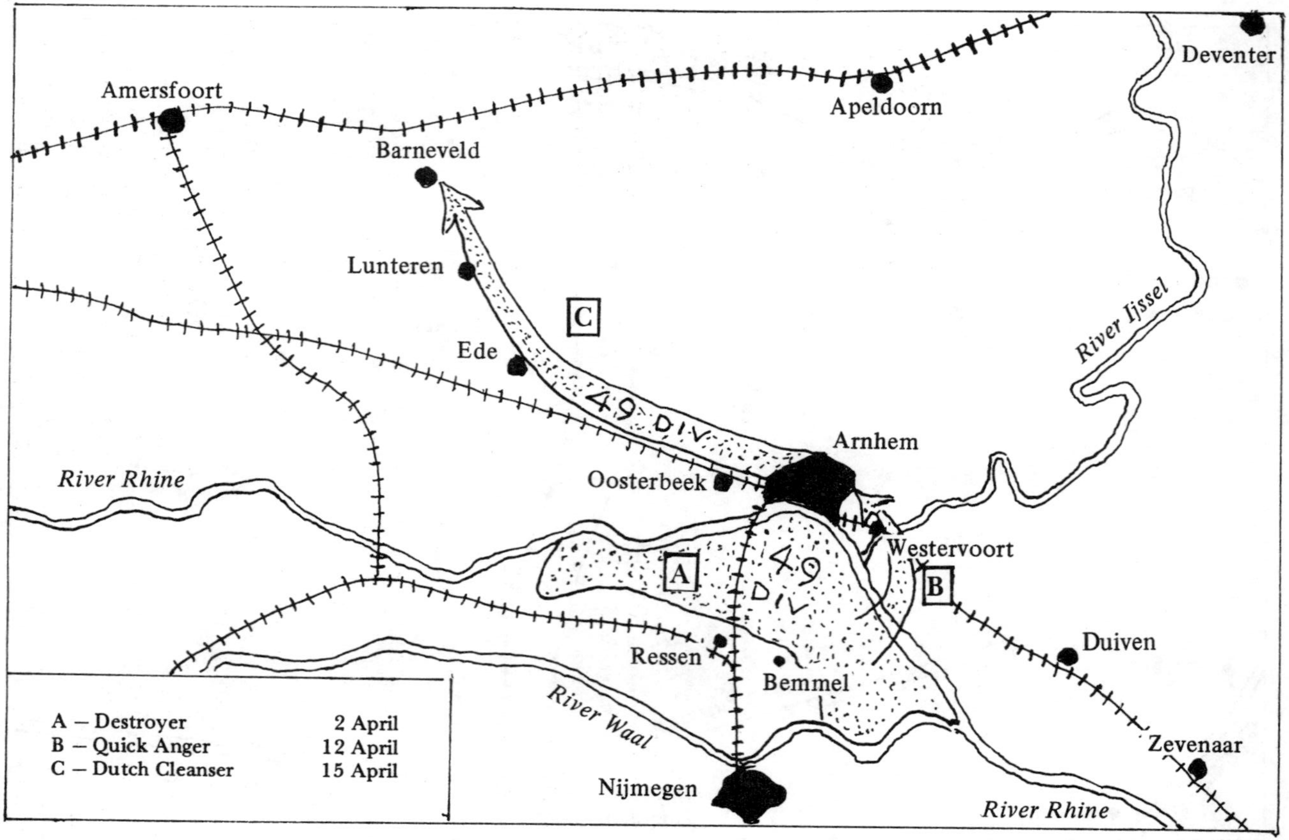

Deventer
Amersfoort
Apeldoorn
Barneveld
Lunteren
C
Ede
River Ijssel
49 DIV
Arnhem
Oosterbeek
River Rhine
Westervoort
A
49 DIV
B
Duiven
Ressen
Bemmel
River Waal
Zevenaar
Nijmegen
River Rhine
A – Destroyer 2 April
B – Quick Anger 12 April
C – Dutch Cleanser 15 April

FIFTEEN – ON THE 'ISLAND'

Stand to next morning was at the usual half an hour before dawn. To combat the chill of the early morning we were dressed in a variety of garb. Some like myself wore their greatcoats with a leather jerkin on top of that, others just wore the jerkin over their battledress. All wore a scarf of some description, the most popular of which were pieces of parachute silk, torn from a 'chute which had been found in a nearby orchard.

As the dawn broke, I could make out the shape of the building in which we were billeted. It was the normal type of Dutch house one sees in the farming areas, with the upper storey and roof covered with the locally manufactured red pantiles. The living quarters at the front of the house were entered from a small hallway inside the front door. The living-room to the right and sitting-room or lounge to the left, were now devoid of furniture, except for a table and a collection of stools and odd chairs which quite obviously had not been part of the original decor of the rooms.

At the end of the hall a door opened into a kitchen and scullery-cum-dairy room, which in turn led on to the outhouses of washroom and storeroom. A further door opened into the barn or cattle byre. The bedrooms were upstairs above the living quarters, needless to say the bedrooms in the top of the house were never used by us for that purpose. The only protection from shells and mortars up there, were the red clay pantiles and thin plastered ceilings. A brief look from the outside showed that quite a bit of the roof was missing.

After stand down, we took it in turns to cross the road to the Quartermaster's Stores for breakfast. The stores were situated in a white farmhouse, standing in an orchard back from the road. A gravel drive led to the barn where the cooks had set up the HQ Company kitchen.

The greeting here was such a contrast to the one I had received the morning before at 'B' Echelon. Here the fare was porridge, done in the Scots way with no sugar but with liberal helpings of salt. Readers may turn their noses up at this culinary delight, but when one gets used to it, and one HAD to get used to it, salty porridge is a good start to the day. Hot Canadian bacon, simply warmed in boiling water, complete with the greaseproof paper around the rolled bacon, a packet of biscuits and a mug of tea comprised the meal.

Paddy, it appeared, had become one of the most liked of the signal section, therefore, as an old mate of his I was accepted without question. I was much relieved by this, as I had a strange foreboding about returning to a rifle company as an ordinary rifleman. I have the utmost respect for these fellows, but as I had been trained as a signaller, I couldn't see the sense of not using the skills for which I had been trained.

True to his word, Colonel Eykin had called to see the Signals Sergeant the night before and also to have a few words with me. His departing remark being, "You'd better get West issued with a decent jerkin, Sgt. Ward."

After breakfast Reg Ward took me across to CQMS Wallace, where I was duly given a brand new leather jerkin in preference to one of the torn blood-stained ones which lay on a pile of hay in the corner of the barn. Due to the stiffness of the new leather, it fitted me rather like a maternity smock. This caused a lot of laughter on my return.

Paddy, seeing me for the first time said, "Be Jaysus, you shouldn't be here in a place like this in your condition — you look about six months gone."

The rest of the day was spent going out to the different companies checking lines and repairing faults caused by the indiscriminate shelling and mortaring throughout the day. I took every opportunity to rub dirt and grease into my new jerkin. Firstly because I looked so obviously a new boy and secondly because of its very light buff colour, I was most conspicuous in a crowd. With a few snipers about, I was only too aware of what my old pal George's sar'nt-major would say. "A bright young cock is easier to hit than a dowdy old hen."

I hoped it wouldn't be too long before I blended with the other dowdy old hens.

It was whilst on our way to 'D' Company that I saw the unmistakable gait of that old lurcher, George. My old Normandy mucker came towards us, thumb stuck into the sling of his rifle as it hung from his right shoulder, tin hat tilted slightly backwards and to the right. A cigarette dangled from the corner of his mouth. His face split into that enormous grin as he recognized me.

"Bloody hell, me ol' mucker! What you doin' back here?" He blew the fag ash off the end of his partly smoked Players free issue and looked me up and down, before continuing.

"I'd a thought that an intelligent bloke like you would have got fixed up with a decent Depot job back in Blighty. Fancy missing a chance like that, silly bugger."

"I had to come back George, you must be getting short of fags by now. Did you ever get my small pack when I got my packet at Frenouville?" I enquired, remembering our pact.

"I never got a chance," he replied. "By the time I knew you'd been hit, someone had taken your bits and pieces to the RAP and by the time I got there, the whole bloody lot had been taken on to Base hospital."

I should explain here that most mates in the rifle companies came to an agreement whereby if one or other should be wounded or killed, the opposite partner would be left the collective unused rations of cigarettes, sweets, chocolates, etc., for his own use. As I had three tins of 50 Players cigs in my pack when I was hit, to say that George was still rather vexed, was very much an understatement.

"Are you still with No. 17 Platoon, George?" I asked.

"Not bloody likely," came the reply. "There's only the Lance-Jack left of our old section. He's a full Corporal now. Paddy Inglishby was made up into a full Corporal, then got killed in Belgium. I never got the Bren-gun though," he said with a wicked smile. "I thought I was chancing my arm a bit too much if I stayed with them, so I'm doing Company Runner now."

I laughed to myself as I thought back to the Normandy days when George had said of the Company runner, "I wouldn't do that job for a bloody pension." Now it appeared that he was doing the job voluntarily, quite happily and without a pension.

"Things must have changed George."

"Arr, it's a different war now, Ken lad — all above ground. Now, if you dig down more than a foot you're in water. I've packed the old shovel away now, the only time we use a shovel is to bury some poor bleeder who's bought it. Hurry up and repair our line, I'm getting blisters wi' all this bloody walking about, see you later."

He waved his hand as he carefully picked his way over the rubble of the shattered wall which now lay scattered all over the road.

Within minutes of George leaving us we had found the break in the line. The shell which had demolished the wall had also taken a chunk out of 'D' Company line. We found the end connecting Battalion HQ and a few feet away, traced the other end to 'D' Company.

"Pull on your end, Ken," said Paddy, "I'll pull on the other."

We stretched the line about three feet, bared the ends of the wire for about two inches and tied a reef knot in the wire. With the earth pin banged into the front garden of the house, Paddy cranked the handle of the handset.

" 'D' Company," came the high pitched voice of the operator at that end.

"Linesman here. Is dat you Nat?" enquired the genial Irishman.

"Yep, Nat here. Where was the fault?"

"At the corner house, about two hundred yards from you."

"Sorry about that," said Nat. "We checked back almost to there, but thought it must be at your end — we've only had one shell here and another some way away."

"Well, dat's de little devil that did it. Before you go Nat, I've got an old mate o' yours wid me."

I took up the hand phone from Paddy.

"Hello Nat, it's Ken West here."

"Thump me," came the voice down the earpiece. "How long have you been back?"

"Came back with John the 'B' yesterday afternoon."

"Well, this is a thumping surprise — are you OK now?"

"Yes, just trying to get back into the routine," I replied.

"How's Leicester these days, any bomb damage?"

"Not really, but the whole town's swarming with Yanks."

"Have you got time to come along for a drop of tea and a chat?"

I looked at Paddy. He shook his head.

"Sorry Nat, not now, got to get back. Bye for now."

Disconnecting the hand-set, I turned to Paddy and asked, "Shall we tape the joint up, now?" He looked at me in disbelief.

"You can forget all that bullshit about taped joints and self-soldering joints out here. They might have been all right at Usselby and on Osgodby Moor. Just make sure that the bare wires aren't earthing then get away before you get a piece of shrapnel or a bullet up your arse. No use making a pukka joint when the line may be cut again before we get back."

This then was to be the pattern for the next week or two. Stand to, line checking all day, stand to at nightfall, and then wireless duty on a rota system during the night.

On the eighth day, we were to be relieved by another Battalion and this was carried out during the hours of darkness. Our new destination was to be Nijmegen for a short rest and baths.

Marching to the rear for about a couple of miles, we then embussed on to Bedford 3-tonners. In these we were carried across the Waal bridge into the town which commences on the immediate south bank of the river. The trucks stopped outside a school situated on the corner of Groesbeekseweg, about 400 yards from the Wintergardens.

On debussing, we were given an address to report to. Laden down with kit, we trudged off along Groesbeekseweg. I rang the bell at No 102 and almost at once the door swung open to reveal in front of us a steep carpeted flight of stairs. From the top of the stairs came a voice in Dutch. We took this to be an invitation to go upstairs. At the top of the stairs was an elderly man, sturdily built and smartly dressed. His slightly greying hair and the smiling face with the gold rimmed spectacles emphasizing his keen sharp eyes, gave one the impression of a self-assured businessman.

He was the owner of an electrical bureau and the room he ushered us into was the first floor room above the work rooms on the street level below. Paddy and I were introduced to his wife, a most homely person, also his two sons and two daughters. The man and his wife spoke no English at all, but the elder boy Wim and the younger daughter Iet did speak a little English. They welcomed us to their house and said that we must have the use of the bedrooms for we were the soldiers who were fighting for the liberation of their country and we must have a good rest. We were shown to the bedrooms and Paddy and I were given the room of the parents.

We left our kit at the house and returned to the school for a bath. These were in fact portable shower units placed in the school playground, but most refreshing. A meal was then taken in the school hall and we returned to the family at No 102.

I don't know whether it was the after effects of the hot shower or all the walking about we had done all day, but we had no sooner got to the house when Paddy asked for the WC or as he put it, "Where de devil is de lavvy?"

Modern day readers will perhaps not know that what he needed was the toilet or the 'loo'. In those days we called a spade a spade so it was either the WC or the lavatory.

I excused myself and went up to the bedroom.

Shortly afterwards I heard the lavatory door close and could hear Paddy coming along the passage laughing. The bedroom door opened and he stood there shaking with laughter and tears running down his cheeks.

"You'll never believe it, Ken, you'll never believe it."

"Believe what?" I asked innocently.

He sat on the edge of the bed still shaking with laughter.

"You'll never believe it, Ken. The pans here are fitted with an inspection plate." He continued to roll about the bed.

"What are you on about?"

"Well, dere I was, having the most comfortable shyte I've had for months. A real seat to sit on, no rickety pole, no trench in the ground. A real comfortable seat. Imagine my surprise after I'd finished. I turned round to flush the lot down and dere," he paused for breath, "dere was two dirty great turds lying side by side on a platform dat goes right across the pan — just like dey was waiting for the CO's inspection."

Still laughing, he got up from the bed, saying, "Here, come along with me. Even John the 'B's never thought of dis one."

We went along to the lavatory and duly inspected this newly discovered exhibit of Dutch plumbing. Every invention has its advantages and also its faults. They were all discussed in full as we stood there, fascinated by the ingenuity of man, then we pulled the chain.

Shortly after this episode, we left the house to pay the first of many visits to the illustrious Wintergardens. In later chapters I shall describe more fully the various activities to be enjoyed in this former concert hall, now transformed into a forces NAAFI.

The next two days were spent inspecting kit and armaments in the mornings. Replacement for clothing, boots, water-bottles, etc. were issued wherever necessary. The afternoons were spent walking around the town looking for bars which may have escaped bombing or shell damage. Very few were in fact open and so it was to the Wintergardens that we usually wended our weary way.

On the evening of the second day, our hosts informed us that we would be returning to the line the next day. I was surprised to hear this from such a source as we had not had any notification from our own HQ.

"When are we going?" I enquired.

"You move off at 11.00 hrs," replied Wim, "and you will be going to Haalderen."

"Just a rumour, I suppose." Paddy nodded in agreement.

"No, please, this is correct." Wim was adamant in his reply, so we accepted the fact and awaited further confirmation.

Confirmation was soon forthcoming. At breakfast time next morning, the RSM called everyone on parade and gave out the notice.

"Every man will go back to his billet and return here at 10.30 hrs with full kit. We shall leave this area at 11.00 hrs to take up another position on 'the island'. Fall out."

So, we now knew officially.

At exactly 10.45 hrs shells began to fall in the surrounding streets. It would appear that the Germans also knew officially.

We embussed at 11.00 hrs and speedily made our way to the Waal bridge where, for reasons unknown to us, the order came to debus. Marching in broken step across the bridge towards the island seemed an eternity as we made our way along the cycle track. Shells travelling in both directions whined overhead. German shells clanged metallically as they exploded in the tree-lined streets of this friendly town which had welcomed us with open hearts, into their trim neat houses and apartments.

It was dangerous at our rear, it was dangerous to our front and we didn't feel too safe here in the middle. It would have shown bad discipline to run, so we marched on — to Haalderen.

SIXTEEN – THE LITTLE WHITE COTTAGE BY THE BUND

As the River Rhine winds its way through Germany towards the Dutch border, it divides and finds its way into the North Sea by two different routes.

The northern arm loops round to Arnhem and on to Rotterdam, entering the sea at the Hook of Holland. This branch of the great river of Europe is called the Nether Rhine.

The southern arm, the River Waal, curls its way in a large delicate 'S' bend before passing through the university town of Nijmegen on its way to the Scheldt estuary. In peacetime, this is the main route from Switzerland to Rotterdam and the high seas.

All along the Waal the flood plains extended in places up to half a mile on either side of the river. To prevent flooding of the rest of the countryside, large earthworks some thirty feet high, line the two banks of the river. These are known to the Dutch as dykes.

Along the top of the dyke is a single track, mostly of stone or gravel but nearer to the villages a layer of tarmacadam is laid on top of the stone surface. To those of us in the 1st Canadian Army Group, these earthworks were known as 'the bund' and obviously the road on top as the 'bund road'.

The 'bund road' was spoken of in some awe. No one walked along there if they valued their lives at all. Up above roof-top height, one stood out like the proverbial wart on the parson's nose, day or night.

Skirting Bemmel, we marched along the small road or farm track which ran parallel to the bund. This led to a small cottage on the outskirts of Haalderen adjacent to the tee junction where the farm road met the bund road as it swept down to join the main Bemmel-Huissen road about 50 yards from the church.

The signals section took up their position in the small white cottage which nestled cosily up to the western side of the bund. Every window was reinforced outside by a sandbagged parapet, or by earth rammed down between the brickwork and old doors which had been staked into the former flower beds ringing the house.

Entry into the house was by means of the barn, the double doors being just wide enough to allow the section's half-track vehicle to enter and to remain under cover during the hours of daylight. A small door led into the kitchen. Two medium sized rooms and a small scullery comprised the ground floor which was devoid of furniture, apart from the table and chair in the scullery. Apple boxes were used for seating during the day when not on duty, otherwise we slept on the bare wooden boards, using the three woollen army blankets for warmth.

The telephone switchboards and wireless set stood on the table in the scullery which had now become the signals office. Telephone wires disappeared through the small window at the back of the switchboard, where they fanned out in all directions to link up with the rest of the Battalion. This window was the only one in the cottage not to be boarded up and from it, one gained a first class view of the village and of the houses in use by our HQ Company. The solitary chair, used as it was by the duty signaller, meant that there were plenty of volunteers to man this vital centre of communications.

The rusting remains of a 75mm German anti-tank gun could clearly be seen from the window. It stood as a silent monument to a short sharp personal battle with the Sherman tank of the Guards Armoured Div. which stood diagonally opposite, on the other side of the field, half in and half out of the ditch. At a distance of some 200 yards and with the barrels of their respective guns in complete alignment they had fired simultaneously. Both rounds had penetrated the respective armour immediately below the barrel, leaving a hole drilled as cleanly as if reamered in their own ordnance workshops. The damage to the machinery behind those two holes is indescribable and the simple wooden crosses in the opposite corners of this field bore testimony to the accuracy of the gunners on both sides. Soon they were to become mere markers used to identify a route to be followed.

"As you leave Bemmel, carry on along the road to Haalderen until you see the knocked out Guards Div. tank. Take the next road on the right and when you come to the Jerry a/t gun, you'll see HQ signals section in the white cottage 30 yards down the farm track on your left."

Looking beyond the a/t gun across the flooded meadow, the houses in the village were quiet. Very little movement could be seen. It was five minutes to four. The 'stonking' hour was approaching. No one was frightened, but everyone was cautious.

Promptly at four o'clock in the afternoon, the Germans would stonk the area of the village, from the church to the little restaurant occupied by our forward company in the northernmost tip of the village. No one moved during the fifteen to twenty minutes in which the mortars rained down, mainly on the church which was soon reduced to a sad pile of rubble. It was during one of these four o'clock stonks that the light on the switchboard flickered, signifying that the RSM's line was still in use.

"Signals office," said the operator.

"RSM here," came the reply. "Have ye any messages for me?"

"Aye, there's two. Ye'd better away an' fetch 'em."

"Ye'll bring them over to my office straight away."

"Ah'll dae nae such thing, Simmonds."

The operator had had many verbal bouts with the HQ Company Runner Fuselier Simmonds, whose skill in impersonating the RSM was well known throughout the company. This time he had no intention of risking his life to jump to the order only to find at the other end a smirking Fusilier Simmonds lounging in an easy chair in the RSM's office. The verbal battle continued.

"This is not Simmonds – this is the RSM."

"Awa' an fass yesel' – ye're nae John the 'B'."

"This *is* John the 'B' – who's that on control?"

"Ye ken fine whae it is, but ye're nae John the 'B'."

"Will you bring those messages?"

"If ye want yon messages, ye'll awa' an' fetch 'em." The phone slammed down on the RSM's line.

Two minutes later the operator saw, to his horror, the unmistakable figure of the RSM striding towards the signals office. Jaw set and his face redder than usual he strode on, seemingly indifferent to the mortaring and the shrapnel flying through the air.

"Jesus! IT WAS John the 'B'. Ye've got tae help me lads. Awa' oot the hoos," he pleaded. "If naebody's aboot, I'll say I couldna tak' yon messages."

We slipped out one by one and hid behind the half-track.

"Where's that man Lafferty?" bellowed the RSM as he stalked into the cottage. Johnnie Lafferty had the presence of mind to pull out the lines to 'B' and 'C' Companies before RSM MacCreadie arrived.

"Come in 'C' Company. Come in 'C' Company," he tried in vain.

"Put down that phone man. What do you mean by disobeying an order from a warrant officer?" barked the RSM.

"I'm sorry sir, I didna ken it was ye. I thought it was yon Simmonds up tae his usual tricks."

"Weel, it wasna Simmonds," he replied mockingly, "it was me – and ye'll be going before the Commanding Officer in the morning."

"Ah've said I'm sorry sir, I couldna leave the exchange and we've lost 'B' and 'C' Companies. The lads are out on the lines now."

We were. We stood on them outside the window as we listed to the irate RSM giving Johnnie a terrible dressing down. Man that he was, the RSM eventually relented.

"All right Lafferty. But next time you are asked to bring a message to my office, ye'll bring it – or send it."

"Aye sir," said Johnnie with great relief and handed the two offending messages over. The warrant officer looked at them.

"All this fuss over these .... Rum ration authorized, and baths unit out of operation." He glared at the operator. "I could have been killed out there by yon mortars just for these."

"Aye sir – an' so could I," retorted Johnnie.

"I'll be away now, Lafferty." He turned as he left the scullery, "An' who gave you permission to call me John the 'B'? Ye'll show proper respect in future." I would swear that I heard him chuckling to himself as he walked back to his office.

Now that I had come into the line with the rest of the signals section I was no longer regarded as a newcomer. We all started off on the same footing in our new surroundings, therefore I became an integral part of the section.

Keeping warm was now of great importance. The cold wet weather, together with the deliberate flooding of parts of Holland by the Germans, soon churned the small roads and tracks into a sea of mud. Wellington boots were worn by everybody. Dry socks were in short supply and wet socks take a lot of drying out.

"Fires, that's the answer," said Jackie Brooks.

"Don't be daft! The SS over there in the brickworks would be over here in a flash as soon as they saw smoke coming out of the chimney," replied Heppy. Jackie cut him short.

"We'll block off the chimney and let the smoke find its own way out the best it can."

"That's a smashing idea," said someone sarcastically. "They won't see the smoke from the chimney — just listen for us coughing our guts up."

"No," said Jackie, "we'll just keep a small fire going night and day. Burn fresh wood at night and then in the daytime we'll use the charcoal from the embers and some of that dried cow muck in the barn."

"Bloody hell," said Paddy. "I don't mind the smell of a nice bit o' turf — but cow muck?"

"It gives off a nice steady heat," replied Jackie.

I thought he should know. During our short acquaintance, our half-track driver had told me that he came from Chipping Norton in Oxfordshire and had worked on a farm before joining the army. Surely he should be given the benefit of the doubt. So it came to pass. We gathered wood from the battered houses to fuel the fire during the night and from the partly burned wood and charcoal we received heat to dry our socks during the day.

At about this time, our daily ration of bread improved slightly. For our midday meal we were issued with a piece of Kraft processed cheese, one tablespoon full of marmalade. On even days we received two slices of bread and on the odd days we had one piece of bread.

The usual practice was to make a sandwich of cheese and marmalade washed down with tea. With our fire we could make . . . toast! I don't know whether any reader has ever tasted toasted cheese and marmalade sandwiches or not. Let me tell you that you haven't lived. Cheese and marmalade sandwiches toasted over a charcoal and cow muck fire produce a flavour which is beyond description.

The aroma emitting from our midday culinary offerings permeated the whole cottage. Our clothing and our hair, smelled of a gentle fragrance of the meadows. It lingered on as we visited former friends in outlying companies who, not just concerned for our safety, entreated us to return with all speed to our little cottage down by the bund, the inside of which was now becoming rather discoloured.

Having overcome the heating problem, our attentions were turned to lighting.

In some parts of the 'island' electricity was in fact being supplied through the civilian system, the source of which was in German occupied territory. There we were, being lit up by kind permission of the Jerries.

'Chez nous', had no such refinements. One Tilley lamp per office was the allocation. Now you can see why the switchboard duty was always oversubscribed by volunteers. A chair to sit on and a Tilley lamp to read by or to write a letter to the folks at home — was there ever such a luxury?

Empty 50 cigarette tins were pressed into use. A hole was pierced in the lid and a piece of 4 x 2 rifle cleaning flannel was pushed through the hole to act as a wick. Paraffin was poured into the tin, the lid replaced and the wick set alight. The result — instant illumination — and smoke.

Other larger containers were used with varying results, but in the main we found that a number of 'fag tin' lights gave off more candle power than one or two bigger models. We all had our own tins which we trimmed and fussed over like kids with a new toy.

After slightly more than a week at the cottage, I was notified that I was to be posted to 'A' Company as relief signaller. I must admit that I was not too optimistic about this new assignment. One reason was that it was a bit nearer the 'sharp end'. It also meant being separated from people whom I had come to trust.

Another thing I would miss would be those crazy Canadians in the fortified position just along the bund road.

About a kilometre to our right as we faced the bund, there was a large building which, from our position, resembled the pavilion at the end of Skegness pier. From this fortified position, the whole of the river Waal and its approaches from the German side were visible and covered by machine-gun fire.

Following an attempt by German frogmen to blow up the bridge at Nijmegen, the Canadians had orders to fire on anything floating in the river. This they did, both night and day.

In order to keep up the spirits of the Allied armies, the American Forces Network broadcast hours and hours of music. All the latest numbers were included, but by far the most popular music was that of Glenn Miller and his orchestra. We all listened to Glenn Miller, including the gunners of the Canadians in the fortress on the bund.

The song 'American Patrol' would come over the airwaves and instantly we would hear the machine-gunners firing in time with the music. *Brrup, ti, brrup, ti, brrup, brrup brrup, ti, brrup* and so on right through the song. 'In

138

the Mood' was also very popular and easy to play on the machine-gun.

These were not just isolated cases. Every day we would be serendaded in this way, so much so, that even if we hadn't got the radio on, we were able to recognize the tune being played.

We didn't mind. When they weren't firing at the river, they would be firing at the brickworks opposite, just to keep the SS on their toes. Yes, I'd miss those happy-go-lucky Canadians. Crazy at times, maybe, but damned fine fighters.

Shortly after dark the jeep arrived to take me to 'A' Company. We turned left at the junction, on past the knocked out Guards Div. tank and on towards Bemmel. Just outside the village we turned off to the right towards a large white farmhouse which stood back from the road about 150 yards. Driving down the tree-lined driveway, I could see in the moonlight another sandbagged and fortified stronghold which this farmhouse had now become.

It was to be the beginning of a long and memorable association with one of the finest groups of men I was ever to have the honour to serve with.

Ossie and his Bren carrier

SEVENTEEN – LEAVE IT TO 'OSSIE'

'A' Company was commanded very firmly and very efficiently by Major John Weir, a tough, granite-faced Scotsman in his mid thirties. Despite his rugged looks and his height of about six feet, he was a very fair man and well liked by his company. He was a schoolmaster by profession, but anyone meeting him for the first time would have thought that he was a long serving regular soldier.

Descending the bricked stairs into the cellar, I was met by the signaller Eddie Fulton. Eddie had been with the Company right through from Normandy and was known throughout the Battalion as the 'Professor'. A tall sandy-haired bespectacled fellow of about 25 years, who had benefited from his education at the Glasgow High School, he spoke in that beautiful soft educated Scots brogue.

"I am Eddie Fulton. And who would you be?" he enquired gently.

"Ken West – relief signaller."

"I'm very pleased to make your acquaintance. Tell me, have you been with us long?" I felt as though I was being interviewed by the Company Commander himself, as he eyed me up and down.

" Since Fontenay," I replied.

"Ah! So you'll know what it's all about then." He looked relieved. "Welcome to our humble abode, Ken."

Humble was indeed the word for it. The three arched rooms were interconnected by arched doorways. Whilst the floor space was quite large, it was only possible to stand upright in the centre of each room. The first room was used as Signals HQ and office, the second as bedroom for Major Weir and his 2 i/c, and the third a bedroom for other ranks. Lighting was again by kind permission of Aladdin and his paraffin lamps.

The air was stale and warm from the fumes of the oil lamps and the personnel, most of whom smoked cigarettes throughout their periods of duty – and I'd thought that nothing could be worse than the little white cottage by the bund.

I spent most of the first night sitting at the switchboard listening through a pair of headphones to all the messages being sent back and forth over the Company network, the idea being for me to put names to voices to be stored up in my mind for future reference. In the fluid situation that we were in, one never knew just what was going to happen from any given moment. Therefore it was necessary to attune the ear to all voices within the whole Battalion network.

It became clear quite early in the evening, that the second-in-command of the Company was now Capt. (pin-down) Dobson MC.

Capt Dobson was formerly a platoon commander in 'D' Company in the Normandy days. He had received the nickname of 'pin-down' through his usage of those words in all his reports of patrol activities undertaken by his platoon.

Whenever his patrol was fired upon by enemy machine-guns, he would report, "We were temporarily pinned down by enemy machine-gun fire." Mostly it was just a case of one's natural instinct to 'freeze' when fired upon. A matter of seconds and then on with the job again. Tonight was confirmation that 'pin-down' was out again with a section. Over the air came an unknown voice.

"Grey Goose reporting ... objective in view ... pinned down by Spandau ... moving to right ... proceeding forward .... Grey Goose, over."

"Hello Grey Goose, message received — listening out, Roger and out."

"That was Arthur Thompson," said Eddie. "He comes from Blairgowrie, hence the throaty dialect."

"Who's he out with, Capt. Dobson?" I asked.

"How did you know that?" replied Eddie. "They've been sitting it out in a house all day — long before you came here, now they're going forward on a listening patrol."

"I noticed that he's still getting pinned down by Spandaus. He doesn't change, does he?" I said laughingly.

"Och, he's OK," said Eddie. "It's just a figure of speech. He won an MC with 'D' Company in Normandy. He's one of the best blokes in the Battalion on foraging patrols — the lads will go anywhere with him. He'll bring them back OK."

Brrrr ... brrr ... brrr ... the field telephone sprang into life.

"Company HQ," I answered — and sensed a pause at the other end of the line.

" 'A' Company HQ?" queried the caller.

"Yes, 'A' Company HQ here," I replied.

"Who the devil are you?" came the pleasant voice from the other end.

"Fusilier West, relief signaller — who's speaking?"

"This is Lt. Dobie, No. 5 Platoon. Any news of the listening patrol by any chance?"

I gave the Lieutenant the news as far as we knew. He thanked me and asked to be informed of their arrival back to our HQ.

"That was 'Laughing Boy'," said Eddie, who had been listening in. "Always got a great big silly grin on his face. I've never seen him upset yet. Always comes up smiling, just a great big overgrown schoolboy really."

We settled down to a listening out situation until about two o'clock in the morning. Eddie said that he would wait until the patrol was back and then leave me to take over until breakfast.

Ten minutes later, the cellar door opened and down the steps came Captain Dobson. He looked surprisingly fresh after his day out in no man's land. His dark eyes glanced to where the Major lay asleep.

"No need to wake him, Fulton, tell him we're back when he does wake up and I'll report to him in the morning."

"I'll do that," replied Eddie, "or rather Fusilier West here will — he's taking over now."

Those dark eyes looked at me hard and long.

"I've seen you before somewhere, West. Where would that be?"

"I used to be with Sgt. Louis Hill in 17 Platoon — left them at Caen."

"That's it, a 'D' Company lad like myself." He mused for a moment. "You'll be pleased to hear that Sgt. Hill is still going strong, still Platoon Commander — never seems to keep an officer for long, they keep getting bumped off. He got a well deserved MM for his part in that ambush at Juvigny."

"I thought we'd had it that afternoon," I said reflectively.

"Of course, you'd be with him. He's carried those lads of his right through, mostly on his own." He yawned, took one last swig of the mug of tea that we had given him.

"I'll take a look at my lads now, then I'll turn in. Good-night chaps, have a quiet night." He went back up the brick steps two at a time, taking care to close the door quietly behind him.

"I'll awa' tae ma wee bed the noo," said the Professor, in the broadest of Glaswegian accents. "Give me a call if you are in any sort of a mess."

I thanked him and started contemplating the letter I would be writing to my wife in the early hours of this December morning. The rest of the night passed quietly and surprisingly it was soon time for stand to.

I woke the Major and gave him the message from Pin-Down.

"You should have woken me," was his gruff rejoinder.

"Captain Dobson said he would report to you first thing sir . . . " He cut me short.

"Remember this, West," he said sharply. "Whenever any of my Company are out on patrol, I want to be informed immediately on their return. Did you inform the Commanding Officer?"

"Yes sir."

"What did he say?"

" 'If Major Weir is asleep, don't waken him . . . I think it will be a quiet night.' " I then gave the usual situation report.

"Very quiet upstairs, sir, only a few doodle-bugs going over. Very little shelling — none around here."

He nodded his thanks and called for the Sergeant-Major to accompany him on the morning's inspection of the stand to points around the Company perimeter. As the cellar door opened, I could hear the sound of the jerrycan cooker being primed ready for use. The first brew of the day would soon be ready. Hot strong tea to warm the lads out there in the half light of a cold frosty morning. Winter was beginning to bite. Little did we know that it was going to be known in Dutch history as 'the hard winter'.

It was about eight o'clock when someone shouted down the stairs that breakfast was ready. Now I could see for the first time what the rest of the farmhouse looked like.

The cellar steps led into the barn adjoining the main farmhouse. The whole place was much bigger than any of the others that I'd been in. The ground floor was being used as sleeping quarters for the members of Company HQ, with the exception of the former lounge which was now the Company Office. It was now apparent that only the duty officer and the duty staff spent the nights in the cellar, and as we three signallers were all duty staff it was going to be each and every night down there in the paraffin fumed cellar for us.

The roaring sound coming from the far end of the barn was the immediate centre of attention for everyone there. This was something new to me. On closer inspection, I saw an ingenious contraption being operated by a swarthy-looking Geordie of about 30 years of age. This then, was the well-known 'Ossie', (the man, not the contraption).

"Porridge?" said Ossie.

"Please." My mess tin was prompty half filled with hot steaming salty porridge.

"Tea's over there, mate." He jerked his thumb in the direction of the steps leading to the granary, where at the bottom stood a thin faced, tatty looking individual in need of a wash and shave.

He paused momentarily between mouthfuls and with a gesture with his dessert-spoon said, "Help ye'self tae the tea." Then continued to devour the remaining porridge in his mess tin.

I sat on the bottom step of the well worn wooden steps and eyed the scene as I ate the delicious Scots porridge.

Ossie was very definitely in charge of this operation. The jerrycan cooker was his pride and joy. It operated thus:

A jerrycan petrol container was laid on its side on top of two house bricks. A small hole had been pierced by a nail into the original base of the can about one and a half inches from the side. Directly above this hole and about three inches apart, a similar hole had been pierced. With the can on its side, petrol was then poured in until a depth of approximately one inch was reached and the filler cap closed.

A paraffin type light was placed underneath the jerrycan. Shortly afterwards, a vapour jet would be observed coming from the nail hole and a further 'fag tin' lighter would be placed in the jet stream of petrol vapour and — hey presto! — a sheet of flame roared into life. Stew pans or billy cans were then placed on an altar of bricks to be heated by this unusual but very efficient flame-thrower.

The delicate art of modulating the pressure of the flame was left in the most capable hands of Ossie. As the pressure built up inside the jerrycan, the 'fag tin' light was withdrawn, thereby lowering the pressure to a managable flame. As the flame became softer, the tin was pushed back underneath. This manipulation of 'fag tins' and the ever necessary rotation of the food being cooked, called for great dexterity from the operator. As George's old sar'nt-major would have said, "H'it calls for great co-h'ordination of the hand and the h'eye."

From my seat on the steps, Ossie was sheer poetry in motion, as he transferred from the porridge to the 'bangers', then to the omelette made from powdered egg. All this being carried out with a continous banter of wit from this Geordie, whose real job at that time was the driver of the Company Bren carrier. The official Company cooks were in another house about a hundred yards away. That breakfast was by far the best I had eaten on the island so far.

Excellent cook that he might be, Ossie was even better at the gentle art of bartering.

With the Bren carrier at his disposal, he had so much territory within the Battalion area that he must cover during his daily routine visits. This he used to the full.

One corner of the barn was stacked high with crates of apples which must have been picked and packed just prior to the Airborne landing and in the subsequent chaos, had been overlooked. All civilians had been evacuated from the area and the apples would just stay there to rot. Not if Ossie could help it. This was his stock-in-hand for bartering for whatever we needed. No one asked where his contacts were, but from time to time he would come back with potatoes, tea and sugar, dried egg, and on one momentous occasion, a sack of flour.

With such a variety of ingredients, very rarely did we have to fall back on to our marmalade and cheese sandwiches for midday 'tiffin'.

Our unofficial daily menu became the talking point of the tight little band of Company HQ. Spud bashing, usually such a drag in the army, became a pleasurable chore. We had potatoes boiled, baked, fried, chipped, scolloped, in fact every possible way. For sweet we used the apples. The introduction of a biscuit tin oven meant that we could now have a variation from the stewed apples. Baked apples with a variation of treacle or raisins in the core hole were very popular until the flour appeared. Then came the *pièce de résistance*, apple tart. A special favourite of mine. My mother used to make a very nice apple tart which was always served up with spoonfuls of thick yellow custard. Ossie's tarts though not quite in the same class as mother's, were nevertheless always most welcome.

Readers may have raised their eyebrows at the Heath Robinson way of cooking and might well think that it was dangerous. It was. Very dangerous. So much so, that after a number of accidents within the Division, one of which resulted in a jerrycan exploding and two men of the Hallamshires being killed, these types of cookers were banned. This however did not deter Ossie for he used his right through to the end of the war.

Our stay at the farmhouse lasted for two weeks, during which time I became more conversant with the way that the Company operated. My previous experiences in Normandy were confined to the furthermost outposts of a company, the rifle section. Here I was viewing things from the top. I was impressed by the overall efficiency and the quiet confidence of everyone to meet any emergency that might arise. Everyone that is, except fellow signaller Arthur Thompson.

Arthur was one of a kind. He was the thin faced chap I had met at the bottom of the granary steps on that first morning. I thought he was looking the way he was, because of the previous day's patrol. The truth of the matter was that he always looked like that.

Originally, he had been in the RAF and had undergone training as a wireless operator/air gunner. But like many others he had been discarded, to be retrained in the army as an infantry signaller for the D-Day landings. Consequent events had brought him to the RSF as a replacement. He was a brilliant reader of morse code and could leave the rest of us standing in that art, so I asked him why he had come out of the RAF.

"I didn't come out of the RAF, I was thrown out — for peppering Blackpool promenade with machine-gun fire."

This needed a little more explanation I thought and he was quite prepared to continue.

"I was training with a Polish squadron up in Scotland. We did our morse course OK and then we had to go down to Blackpool for the gunnery course." His pale blue eyes twinkled as he relived in his mind an incident as bizarre as it was hilarious.

"After the theory, we had to go up in a plane to do the practical," he continued. "An old plane towed a canvas target out over the sea on a course parallel to the beach. Our plane had to fly between the promenade and the target plane and fire away at the target over the sea. When it came to my turn to fire, we were coming to the end of the run and the plane turned as I fired. Instead of hitting the target, I put a few shots through the fuselage of the towing plane, the crew of which were also Polish. Everyone was screaming at me in Polish and broken English — Hold the Fire! Target to starboard! Fire! I fired, but got my starboard and port sides mixed up. *Brrr* .... *brrr* .... *brrr* .... *brrr*. More screaming from the Polacks — then I looked down, and there all along the promenade, everyone was lying flat out. I thought I'd killed the bloody lot. Fortunately no one was injured, but it was decided that as I couldn't hit a target out at sea or even hit the stationary Blackpool Tower,

I wouldn't have much chance of knocking down a Messerschmitt over Germany in the dark."

He didn't seem too hurt by being seconded to the army and was quite philosophical about the whole thing. But he did warn me.

"If I ever have to fire this bloody Sten gun in a hurry, make sure ye've got the head well down, Kenny lad." Fortunately for me the occasion never arose but he very nearly scared the pants off me one day when we were on a line break job.

Slight mortaring had taken place, hence the break in the line. We had repaired the break and I was just moving off when I saw Arthur, tip-tapping about with his foot. Thinking that he'd maybe found a little mouse or something similar, I waited for him to pick it up. He rolled whatever it was, around with his foot for a time and then stooped and picked it up. He walked towards me and there in his hand was a mortar bomb.

"It was a waste o' time for the Boche to send this one over, Kenny lad — it's a dud."

I froze in my tracks.

"Now look Arthur," I said as calmly as I could. "That thing could still go off. Put it down gently. Don't throw it down — we don't want another line to repair."

I think the sheer stupidity of my remark saved the situation. Arthur chuckled to himself and instead of throwing it away, as I'm sure he would have done, he placed it carefully by the side of the road. I gave a sigh of relief.

"That's the idea Arthur, leave it there. My old mum always told me as a kid, never pick anything up in the street young Ken — you never know where it's been."

We walked back to the white farmhouse in silence, but I had learned my lesson. Whenever I saw Arthur kicking anything on the ground, I always walked off in another direction.

It's a funny thing, self-preservation.

EIGHTEEN – SECRET WEAPON

Thoughts were now beginning to turn towards Christmas. Only another ten days to go and there were so many rumours and speculations about where we would be at this festive time.

Another general turnaround on the Battalion front meant that as 'A' Company had been in the line for some four weeks, they would now go into reserve. This meant that one signaller would be surplus to requirement. As the newest lad, it would be my turn to return to Battalion HQ.

Our old billets at Bemmel were the new location for us. It was not quite the same as when we had left them some weeks ago. Shelling and mortaring had paid their toll on the buildings. The back of the signals section house had almost disappeared, it was little more than a pile of rubble. The orchards around the part of the village adjacent to the HQ were now looking decidedly battle weary.

The cookhouse had luckily received far less attention than the other building, although it was directly opposite the signal office. The beaming face of CQMS Wallace met me as I called for a mug of tea shortly after our arrival.

"Back again eh, laddie? I bet you're glad to get a good cup o' tea again after that muck at 'A' Company." I thought about those super meals of Ossie's, but I knew he was referring to the 'A' Company cooks, Morrison and James.

"Aye, ye make a fine cup o' char, Colour," I found myself answering in an adopted Scottish accent.

Sitting in the side room of the signal office as we ate our midday 'tiffin', we weighed up the pros and cons of Christmas in Nijmegen. Suddenly from overhead came an unusual whine. Silently we waited for the expected explosion. The whine receded but without the resultant bang.

"They've not only fired one from the train, they've sent the bloody wagons over as well," said Jackie Brooks. He was referring to the long range shells that the Germans were reputed to be firing from the main railway line north of Arnhem.

"That was no ordinary shell," interposed Sgt. Reg Ward.

"Another one of Hitler's secret weapons," joked Bill Brown, little knowing how near he was to the truth.

A few minutes later we heard the whine coming again. It may sound ridiculous, but everyone in the room dumped their mess tins on the floor and ran out of the front door. Looking to the west of the church tower we could see a plane disappearing in the direction of the Reich. A blueish-black column of smoke came from its rear as though it was on fire.

We stood there trying to fathom out what kind of plane it could be. We soon found out.

Back came the screaming, whining plane. We looked up in disbelief. The plane passed over us only a few hundred feet above the ground and we could see the sleek silver belly of the fuselage as it sped along.

"It's got no bloody propeller," said Paddy. "An' its arsehole's on fire," he shouted incredulously. "It must be a piloted rocket of some kind — it's not a buzz-bomb and the V2 is a rocket fired from the ground."

We awaited the return of this new fangled form of Nazi destruction. Our wait was in vain for it didn't appear again that day, but we did see it again on two or three other occasions.

What we had witnessed was a piece of aviation history. The screaming, whining object in the sky over Bemmel was indeed the Me 262, the first operational jet plane in the world.

Much later we were to find why the plane did not attack us. Field Marshal Hermann Goering had decreed that the new jet plane must only be used for reconnaissance work over the front lines.

Much to our chagrin we discovered that we had fallen right into the trap. In our eagerness to inspect this new flying weapon, we had been photographed out there in the open, thereby giving away our positions and, as we were to learn later, our identity, to the low flying intruder.

So great was the air supremacy of the Allied Forces, that although we were only about 12 miles from the actual border of Germany, we never saw an enemy plane flying over the 'island' during daylight. This new plane was in a class of its own, because of its much higher speed, there were no British or American planes which could get within striking distance of it.

The sudden increase in reconnaissance on their part, was necessary in order to build up a complete picture of the disposition of troops along the northern end of the Allied front.

The unforseen offensive in the Ardennes was being built up painstakingly by the enemy. Had the new well-known 'Battle of the Bulge' been won by the Germans, we in the Canadian Army would have been cut off from the rest of the 21st Army Group, and this story may well have taken on another perspective. Fortunately for us the line was held at Bastogne, but all this would be happening after Christmas and here we were, just a week away.

Letters from home told of our loved ones preparing for the anniversary of the birth of our Lord. We hoped within our heart of hearts, that this would be the last time we should be separated, and that we could look forward to peace on earth and goodwill to all men.

The hard facts were that it had taken us six months to get from Normandy to Holland and we were not yet half-way to Berlin. Christmas at home was just fanciful thinking.

We would have to make the best of what we had.

Ressen Church, December 1944

NINETEEN – SILENT NIGHT

"We'll no' be spending Christmas in Nijmegen." John the 'B' poked his head round the door as he spoke. "Instead, we'll be away doon the road tae Ressen. The Commanding Officer and I have agreed that we should let the Sassenachs get away tae Nijmegen for Christmas — but we'll be there for Hogmanay." I saw the glint in his eyes of expectations of much merriment yet to come.

"When do we move?" everyone asked together.

"We go tonight — move off at dusk. Their advance party will be here in half an hour."

I looked across at Paddy. He took the news quite philosophically.

"When you're serving with a load of heathens, I suppose you must expect to conform with their pagan rituals."

There didn't seem to be any point in arguing with that profound statement, so we packed our kit in silence.

I scrounged a lift on the half-track with Jackie Brooks. No point in straining oneself even though the distance was no more than a couple of miles. We proceeded at a walking pace, but it was nice and warm in the cab. Four of us were crammed in tightly and Jackie got some very funny looks as he fumbled for the gear lever amongst the conglomeration of legs and kit.

The little village of Ressen was a small oasis in a countryside which had been transformed from beautiful fruit orchards and glasshouses with their lettuce and tomato crops, to a churned up, shell pocked battleground where the trees in those orchards had been snapped off in full fruit. Glasshouses no longer held the glass in their frames, and cattle and pigs had long since left the scene.

Most of the shells landing in Ressen had miraculously missed the houses and had found their resting place in the field in the centre of the village.

The half-track pulled up outside the vicarage, or Pastorie as it is known in Holland. The vicarage stood in its own trim garden, a large squarely built house, with two large beech trees in the front garden. Two gravel paths allowed entrance to the front door which stood at the top of three stone steps. At the back of the house was a large pump which stood half-way down the path leading through the vegetable patch. Someone had thoughtfully protected this pump with straw to keep out the icy blasts which blew from the north with ever more penetration. A water supply such as this was very welcome. Here we were to have the pleasure of a wash and shave using our own clear water direct from the well.

Looking from the front steps of the house, one could see the neat layout of this small village.

A rectangular field measuring some 200 yards long by 100 yards wide, was surrounded by a neat row of trees ten yards apart which had been planted around the perimeter. Outside the trees, a ditch filled with water prevented access, apart from one single gate on the southern side. Another rectangle of trees, symmetrically opposite the inner line, stood between the ditch and the roadway which skirted the village green, as it came to be called.

The vicarage stood on the northern side of this rectangle and a collection of neat detached houses, each with its own individually designed front garden, could be seen on the western side. At the southern end there were three farms, or smallholdings, of which the centre one was by far the largest.

The eastern side of this delightful little Dutch landscape was dominated by the church. Not a large church by any standard, just a small stone built one with the old square tower nearest to the road. A short stunted steeple sat on top of the tower. A neatly trimmed evergreen hedge completed the boundary from the church to the road leading to Bemmel.

The white Polar Bear with the number 61 in white on a green background could be seen outside most of the houses. The 'Scottish Polar Bears' had arrived for Christmas. For me it was to be a most memorable one, indeed even now when the festive season is upon us, my mind goes back to that wartime experience and 'a wee bittie tear stings the eye'.

Whether it was because we were in the Pastorie or not I don't know, but somehow I had never felt so safe in a house before as I did in that house. For the first and, let me add, the only time, I slept upstairs at night.

The large bedroom at the front left hand side was probably the main bedroom. Now it was just a bare room, so we slept on the wooden floor boards, but it was one of those warm friendly houses and we felt comfortable within its embrace.

One of the occupants of the room was a north country chap by the name of Hartley. Like most of the despatch riders in the army, he was an adventurous bloke who used his motor bike to his best advantage.

Ben's peacetime hobby and interest was organs. He had an overriding passion for the things. Anything with pedals, stops and pipes, would attract Ben like a bee to a hive. There were many tales of him being reported missing or overdue, only for him to be found by someone noticing a motor bike outside a damaged church or a house. Inside, Ben would be found pumping or pedalling away at some old organ or harmonium.

As one of our less literate colleagues was heard to say, "There he was, sitting at this harmonious commode, playing away."

Ben's answer to that had been, "I know I might sometimes play a load of rubbish, but I've never played a load of shyte."

I had got to know this Lancashire lad quite well by now, so it came as no surprise when one day he said confidentially, "Come and see what I've found, Kenny lad."

We turned left as soon as we went out of the gate. I knew then that it was going to be a visit to the church. Once those long legs of his got into motion, I almost had to run to keep up with him. I sensed there must be an organ at the end of this. I would not be disappointed.

The door on the right hand side of the church was wedged half open. As we entered, we saw that direct hits on the window of the nave, had caused severe damage to that end of the building. The lectern was smashed and lying on its side amongst the rubble from the window. The font was sitting foolishly askew on its shrapnel-scarred base. Gaping holes in the roof showed that this was not just an unlucky strike. This had been premeditated.

There was a mistaken belief, on both sides, that all church towers and spires were used as look-out towers or vantage points for snipers to use. This may have been the case in some instances but not always was it so.

We looked up to the left. There at the top of a spiral staircase was the organ. Ben went up those stairs two at a time. A quick look told him that the organ was a pump operated type. He nodded his approval.

"I thought it would be one of these, Ken — that's why I wanted you to come along. Will you pump, while I try out the keyboard?"

I started to pump. The old contraption wheezed and blew. Ben looked down at the yellowed keys, old and irregular. He rubbed his hands, whether in delight or to warm them, I knew not. He started to play what should have been 'In the Mood'.

"Christ, it's had a hell of a battering."

He got up from the stool and leaned forward for a closer look.

"Just look at these pipes, Kenny lad, they've had a right spraying with shrapnel." Sure enough, most of the pipes had holes in them of varying sizes.

"Looks to me as though it's had it," I said.

"Have you got any adhesive tape on you?" he asked hopefully. I searched my pockets.

"Yep, I've a part roll here."

"Right. We'll tape over some of these small holes and see if that does any good." The next half-hour was spent taping over the small holes.

"Righto Ken, we'll try again." The maestro placed his hands on the keys once more. "I think I'll play something a little slower this time."

Pumping with all gusto, I managed to provide enough air for the organ to wheeze and groan out a tune which faintly resembled 'Silent Night'.

Now Ben was a perfectionist. In civvy street he had been one of those part-time organists, so popular in the 1930s in the cinemas. He played in one of the Lancashire towns and was quite proud of the fact that he could play practically any tune you could name. To say he was disturbed at what he'd just heard, was putting it mildly.

"Jesus — did you hear that? It sounded like the Battalion latrines, with every other bloke farting out of tune."

I thought of our companion and his harmonious commode and quickly changed the subject.

"How can we seal the holes?" I asked despairingly.

Ben thought for a minute, then played a note. It came out flat. Leaning over the rail, he took a gob of chewing gum from his mouth and smeared the gum into the hole. He then bound the pipe and gum with the tape and tried again. The note came through pretty much on pitch.

"That's the answer, Kenny lad," he said, rubbing his hands with glee. "Come on — we need lots of chewing gum."

The first job on our return to the Pastorie was to ask everyone we met, to save their chewing gum. For the next two days, everyone was chewing the cud for all they were worth. As soon as we had a bit of spare time, we would be across to the church, re-chew the gum, and patch up a few more holes.

It was late in the afternoon of the second day that eventually we got the organ working to Ben's satisfaction. A quick rendering of 'In the Mood' and then on to the serious stuff.

Appropriately enough, he started with 'Bells across the meadow' and then with the Christmas spirit welling up inside him, the carol 'Silent Night'.

I pumped away like billy-o and like Ben, got carried away with the excitement of the moment, as we sang:

"Silent night, holy night. All is calm, all is bright.

By yon virgin mother and child,

Holy infant so tender and mild,

Sleep in heavenly peace, sleep in heavenly peace."

We had just got started on the second verse when we were rudely interrupted.

"What the hell's going on in here?"

We looked down at the British officer's uniform below and saw the three pips on the shoulders.

"Christ — it's the adjutant," whispered Ben through his teeth.

"Who the devil's playing up there? Stop playing that confounded thing at once! I've just come along the road from Bemmel and you can hear that bloody noise all the way here. It's echoing across the countryside — they can probably hear the bloody thing in Berlin."

Ben sat his ground.

"It's Hartley here, sir — we're just trying out the old organ now that we've patched it up."

"Come down here you bloody fool," said the adjutant.

When we got downstairs, Ben explained how we had spent our spare time repairing the damaged pipes. Much to our surprise, the adjutant went up in the murky light to see our handiwork for himself.

"Damned ingenious, Hartley, I didn't know you were an instrumentalist —

what else can you play?"

Ben sat down and as I pumped, he played softly a little bit of 'Poet and Peasant'. The adjutant nodded appreciatively.

"Can you play carols?"

"How about 'The First Nowell'?" offered the maestro. Half-way through, the captain stopped him.

"You'll get me shot, Hartley. I came in to give you a bawling out and now I'm aiding and abetting you. You'd both better pack it in for today, but I'll have a word with the CO and see if we can't hold a carol service the day after tomorrow — on Christmas Day."

December 24th was a quiet day, until the hours of darkness. The evening's rum ration probably started the ball rolling. This little tot each evening was always very eagerly awaited. Tonight was something special.

John the 'B', entering into the spirit of things, was able to give out a double ration with which to bring in Christmas Day. Some of us couldn't wait that long.

The first sign of things going awry was the call from the platoon nearest to the Waal bridge.

"Jimmy Logan here. I'm taking over this post — giving the lads a break." This was followed by another call shortly afterwards from the bridge.

"Jimmy Logan here. I'll be taking over for an hour or so — just to give the lads a wee break."

We tried to raise both positions, but to no avail. What had happened, was that Jimmy, with his delightful bit of Irish blarney, had offered to take over their telephone for a short time, in exchange for their rum ration. Having received the ration, he had downed the lot and then rung through with his repeat offer. As the patrol was only just down the road from Nijmegen, they fell for his assurances that a relief patrol would be along to take their place. This was a pure figment of his imagination. Luckily enough, the Germans were probably celebrating in a like manner. The danger to the bridge was not as imminent as one might have thought. It was the end of Jimmy's Christmas though, he was paralytic by midnight, and it took two days in the RAP to get him back on his feet again.

Meanwhile back in the village of Ressen, old scores were being settled, or attempts were being made to settle them.

The light flickered on the switchboard.

"Have ye no seen the RSM?" came the slurred voice.

"Did you want him urgently?" enquired Bill Brown.

"Aye, I did that — an' when I find him, I'm gonna kill him."

"Charming," replied Bill, "and a merry Christmas to you too."

"I'll have none o' your cheek, laddie. I've no' forgotten what the man did tae me in India in 1938 . . . . " The rest was lost.

"Better get someone out quick," said Bill. "That silly idiot is trying to settle some old score that's years old."

After a quarter of an hour's frenzied activity, all was quiet. Someone had biffed the Sergeant and put him out cold.

As the hour of midnight arrived, we raised our mugs and drank the toast.

"Merry Christmas to us and to the folks back home."

The adjutant was as good as his word. A message was broadcast to all companies.

"All men not on urgent duties, may attend a carol service at Ressen at 11.00 hours."

The little church was full as the Colonel and the Company Commanders took their places. They sat on the only chairs available. So many wished to attend, whether voluntarily or not, that standing order only was the order of the day.

For Ben and myself there was a little disappointment. The Colonel had decided that as we had a church organist in our midst, he should be the one to play the organ. Ben and I were left to make sure that the old girl performed in a smart and soldier like manner.

The organist turned out to be none other than a mate of ours from the signal section, John Boult. In case the name sounds familiar, it can be revealed that John was the nephew of the celebrated conductor Sir Adrian Boult. Yet another dark horse in the squad.

Looking down on the assembled congregation, we could see two youthful figures at the front amidst a sea of khaki army uniforms. The two young men were the only two civilians in the village. They had been found in the pigsty at the back of the house next to the church. Thinking that they were enemy left-overs, they had been ferreted out, only for our lads to find two startled youngsters who had been left behind to look after the livestock in the barn.

Guy Lammers and his cousin Jan, had become mascots to the RAP staff who had taken over their parents' house. They were unofficially taken on ration and issued with red cross armbands of which they were very proud.

The two youngsters joined in the singing of carols in their own language, whilst the rest of us enjoyed the opportunity to sing a good selection of the well-known favourites. The service was conducted by our Church of Scotland padre and the lesson read by 'Dad' Eykin. The old organ did us proud and John even had enough faith in our 'chewwy and tape' bandaging, to play everyone out.

It is a service I shall never forget. Everyone standing under the roof that opened to the sky. Wisps of snow and sleet fell on to the lads below and we all forgot for a short time the ravages of war. Our thoughts were not only of the occasion we were celebrating, most of us, in our minds, were at home with our loved ones.

To celebrate the great day, Bill Brown had somehow obtained a camera with a film in. We must have a photograph taken on the front step and those not on duty filed outside. Cpl. Jackie Thompson did the honours. Bill decided that he had better take another photo in case of a bad exposure. We lined up again.

"Smile please." . . . . *wheeeeeee* . . . . . . *crrrrummmp.*

The only shell to be fired on our front that day landed slap between the two beech trees. Everyone hit the deck. On the resultant photograph, which I still have, we can be seen taking off in all different directions. Amazingly enough, no one was injured. We returned inside for a mug of tea and our marmalade and cheese toast.

In the evening we made our way round to the big farmhouse for the main meal. Our Christmas dinner was stewed steak and potatoes with Christmas pudding – and a can of beer.

Ressen vicarage – Christmas Day, 1944 with (l. to r.) Ken West, Harry Harper, Paddy Deegan, Ben Brenner, Bill Brown, and 'Heppy' Hepworth

TWENTY – HAPPY HOGMANAY

The great iron structure of the Waal bridge loomed in the distance, its dark outline clearly visible in the pale moonlight. It stood defiantly intact as though it was waiting to welcome us into its heart, bringing warmth and succour to the tired and dirty file of men getting nearer and nearer.

Our footsteps made very little sound as we made our progress along the small country roads. The thin carpet of newly arrived snow cushioned our feet from the sharp gravel which covered the roads. Wellington boots are not the best of footwear in which to march, but as they had become our mode of dress on this wet and sloppy island, it was necessary to give ourselves the maximum amount of protection to our feet, so, silently we came nearer and nearer to this colossus from the Clyde.

It was an eerie journey, not a word was spoken. No one was allowed to speak whilst on the move at night on the island. Voices carry a long way on a still winter's night. Here and there was heard a jingle of equipment as someone slithered on the uneven road, fast becoming padded down, for the snow was pounded flat as it fell.

Eyes became tired as we kept a clear look-out for the black shape of the comrade in front, carefully keeping the required distance. Bunches of soldiers tend to become a clack of chatterboxes after a time. A mortar bomb or a shell can also wipe out half a dozen men if they are too close together. We didn't want any accidents this night. After four weeks in the line, we were at last on our way to Nijmegen for a rest.

A shrapnel-scarred sign with the name LENT written on it in bold black letters cheered us a little. We know now that this was the beginning of the long approach to the big bridge. I felt a new spring in my step as we marched on eagerly into the yawning mouth of the road bridge. Someone started to sing softly. I quickly recognized it as 'Good King Wenceslas'. One by one we all joined in. We sang carols all the way across the bridge and on by the Citadel. As we passed the Wintergardens and along to Groesbeeksweg we sang 'Silent Night'. Somehow this seemed quite appropriate. Coming back to this part of the town was like coming home again. We hoped that we would spend some time with our friends whom we had met on the previous occasion.

We rang the bell at No. 102 and the door opened as before in that mysteriously silent way. Mynheer and Mevrouw stood at the top of the stairs in a state of happy expectancy; their beaming faces looking down at us showed that we were indeed welcome.

Greetings were exchanged in Dutch and English and formal hand shakes extended to Paddy and myself from all members of the family.

"Thee?" asked Mevrouw.

"Dank U," we replied in our newly learned Dutch.

Mevrouw went to the chimney. Her hand disappeared up the flue, reappearing with one tea-bag held between forefinger and thumb. The teapot was ceremoniously warmed. The tea-bag dropped inside and hot water poured into the pot until it was full. Tea was made.

From the cabinet on the far wall, a cup and saucer was taken and placed before each person. I looked at the exquisitely delicate china. Each piece looked so frail and transparent, I doubted whether my coarse fingers with their tips still without feeling would be able to pick up these frail cups when they were full of tea. My fears were allayed, the cups were only slightly more than half filled with tea. I looked into the cup. The water had only changed colour very slightly. Mevrouw beamed her motherly smile across the table towards Paddy and me.

"Zukker?" she enquired, as she proffered some cubes of sugar.

I looked sideways at Paddy as I replied, "Een, dank U."

Paddy followed my example and took only one lump of sugar. My intuition had told me that this sugar had been kept for a special occasion. Many weeks later this was confirmed by Wim the elder son. We were honoured.

There were two days to New Year's Eve. We took our leave of the family and retired to the bedroom where we slept like a couple of logs in the large double bed.

Baths, a change of laundry and haircuts were the order of the day. We were able to partake of these luxuries in a leisurely manner. No need to rush things for a few days.

The Wintergardens beckoned us after 'tiffin', where we joined the large queue as we waited for the vouchers needed to enable us to purchase the 'char and wads' on sale in the main hall.

"One mug of tea and two cakes," said the NAAFI waitress when we eventually reached the counter. That was it! We paid the girl and found a clear space at one of the tables on the side.

The large Concertgebouw had been commandeered for us to eat our char and wads. Where once had played the most famous orchestras in Europe, conducted by all the most celebrated maestros of the twentieth century, a mass of men from all corners of the British Empire, sat devouring cakes, as they listened to a young group of Dutch musicians playing all the latest popular wartime songs. 'White Cliffs of Dover', seemed to me to be so very much out of place. Paddy as usual, brought things into proper perspective.

"If the Royal Palace in Naples is good enough for the Eighth Army and the Yanks, I reckon this is good enough for us."

We pushed our feet under the table and joined in the eating.

Table-tennis, being so popular, was out of the question. You also had to deposit your belt and hat in return for the bats and a ball. That seemed decidedly risky, so we adjourned to the writing room and library.

I had saved up two of my 'censor free' envelopes for this sort of occasion. Now I was able to write to my wife Margaret freely, and tell her things that I had been keeping bottled up for weeks. The words flowed from the pen of a love-sick swain.

Margaret had joined the Women's Land Army shortly after her eighteenth birthday in 1940. For two years she had worked in that lovely part of England, the county of Rutland. Both of us had made many friends in those villages in the vale of Hambleton, now sadly under the waters of a reservoir.

My mind went back to those picturesque ironstone farms and the rugged characters who tended their animals and tilled the rich reddish-brown fields. I thought too, of the times we had picked bunches of rich yellow primroses in amongst the silver birches of Hambleton Woods.

Here in Holland, I was living within a farming community and I knew that Margaret would be interested to hear about the kind of people I had met and who now were permitting me to share their home.

I had been fortunate to spend every Christmas with Margaret for the past four years. We had married in September 1942 and so this would be our first Christmas and New Year apart. This was an experience which we must share with many millions of people who were also separated from their loved ones, some of whom were never to be reunited. I wrote only of the cheerful things and of my deep love for her.

New Year's Eve was spent at the special concert at the Wintergardens. An ENSA group comprised mainly of continental performers, had provided splendid entertainment. Each act had been well received, but the most vociferous ovation had been for the Belgian couple who performed an adagio act. Not so much for the brilliantined gent who did the throwing, but for the curvacious blonde in her minute sequinned costume, as she posed in the most graceful positions between the spells of rotation on the stage.

"An' her sister's a big girl too," interjected my Irish pal. Paddy had awakened from his after-dinner meditation. Unfortunately we had not had dinner, just tea and cakes — twice.

Our hopes that the NAAFI would celebrate the turn of the year with an issue of beer were, however, sadly dashed.

Following the stage show, a dance had been organized in the main hall. It became very obvious that we stood very little chance of a partner, as the 'back room wallahs' had brought their own girl-friends with them and they were going to keep them to themselves. After about half an hour we decided to leave and spend the rest of what was left of 1944 with our host family at No.102. On our way, a small party of us sang on our way around the giant roundabout, wishing all and sundry a happy new year as they passed by.

The Van Beukering family were expecting us to return in time for the sounds of Big Ben as they received them on their wireless set, no longer hidden from prying eyes, but here on the family dresser for everyone to see and to listen to in perfect freedom.

Small presents were exchanged, in between the speeches of thanks which were translated carefully and painstakingly by both Wim and his sister Eit. We gave some tea and sugar and one or two items of 'government surplus', socks for father and gloves for mother.

We were joined in the family celebrations by a Canadian Corporal named Roy whom we had met at the house from time to time. We formed the impression that he was rather sweet on Dot, the elder sister, but mother wasn't too keen on her daughters being too friendly with the soldiers. I don't blame her.

Roy, being in the Canadian forces, had access to a liquor supply. Unlike the British Army, Canadian Corporals were allowed an issue of spirits. Roy had saved his ration to share with us on this festive occasion. One bottle of gin went to Mynheer and Mevrouw and a bottle of Scotch was shared between us.

The last hour of the year was spent talking of home and our hopes and aspirations for the future. We laughed and sang until the familiar tones of Big Ben rang out. A new year at last.

Arms were linked in the true Scottish tradition and we sang "Auld Lang Syne" as we ushered in the New Year of 1945. Our good wishes for the new year were answered by the Dutch with "Gellukkig Nieuwjaar," then, for the first time, we put our arms round the ladies in turn and kissed them as we wished our own private wishes to each other.

Roy filled the glasses and proposed the toast, "Het Nederlands."

Mynheer returned the compliments with "Our Liberators." The names of Winston Churchill and Monty were also mentioned before I proposed the toast, "The folks back home."

I detected a wee bit o' tear in the eyes of our Canadian friend as he grasped my hand firmly and said quietly and firmly, "Praise God, this may be the last year of this horrible war. May we all be back with our loved ones next year."

"Amen to that," was my reply.

The first hour of 1945 was celebrated from within followed by serious predictions of when we might see the end of hostilities in Europe.

"I don't think the Germans can last longer than the beginning of June," said Roy.

I couldn't see how we could possibly finish the task in front of us by then, but when Wim asked for my opinion, I could not bring myself to deflate the air of expectancy that Roy had created by his optimism.

"Oh, I can't see how they can possibly go on much longer than that —

perhaps July," I found myself saying.

This statement from me seemed to substantiate all their hopes and so we danced around the room to the Scottish music from the BBC.

By now all etiquette had been completely forgotten, and the night finished with an impromptu sword dance.

With the aid of an umbrella and a walking stick laid on the floor in ceremonial fashion, I poised as Paddy stuffed a cushion under his arm in the fashion of a 'doodlezak'. Imitating the bagpipes we commenced. The tots of whisky within me fanned the fervour with which my stockinged feet crossed and pointed their way through a memorable display of this noble art. We were a very happy group of people as we went to bed that night.

Our dining hall during all our stays in Nijmegen, was in the main hall of the school situated on a crossroad, about 200 yards from the van Beukering house. Most of the school buildings were used as billets for the HQ staff, so we were very fortunate to be placed in civilian houses.

As is customary in the British Army, Christmas dinner is always served to the men by the warrant officers and officers of the Battalion. For our New Year's Day dinner, we were to receive the full Christmas Day fare.

Soup was served into our mess tins by the RSM and RQMS, with quite a lot of ribald comments about the quality and quantity of the helpings provided.

The turkey was of course served by Colonel D.A.D. Eykin, whilst the rest of the vegetables, apple sauce and gravy were served to us by the second-in-command and the adjutant. The stuffing caused much merriment. Our own Signals Officer, Capt. MacLeod was in high spirits as he proffered the steaming plateful.

"And who wants stuffing?" he enquired politely.

"Present company excepted, most of the officers," came the expected reply. This was countered by a wry smile and a friendly "tut-tut", as spoon met plate.

The Christmas pudding received the full treatment. This was piped in by the Pipe Major. The adjutant, in full dress uniform with Glengarry and tartan trews, carried aloft a large black pudding to the table at the end of the room, whereupon brandy was poured on to the top and duly set alight. All officers helped to serve the delicious pudding and the warrant officers did the rounds with the brandy sauce.

"Beer will now be served," announced the RSM, to loud cheers.

Each man received one can of beer. Written on the side was the amount of its contents, 'Light Ale – one imperial pint'. The brewer's name has been long forgotten, but I savour the taste of that beer to this day. It was something we would come to look forward to each week from now on.

The RSM called us to order and the Colonel gave a short speech which covered the last six months of the year and went on to ask for the same outstanding effort for the coming year. He ended by wishing most sincerely for a peaceful ending to the year.

The loyal toast was then proposed and the answer echoed round the school hall — "THE KING."

Plates and mess tins were soon washed and stacked on to a table out of the way and the floor cleared ready for the festivities.

In honour of the occasion, the Pipe Band had been summoned together and we had a programme of Highland tunes and a competent display of sword dancing was performed to finish off the official entertainment.

The strains of 'I belong tae Glasgie', set the mood for what was to follow. All the Harry Lauder songs were sung. The brash 'Highland fling' was flung and a few brave souls whirled and shrieked in the 'Gay Gordons'. The favourite song of all Scottish soldiers 'The ball o' Kirriemuir' was sung in its entirety on a number of occasions before the party petered out at about five o'clock in the afternoon.

In the early evening, we sat around the dining-table at our hosts' house, talking animatedly as we tried to gain permission from the mother for the girls to go to the special dance that had been arranged at the Wintergardens.

Roy eventually persuaded the mother that her daughter would be safe in our care for the evening. I think the soft North American drawl had found a soft spot in the dear lady's heart.

"I t'ought the Irish were the ones supposed to charm the birds off the trees? This chap's the one who charms dem up there in de first place," said Paddy, indicating Roy.

"I think it was the army surplus gloves that did the trick," was the reply from the Canadian.

To anyone under the age of thirty, I would imagine the words 'jitterbug' and 'jive' must seem very old-fashioned. To the teenagers and young people of Britain, this form of dancing was unknown to them until the Americans came to Britain. I first saw jive in early 1942 when the American forces started attending the dances at the De Montfort hall in Leicester. Of course, the girls soon took to this new craze and it swept the country.

The Canadians were also very fine exponents of this new craze and this New Year's dance was to really bring this new style of dancing to our Dutch friends. They were not the only ones to make a new discovery.

We had never quite discovered what had happened to the many hundreds, nay thousands, of parachutes which had been discarded by the airborne forces in the areas around Nijmegen and Arnhem. Apart from a few odd pieces that we had found to make into scarves for ourselves, all the other silk 'chutes seemed to have disappeared completely — until tonight.

As the couples gyrated around the floor, each one improvising new and more difficult steps, the great silk parachute mystery was unveiled before our very eyes. The answer was to be found in one word:

Knickers!

There were orange knickers, green knickers, blue knickers, in fact knickers of every colour of parachute that had been dropped. The knee-length skirts of the girls lifted as they swirled around, exposing a bare piece of leg above the stocking top and above that pure silk underwear provided by kind permission of the 'Red Devils' and the 'Screaming Eagles'. Subsequent enquiries revealed that when the paras had landed, the Dutch civilians had run out of their houses and taken the parachutes away and hid them. Later, the industrious and resourceful females had turned their spoils of war to a very practical use.

Paddy and I sat for most of the evening admiring the view.

The Wintergardens also provided a good supply of films for us with the programmes being changed twice weekly. Most of the big American films were shown very quickly after release. The 'Road' series starring Bing Crosby and Bob Hope were always very popular, and the musicals were also quite well received.

It was in this cinema, probably some time in March, that we were fortunate enough to attend a world première of the film *Henry V*, starring Laurence Olivier. When the time came for the release of this picture, the powers that be determined that the world première should be shown to a forces audience in the front-line zone. That is how Nijmegen came to be one of the towns chosen and I was fortunate enough to draw a winning ticket in the company ballot.

Now that the Hogmanay period was over, we sensed that we would soon be returning to the 'island' once more. Medical checks and dental attendances were required. Inoculations were administered where required and some poor souls had smallpox vaccinations to contend with. The barber was also kept very busy, after all we wanted to look as presentable to our new friends as we possibly could.

One evening we returned to the house to find the younger son Kan quite excited. He tried to avoid his mother during a family discussion and later whispered to Paddy and me in the corner of the room.

"Today, I fire the big gun." His eyes were bright and as big as saucers. We knew what he meant.

At the rear of the house was a large open space on which were sited five Canadian artillery pieces.

On their way home from school, the young boys would stop and talk to the gunners and sometimes when firing permitted, they would allow the boys to chalk messages on the shell cases and then fire them at the German lines. All very improper, but for the young boys, all very exciting stuff. We were sworn to secrecy, because if his mother got to know the truth she would have been most upset. The ladies had been talking in the shops apparently, and she didn't want her boys to be involved in any way. But the family discussion was not about this, it was about our forthcoming move.

Wim cleared his throat and swallowed before telling us that we would be returning to the 'island' next day. We would be leaving at two o'clock in the afternoon and would be going to Andelst.

This was a new name to us. We had not been there before, but a quick check on the map showed it to be a village on the left of the salient next to Zetten and that wasn't a very healthy place to be in at times. Most of us had heard about Zetten Castle and the 'punch-ups' that had taken place there.

A visit to the Wintergardens was called for, so off we went to enjoy our last night of freedom for the time being. Betty Grable did her best to keep our attention on the silver screen, but our minds were on other things that night.

For more than a week we had been able to put the war and all its discomfort from our minds as we enjoyed the kind hospitality of these nice folk, along with the warmth and the entertainment of this oasis, in the middle of a front-line town which was becoming more and more devastated by the steady shelling of the German big guns. No doubt there would be more as we departed, it was common knowledge that the Scottish Polar Bears were leaving.

The clean white sheets were most welcoming that night. The simple pleasures in life are all too often taken so much for granted, but those days and nights spent in someone else's house had taught me to be grateful for those simple things.

The Beukering family, Nijmegen — (l. to r.) Wim, Doh, Iet, Father, Mother, Kan

TWENTY-ONE – BETTY

The German offensive in the Ardennes shortly after Christmas, had caught everyone by surprise. The 'battle of the bulge', as it has now become known, was the final fling of the German Army to drive a wedge between the Americans and the British 21st Army Group and advance between Brussels and Antwerp through to the sea, thereby cutting off the whole of the 1st Canadian Army. We were up at the sharp end of the salient and so would have been placed in a serious predicament, had the plan succeeded.

Progress forward on the 'island' was out of the question. Most of the countryside was flooded and only a few of the more major roads were at all passable to vehicles. The snow showers and the interminable frosts at night, made even the infantryman more or less immobile. But not quite!

Patrolling was the answer. Here at Andelst, we must have been out on patrol every night and every day too. It is not good for a fighting unit to sit on its backside for too long and the Colonel had not the slightest intention of letting us do that.

Listening patrols I have described in a previous chapter. We had our fair share of these and of course each one needed a signaller in attendance, so the signals section was kept quite well occupied.

Standing patrols were the worst kind to endure. Houses were selected in no man's land for their position, giving good observation of the enemy and for the best possible fortification for defence in case of attack.

Top of the hate list at Andelst was 'Betty'. I never did find out why these strongpoints were always given a girl's name, least of all Betty. I had a sister called Betty and she was a most happy, cheerful and friendly girl, so perhaps I was under some sort of misconception when it came for my turn to attend the next party leaving for the fortified house.

"It's a good job there's only nine of you," said the driver of the jeep as we assembled outside 'A' Company HQ.

Looking around I could see the familiar face of Cpl. Dawson, with another L/Cpl and six riflemen. They were all loaded up like Christmas trees, with supplies of food, water, ammunition and a variety of weapons, including a PIAT (anti-tank weapon).

Our job was to relieve the patrol already at 'Betty'. We would then stay there for 24 hours until relieved by yet another group, hence the need for so many supplies.

"If two of you sit on the bonnet, Cpl. Dawson and L/Cpl MacDonald sit on the front with me, the rest of you can sit with your legs over the side and lean back into the centre and hold the kit down." Fusilier Nimmo had evidently done this run before.

"Are ye ready lads?" enquired the Corporal. "Away we go."

The jeep pulled away and the driver picked his way carefully and quietly along the narrow road. Once we had moved off, strict silence had to be observed. It was surprising how little noise that American made Willys jeep made that night. Usually they were renowned for their throaty roar as they sped about their daily tasks. Most drivers gave them quite a bit of 'wellie' and if a silencer dropped off now and then, no one seemed too worried. The jeep had become the twentieth century army mule and a very welcome animal it was too.

We turned quietly into the driveway of a large white house which stood at the end of a row of detached houses. There must have been seven or eight such houses in a stretch of about 500 yards, all on the same side of the road, with a water-filled ditch in front of each one and the water now covered with a good coating of ice.

An inch or two of snow lay on the ground and the houses stood out, black and gaunt without light on this dark and moonless night. Although the time was only just after six o'clock, the cold wind bit deep into our gloved hands. We were glad to get inside that house away from the penetrating wind.

The outgoing party was equally pleased to get away from the house. I could understand why. The whole place had a sense of foreboding about it. It was strange how some places gave one this second sense that all was not well. I felt uncomfortable and ill at ease as I made my way up the stairs to the little closet in one of the bedrooms where the two wireless sets stood on the floor. A pantile on the roof had been dislodged slightly to give access to the twenty foot aerial from the 18 set.

Curtains and any other sort of covering to be found had been used to black out all the windows, and the room was lit by a single hurricane lamp standing on the table behind the door leading to the stairs. I settled down for a long, cold, uncomfortable night.

Very little happened during the night. The two-hourly reports were the only contact with the outside world and it was with relief that we noticed that dawn was breaking.

With the light of day, it was now possible to take stock of the house and its surroundings. The black-outs at the windows were slowly moved back to give just the faintest of gaps to enable us to look out and observe the rear.

The house stood on a smallholding of perhaps three-quarters of an acre of land used for horticultural purposes. Three greenhouses stood in the middle of the area, looking strangely intact. Bamboo cane covers were stacked neatly under a lean-to shed.

All was quiet — it all seemed a little bit eerie.

Two of the Battalion snipers had come up shortly before dawn and had now gone further forward to do a little bit of personal pot-shotting at whatever might be moving about in the enemy held ground to the north. We settled down to a breakfast of porridge, bacon sandwich and hot strong tea.

Our method of heating up the food was one which had been passed on from the old Desert Rats of the Eighth Army. A 7lb jam tin was half filled with sand and then petrol was poured on to the sand and allowed to sink in. A match was then dropped into the tin and the vapour ignited. A nice steady heat was generated, enough to boil water fairly quickly. When the flame dimmed, a stick was used to stir the sand, more vapour was released and away went the improvised cooker once again.

During the course of the morning, Cpl. Dawson took a small party out to check the houses in the row and came back to report that all was well, with no trace of any of the houses being used by the enemy.

It must have been about three o'clock when, through my little spy hole in the roof, I noticed movement in the downstairs room of the house next door.

"Somebody moving in the next house," I called out.

"Probably the two snipers on their way back," said the Corporal. "Everyone on the alert." We waited for further movement.

Two people emerged from the side of the other house, then a third, then a fourth ... five ... six!

"Bloody hell, it's a Jerry patrol," spat out MacDonald. "They're coming to check on us now lads .... Wait for it, don't shoot — wait till they come in the gate."

Dawson and MacDonald took up their positions from behind the sandbagged window of the downstairs front room and waited.

The first two of the patrol came cautiously to the gate. They beckoned their mates to wait as they came stealthily into the drive.

Click, went the Corporal's Sten gun.

Click, went the Lance-Corporal's Sten gun.

"Sod it! This bloody Yankee ammo's jammed again, fire the Bren."

Too late. As soon as the Jerries had heard the click of the Stens, they had dived round the back of the gatepost to find cover behind the small hedge.

'Crack'. We heard the ice break as they both slid into the water-filled ditch below. Their compatriots took this opportunity to scurry back to the house from which they had recently departed and promptly opened fire. Our Bren-guns returned the fire as I reported the state of affairs to HQ.

The two men stuck in the ice cold water could move neither backward nor forward, and they remained there for some twenty minutes before we heard the plaintive cry of *"Kamerad, Kamerad."*

We knew that they must come to us to surrender, but to my great surprise, not one of us could speak any German. It seemed ludicrous to me, after all the months of training in England on how to fight and beat the Germans, no one had thought of teaching the troops a single sentence of the language of the fatherland. Apart from *Heil Hitler, Kamerad* and *Kaput*, we knew nowt.

Eventually someone shouted out a couple of words that sounded like "Hendy hock."

From the ditch came the plaintive cry again, "*Kamerad, Nicht shissen .... Kamerad.*" The shooting from the other house had by now stopped and a look-out from my spy-hole reported that the other Jerries had withdrawn.

Cpl. Dawson went out with a couple of the lads and after some minutes, coaxed the two out of the ditch. They came into the house, their field-grey uniforms dripping wet and they stood there shaking with a mixture of the intense cold and fright from their ordeal.

A quick prod from the L/Cpl and they came up the stairs into my room where they were searched. Two stick grenades and four black plastic 'egg' grenades were found about their persons. Pockets were emptied, but only a collection of the usual paraphernalia carried by soldiers came to light. The grenades were placed on the table. Both men offered their watches, but these were not taken, all our lads wore a watch already.

Brrrp ..... brrrp .... The sound of a Spandau brought instant action from our squad. Everyone dashed downstairs to man the defences. Suddenly the 18 set burst into life.

"Hello Betty one. Hello Betty one."

I half moved to the set, then I realized that I was alone with these two characters. The table with 6 grenades was between us. I had a rifle in one hand with a round up the breech, in the other hand I held the microphone to the 18 set. From the headset on the floor I could hear Eddie's voice calling.

"Hello Betty one. Hello Betty one."

I looked across the table at the two Jerries on the other side. One was a youngster of about eighteen years and the other was about my own age. Both were blue with cold and their hands by now were barely shoulder high. I flicked my rifle in an upwards motion and their hands shot up again above their heads. My eyes met theirs and I put on the meanest and most beligerent expression I could muster, more for my own defence, for I'm sure that by now they were still in a state of shock.

I depressed the pressel switch on the mike and reported.

"Two prisoners taken — will hold until relieved."

"What about the Spandau fire?" enquired Eddie.

"Speculative fire ... not replied to ... observation being carried out ... Roger."

I dropped the mike on to a chair and shouted for the Corporal to come and move the grenades. He bounded up the stairs two at a time.

"Bloody hell, they could have wiped us out with that lot! it's a good job that they were scared stiff."

He collected the small armoury and took it downstairs. I breathed a little more easily after that.

Minutes later, a rifleman came up to the room with a mug of hot tea, followed by the Corporal with two mess-tins of tea. He made the prisoners take off their boots and then sat them on the floor and passed the mess-tins of hot tea to them. A look of disbelief came into their eyes, but a quick drinker's motion of the right hand reassured them and the mess-tins were soon empty.

Promptly at six o'clock the jeep arrived with the new patrol. Paddy Cunningham was my relief and I quickly put him in the picture.

"Sure, I don't think oi'll be gettin' a lot o' sleep tonight," he drawled in his northern Irish accent.

"Sooner you than me tonight, Sammy lad," I said.

We made our way back to Company HQ, with the two prisoners walking in front of the jeep. Oh for a hot meal and a good sleep in those woollen blankets.

I was just slipping into the arms of Morpheus when the fun started. At first the sounds penetrated the subconscious mind. Was it a dream following on from the events of the past day? I stirred and listened. No, it wasn't a dream. There were Spandaus and Bren-guns blazing away and the unmistakable crashes of grenades exploding. It all sounded so near. The other lads were now outside the door listening.

"Christ, there's all hell let loose over at 'Betty'."

"Who's the signaller with them tonight?" asked another. I got out of bed and joined them at the door. The noise was indeed coming from the right direction and over the still night air it sounded much nearer than it really was.

"Sammy Cunningham's on tonight," I said, "but I don't fancy his chances in that lot. I'll go and see what the position is," I said as I walked off towards the signal office.

The duty signaller reported that Sammy had been giving a running commentary from his little closet underneath the roof.

"Dere's Jerries all round de house ... t'ree of dem wid Spandaus and anodder one o' dem is t'rowin grenades, but he can't t'row for toffee — dey're all landin' short."

A short pause and then .... "Can youse ask de mortars to put down a stonk all around de house?"

The mortars opened up just behind us with a salvo on to a predetermined shoot.

"Keep 'em dere lads," said the cool Irishman, "as long as you don't hit us wid ony strays," he added laconically.

Despite all the noise from the enemy side, our patrol was giving as good as it received. Some fifteen to twenty Germans had surrounded the fortified house and the nine Scots laddies had kept them at bay. At about one o'clock in the morning a Platoon was sent out from the nearest Company to clear up the nuisance. When the enemy realized what was happening, they disengaged and withdrew to their own positions. Enemy mortaring continued for some time afterwards, but by morning things had quietened down and at last I managed a few hours' sleep.

We awaited Sammy's arrival as the daylight faded and another long winter's night began. The sound of someone whistling softly, heralded the approach of the quiet Ulsterman. He came through the door and threw his kit on to his bed-space.

"How did it go then, Sammy? What happened?"

"Not a lot," replied Sammy. We were used to his non-committal sentences, but this was ridiculous.

"What d'ye mean, not a lot?"

"Like I said, not a lot. After all dat shenanigan, dere wasn't a casualty on either side — leastways, we had none. And d'ye know what? Dere wasn't a sign of blood in de snow outside, an' dere wasn't a pane o' glass broken in dem bloody greenhouses."

This was incredible. After three hours exchange of small arms, plus two hours of intermittent mortaring, nothing had been gained and nothing lost . . . . apart from a good night's sleep.

TWENTY-TWO – THE BELLS OF ST. MARY'S

We could hear the Bedford three-ton lorry coming towards Andelst long before we could see it. There was no mistaking the high pitched whine of the prop-shaft as the driver urged the vehicle along at the highest speed possible. What did puzzle us was why it was coming from the direction of Zetten. No one in their right mind would use that particular road during the hours of daylight. Running as it did, across more than a mile of open countryside with very sparse cover, one became a sitting target, rather like the ducks which proceed across a stall of a fairground shooting gallery.

The Bedford came round the bend at the end of the village street and screeched to a halt beside the small knot of men as they returned from the cookhouse with their midday 'tiffin' and tea.

We noticed the 21st Army Group sign on the front wing. Back room boys! In the front line area? They must be lost. We looked at the Corps sign on the other wing, but no one recognized it.

"Army Film Unit," said the driver as he wound down his window. "Where's this place?"

We looked at him in disbelief, thinking for a moment that he must be joking.

"This is Andelst . . . you've just come from Zetten, where are you looking for?" asked Jackie Brooks.

"Not quite sure, are we Corp?" admitted the driver. "We were booked to do a show for the Leicesters, but their CO said they were a bit busy at the moment – do you know anyone who could do with a show?"

This was said with such off-hand manner that we were slightly nonplussed by the offer, also for the reason why the Leicesters were rather busy at that time.

Some thirty-six hours previously, a company of the Leicesters under the command of a Capt. Saunt, had set out to clear up the ground around the Zetten Castle area. The Germans had no intention of being dislodged from the houses they had held from the time of the Airborne withdrawals. Not only did they defend well, but also put in a determined attack which called for a more concerted effort from the Tigers, whereupon the whole Battalion had become embroiled in a most ferocious scrap over the aforementioned castle. No wonder they were not able to attend the film show which had been booked for that afternoon.

All this activity was taking place less than two miles from where we now stood and could be clearly heard by all and sundry within a five mile radius.

We felt that we couldn't disappoint the film unit, so we offered those gentlemen the privilege of putting on a show for us — but where? Heppy solved the problem.

"How about that big building opposite the church?"

The lorry turned down the small road leading to the church and we all went into the building which resembled a village church hall.

"This is fine," said the Corporal. "How many blokes do you think you can whistle up?"

"Have to check with the adjutant first," said Heppy.

"Oi'll come wit ye," offered Paddy.

They returned after a quarter of an hour with the news that the adjutant had given the OK and those lads who could be spared from the nearest Companies would be allowed to attend, with the proviso that if needed they must return to Company immediately.

Everyone from the signals billet rallied to the call, screen, projector and sound equipment were soon installed in the hastily improvised cinema; apple boxes, planks, and all manner of seating was arranged to give good viewing to as many as possible, the rest could stand at the back.

An hour after they had arrived, the two men from the Army Kinema Corps were starting their film show to a packed house. All seats were taken and men were standing not only at the back, but all along the sides too. Fire regulations and adequate access to exits were not even considered. We had come to see Bing Crosby.

A 'Popeye' and 'Donald Duck' cartoon set the whole thing off to a good start. Two newsreels, one from Pathé and the other from Movietone gave us a little taste of what was happening in other parts of the world as a prelude to the big film.

"Programmes, ices, choc-ices," called some wag from the back of the hall as the reels were changed ready for the main feature.

This is to certify that . . . . 'The Bells of St. Mary's' has been passed by the British Board of Censors. A great cheer rang out as the customary notice was shown.

"Good old Bing."

The audience settled down to see this old Hollywood weepie as Bing sang, aided and abetted by an ever warming group of Fusiliers, interspersed with some ribald comments during the romantic parts. With all those closely packed bodies in such a small building we became more and more relaxed and the sounds of battle were either ignored or pushed aside by this unexpected pleasure of both the free show and the warmth provided by our comrades.

The film rolled on to its predictable ending. I have vivid memories of old Bing standing in his dress of a Catholic priest, as he sang 'The Bells of St.

Mary's', outside the church, with the snow falling all around him unbelievably thick in such a short time, but these things happen in films, not in real life.

The film closed as he sang the last high notes of the song. The show was over. We sat for some minutes, savouring the warmth and the chance to chat with friends we did not see very often.

The first two or three went out of the hall, only to return promptly.

"There's more snow out here, than Bing had in the film."

"Take no notice of them, they're always joking," said one of the 'D' Company Sergeants as I left with him. We opened the door to be met with a blizzard howling outside.

"Bloody hell! There must have been about nine inches of snow whilst we were in there," said the Sergeant. He was right.

The snow, which had just been a light covering of an inch or two over the last few days, was now well up to the top of our wellington boots. Visibility was only a matter of yards in the dwindling twilight of the afternoon. I was pleased to reach the shelter of our house, only a hundred yards away.

Over Zetten way mortars and shells still fell from the sky together with the snow. During the night, the snow won and by morning there was little noise from that area, apart from a few sporadic bursts from machine-guns as old scores were being settled.

I looked across the orchard as I stood by the hedge at the end of the churchyard. As far as one could see there was a wonderful carpet of pure white snow. All the old scars of war had been obliterated overnight. Gone were the shell holes. The debris from the battered orchards had now been buried deep under this deluge from the heavens. Even the American Flying Fortress, lying on its belly where it had crash landed, half-way between Andelst and Valburg, no longer stood out gaunt and black, but had blended into this new landscape fit for any one of the old Dutch masters to paint in his inimitable style. It seemed a pity to me, that we couldn't just tiptoe away and leave this beautiful scene untouched and untarnished by man's inhumanity to man.

"Better get that snow out o' that slit trench laddies." I looked up. The RSM was on his rounds.

"Get the snow off those breastworks too, West. Make sure you can still get a good field o' fire."

My visionary dreams of an untouched land were instantly shattered. The realities of war had decided against it. We cleared the snow with our rifle-butts and jumped down into the trenches, inches deep in gooey mud.

A new way of life had now begun.

Soldiers soon accommodate themselves to any change in their environment. In this case the snow, although by now knee deep, was in many respects less troublesome than the heavy rains and floods which followed.

We were careful to keep to set paths and tracks, thereby avoiding the pitfalls of deep ditches and other such obstacles which were hidden under this flat carpet of snow. Also, one cannot walk in snow without leaving a track, so we were careful not to break new tracks unless absolutely necessary.

Patrolling became more stereotyped. We used civilian sledges quite a lot to transport kit and stores in conjunction with the ever reliable jeep which, with its four-wheel drive, had the ability to overcome almost every obstacle put in its path.

During the whole period of the snow, which lasted many weeks, we were never issued with any sort of camouflage equipment. Improvisation met the needs of the day and many and varied were the items used to adorn ourselves, as we tried to blend with the winter wonderland in which we lived.

Scraps of old sheeting, table-cloths, pillow-cases, an old shirt, tattered and torn — anything to break up the sharp outlines of the body and equipment.

One comedian always used an old-fashioned flannelette nightgown together with a white bonnet to cover his steel helmet. Naturally from that day he was always known by the nickname of 'Old Mother Riley'.

Imagine our reaction to official photographs which appeared some time later in *The War Illustrated* magazine, showing members of the Royal Scots Fusiliers dressed completely with the official army issue white camouflage suits, purporting to be on patrol in the snowy wastelands of Holland.

With the snow came the more intense cold. It was now January and no matter how we wrapped ourselves up at night the cold seemed to penetrate our clothing. We could sleep reasonably warm in our various houses and farms, but the standing patrols were so cold that sleep was nigh impossible.

The usual rum ration was doubled for anyone on the standing patrols, also we managed to take with us more than the issue of tea and sugar mixture, but that of course meant that more water was needed.

After a particularly cold night, during which we found that even our 'wellies' had frozen together, we had mashed so many times that the water ran out.

"Don't worry about a small thing like that," I said. "There's plenty of snow about. We'll just melt some snow and we'll soon have a cup of char."

I remembered reading about the Canadian trappers using this method out in the Yukon. Perhaps their snow was not so loosely packed as ours. We used bucket after bucket of the stuff, each bucketful producing about half-an-inch more liquid in the biscuit tin on the petrol fire.

There is a saying 'Pure as the driven snow'. Let me put that statement in its true perspective. Snow may look pure and white and innocent, but when it falls through the atmosphere, it collects minute particles of dirt and dust which only come to light when the snow melts.

Our biscuit tin became half full of a greyish evil looking liquid as so slowly it began to heat up. When it started to simmer, the tea mixture was sprinkled in and stirred along with the powdered milk. The whole mixture now took on a light brown appearance, so we dipped our mugs into the tea and drank.

There was a quaint piquance not easily discernible to the palate at first. A rather bitter taste, though warming as it went down. I recognized it, but decided that discretion was the better part of valour.

"It's got bloody cordite in it," said one of the riflemen. We tried to dissuade him, but he insisted that he was correct — he was too.

Not only had the snow brought down with it the usual dust and dirt, it had also brought down all the other foreign bodies that two armies had been throwing about for the past three months. I think I had the backlog of the Red Devils' last stand at Oosterbeek in mine. However, one has to put on a good face in times of emergency and so I said mine was quite palatable and had another helping. It was horrible, but it WAS warm and I could feel it circulating inside me as we played out the remaining hours of the patrol.

The hot meal was ready when we returned to our Company. Just a simple stew made up of a selection of the various tins from a 14-man pack. Very tasty and quite filling, these stews were to become an almost daily fare on our menu. Best of all was the well brewed mug of tea. Preceded by a generous portion of treacle sponge pudding, the tea was without doubt one of the best mugs I had drunk for some time.

It was later in the evening when the chickens came home to roost.

Suddenly I was convulsed by wind. There was nowhere to go and discreetly discharge this hurricane within me. So out it had to come.

Not gentle flowing breaks of wind, but sharp staccato outbursts of quite a revolting nature. Many friends were lost that evening. The whole episode was summed up quite succinctly by Jimmy Logan.

"If ye've to keep on farting like that, make sure ye're well awa' frae cny naked lichts, or ye'll maybe be blown tae tiny wee pieces."

With mutual consent, I slept that night in the far corner of the room.

Some days later our Battalion was called to relieve the 1st Leicesters from their positions at Zetten and Valburg. The dangerous road conditions made this formerly simple exercise, into a tricky slippery operation with some vehicles sliding off the cambered roads, into the ice-covered ditches which ran alongside the roads on both sides.

'A' Company, whom I had now rejoined, marched through Zetten and on to a small road running at right angle to the main Zetten-Randwijk road. We took up our position in a row of houses quite remote from the rest of the Battalion. Little did we know at that time, that we were in fact, the most northerly unit of the whole Allied Army.

The approach to the houses reminded me of those along the road from 'Betty'. But the feeling was different. There was a quiet serenity somehow and one got the feeling that we would not be unduly upset during our stay.

"Nice of someone to clear the snow away for us," said the Sgt.-Major.

"They might have cleared all the others, but they've piled all ours across the entrance," said Eddie Fulton.

I thought it strange that whilst most of the other gate ways had a pile of snow away from the path, our pile was directly on the pathway to the house. I shrugged the thought from my mind as I followed Eddie over the hump and into the house.

Now this was more like it. The main entrance to the house faced away from the keen biting wind and a lot of effort had been made to make the whole house as draught-proof as possible. We made ourselves nice and comfortable in our new surroundings.

The line to our Platoon out on the left of our perimeter suddenly went dead.

"Sgt. Duncan's lot has gone off, Ken."

We tried all we could to trace the fault near at hand, but it was no use, someone would have to trace the whole line and get it repaired. It was my turn as linesman.

"Ye canna go out on ye're own, laddie," said the Sgt.-Major. "I'll get a rifleman to escort ye."

A youngster of barely nineteen joined me as I set out along the line. I ran the yellow cable through my gloved hand as we made our way towards the snowy wastelands which separated us from Sgt. Duncan's Platoon.

We had gone about half a mile when suddenly, the cable ended. I retraced my steps until I found the end once more and handed this to the rifleman for safekeeping.

"I'll go and find the other end — don't let go of that," I said as I walked forward.

I had gone barely ten yards when I saw two sets of footprints crossing our intended route. They came from the direction of the Jerry lines. Ahead was clean unbroken snow. To the right and to the left, the same unbroken snow -- apart from the footprints which went out of sight towards Zetten. I walked on and found the yellow cable amongst a conglomeration of other signal cables. No matter how I pulled, the cable wouldn't join up, so I knotted in a piece of spare from my belt.

We both gave a sigh of relief when we heard Eddie's voice from Company HQ, but there was still nothing from the other end. I looked at the youngster.

"Nothing for it Bill but to go on."

The line was traced right up to the ruins of a house where the Platoon were in position in the cellar. Despite a most diligent check, nothing seemed to be out of order.

"Have a cup o' char while you're here?" asked the genial Sergeant. I drank the tea and rechecked the phone. The type of telephone used was a single line with earth return. Silly fool, I thought, check the earthpin.

The earth wire dropped out of a small window and had been fixed firmly to the pin and the pin wedged quite firmly into the bricks and rubble in the snow.

The cold north-easterly wind penetrated through the body right to the bladder. Time to empty the contents I thought as I stood astride the earth pin.

My mind flashed back to Usselby Hall in Lincolnshire, I could hear old cow face, Cpl. Evans saying . . . .

". . . out in the desert once . . . . not a flicker on the phone . . . . earth pin well into the sand, but the sand was dry . . . . water the earth pin, but how . . . . so I pee'd on it . . . . and it worked perfectly."

There was my answer. My bladder was duly emptied and as I went into the cellar, Sgt. Duncan shouted, "The line's OK now Westie, what did you do?" When I told him he roared with laughter, adding, "I think I'll go and make sure it keeps working."

Bill and I made our way back most cautiously, especially near the break and the footprints, but luck was with us. Whoever had gone across earlier had not returned and the line held for sometime afterwards.

Following my report to Major Weir, a memo was issued to all Platoon Commanders to the effect that should the phone ever go 'dis', members should be requested to urinate upon the earth pin. I never did find out who eventually extracted the earth pins of 'A' Company.

Both Bill and I had noticed on that eerie night, how difficult it was to stare for long at any given object, without the eyes beginning to water and impair one's vision. Staring at the snow for long periods caused many illusions of movement in all sorts of inanimate objects. Especially trees in the orchards. On a windy night, things got a little out of hand.

" 'B' Company here. Capt. Murray has reported that his patrol has observed a party of 57 enemy passing through a gate in the orchard between you and us."

Eddie called the Major. This was serious. A party of over fifty men could cause untold havoc if they drove a wedge between two Companies. Major Weir acted immediately by putting everyone on full alert and asking all Company HQ personnel to man the stand to posts.

Eddie and I tuned in the standby set ready for use. The time was about ten o'clock at night.

Within the next hour all the Battalion and shortly afterwards the rest of the Brigade was put on alert. We listened in to the buzz of conversation on the air. Direct phone links within the Battalion were also buzzing. No one else had reported anything to follow up the sighting. The fifty-seven men had disappeared, but where?

The Colonel came on the phone.

"Can you send a Platoon out, John, from your end? I'll get 'B' Company to send one from the other side of the orchard, we should pick up some footprints in the snow. Fire a red if you spot them and we'll give the area a stonking."

"I'll take a Platoon myself, sir — and a signaller," he replied. "You had better come with me Fulton," he added as an afterthought, "West's already been out tonight."

It was well after midnight when they returned. The Major was fuming.

"There's never been any ruddy Boche out there tonight, not one — not a ruddy footprint anywhere. Get me 'B' Company please. Hello Alex, we've checked the whole orchard, there wasn't anyone jumping through or over any gate tonight. Your 2-i/c must have been counting bloody trees."

Major Alexander replied to the effect that fifty-seven men couldn't vanish into thin air. He would wait for his Platoon to report. This they did shortly afterwards and their report was the same. No footprints and no Boche.

The Colonel came on the line about one o'clock, he sounded tired and one sensed that he'd had a rocket from Brigade, but ever the gentleman, he politely asked me to give the Major the message 'stand down'.

As Major Weir came into the room, I told him of the message from Colonel Eykin and added, "The Colonel said he was sorry for all the trouble you'd been caused but would you please leave strong look-outs, just in case."

"Aye, I'll pick men who can tell a man from a tree." He wanted to say more, but it wasn't the done thing to criticize another officer from another Company within the hearing of other ranks.

The other ranks were not so reticent. From that night the illustrious Captain Murray MC was known to all ranks as 'Heinz', after the famous British company who advertised that they proudly produced 57 different varieties of tinned food.

About a week after the 'Heinz' incident, we had a sudden thaw. Quite often in the middle of a very hard winter this sort of phenomenon occurs. Twenty-four hours of rain began to erode the top layer of snow from the roadsides. On the morning of the second day, two black objects were observed in the pile of snow leading to the next house. Later a larger black object became visible at the other end of the same heap of snow — this required further investigation.

On arrival we found to our surprise that the two black bits were boots — jackboots.

The other end we saw a German helmet. It was not just a pile of snow, but a body which had become covered in snow.

We looked down the road. Incredulously all the other heaps were thawing out to reveal other bodies. We counted them — nine in all. We must report this to Battalion HQ.

As we approached the gate to our house, we saw with some horror that the heap that we had been walking over for more than ten days, also contained a body.

We felt ashamed and at the same time very sorry for the unknown man over whom we had unknowingly walked for all that time. Respectfully, we passed round him and phoned the Padre.

"With the thaw, we are finding under the snow, a number of dead Germans."

There was a short pause at the other end of the line.

"How many have you found?"

"Nine so far sir — but there may be more further along."

"I'll be along as soon as possible, have a good look round and I'll contact the Colonel."

Subsequent searching brought to light a total of fifteen bodies on the roadsides. We then searched the outlying houses where four or five more were discovered.

At the last house in the road we came across three British lads laid on stretchers as though they had been wounded and were awaiting collection, but now frozen stiff.

Whilst we had been enjoying the pleasure of Bing Crosby in the film 'Bells of St. Mary's', the blizzard had not only brought the fighting to a halt, but also denied any of these men, friend or foe, any chance of survival from the elements as they lay in their last moments of life, hoping for someone to return and bring help.

It took men from the Royal Engineers the rest of the day to gingerly check for booby traps and then to carefully prise the frozen bodies from their temporary resting places along the road for which they had fought, and lost.

The Padre and his staff carefully tabulated all the bodies and then they were taken to a plot of ground near the Waal which had been designated as a burial ground for the German troops. Here they were respectfully given a Christian burial conducted by the Regimental Padre, a Church of Scotland minister.

In the early hours of the next morning it began to snow heavily and by midday a new carpet of snow covered the roadside, hiding from view the scars left by pickaxes and crowbars.

TWENTY-THREE – THE 'ISLAND FOLLIES'

To alleviate some of the boredom during periods of inactivity we read a lot of newspapers and periodicals. Local papers from all parts of the British Isles were scanned eagerly, gleaning scraps of information about towns and counties hitherto unknown.

'Black Bob' was the greatest favourite of the Fusiliers. Each week the adventures of this Scottish sheepdog were featured in a serial about a Highland shepherd and his way of life in northern Scotland.

Published in Glasgow, Thompson's *Weekly News* was circulated around the Battalion, bringing news of home for the Jocks in our midst. We Sassenachs also became regular readers of this excellent newspaper which was renowned for its short stories and very good sports coverage, but it was the back page which always captured our attention first.

The wonderful adventures of the faithful Black Bob as he helped his master round up the sheep, saved children from flooded streams, rescued old women from blazing crofts, all these and many more were avidly read each week.

It didn't really matter what the Russians were doing on the eastern front, not until we had found what brave deed Black Bob had performed that week.

It was to satisfy partly this clamouring for reading material that 'A' Company decided to start a company news-sheet on a weekly basis. Company signaller Eddie Fulton took on the job of editor and for some weeks it flourished, mainly due to his own efforts. So much so, that it quickly came be to known throughout the Battalion as 'Fulton's Weekly'. His remarkable wit, together with his scathing comments on Army procedures, made very good reading. More contributors were however urgently needed for the continuance of this news-sheet.

"Why don't you write an article for next week's news-sheet, West?" asked Capt. (Pin-down) Dobson one afternoon. "You write a very interesting letter to your wife, full of description – I rather look forward to them coming to me for censor in fact," he continued.

"I don't write them for your satisfaction, sir," I replied acidly.

"Come now West, someone has to censor them and it's a lousy job having to read some of those letters."

"I'll make sure you don't read any more of them in future, sir," I said adamantly.

"Now look here, West, all I'm trying to say is that I think you could write something about your county of Leicestershire. We intend to cover as many counties as possible and I think you could get it off to a good start – how about it old man?"

"OK sir, I'll write something up and let Fulton have it in a day or two."

"That's the ticket old man, I'll look forward to reading it." He seemed satisfied and walked off.

I wrote the article a day later, starting off 'I was pinned down the other afternoon by the 2-i/c ......'

'Fulton's Weekly' prospered and went on to be praised by the Colonel as a good morale booster until it became almost the Battalion news-sheet.

We thought that our little news-sheet had reached the outside world, when, one day 'Laughing Boy' Lt. Dobie came bounding into the Company HQ.

"Is Fulton about? I've got a war correspondent here. He needs a few facts about some of the activities we have been engaged in."

We replied in the negative. Eddie had gone out on his walkabout, collecting items for the next publication. But where was this war correspondent?

Standing outside the door was a small man, about five feet six inches tall, slimly built, sallow complexion, with black hair and a thick black moustache. On his shoulders he wore three pips, according him the equivalent rank of captain. He looked so forlorn and ill at ease, I don't think I have ever seen anyone look less like a soldier than he.

"Ask him to give me a ring when he gets back, will you?" Laughing Boy bounded out the same as he had bounded in. The little man followed him like a faithful dog, trotting to keep up with the long striding Lieutenant.

"Who the 'ell is he?" asked the storeman.

"Yon wee fella looks like Black Bob," replied the Sgt.-Major – and that was the nickname by which our newshound was known for the many weeks he spent with the Battalion.

About three weeks after our first encounter with 'Black Bob', our genial Lieutenant breezed into the office one bright frosty morning and threw down onto the table the latest edition of Thompson's *Weekly News*.

"Look at that laddies," grinning all over his face. We turned to the back page to read about the sheepdog.

"No, not that ye fools – see the front page." We looked at the front page.

Right across the headlines read *Report from the front in Holland by our own correspondent*. There was a meticulous account of life with a famous Scottish Regiment. Our Regiment –our Battalion.

"Here, read this bit," said Laughing Boy. We read ....

This fine fighting battalion has seen action all the way from the beaches of Normandy . . . led by young, dashing and frighteningly efficient officers, is still there, in the vanguard, at the very spearhead . . . . . etc.

We hooted with laughter.

"Where the hell has he got all that bullshyte from?" asked the Sgt.-Major. "He's never spoken a word tae anyone since he's been here."

"An' what's all this aboot — young dashing and frighteningly efficient . . . ?" asked Jimmy Lafferty as he looked at the Lieutenant. "He canna be writin' aboot you, Laughing Boy."

The young Lieutenant's pink cheeks turned quite rosy at this riposte, but he countered, "You are only jealous, Lafferty, because there's not a mention of the signallers."

"There's no mention o' the likes of us because ye've only tell'd him aboot yesell," retorted Jimmy.

"I shall have to write home and let the folks know that we were the ones he was writing about," said the cheerful young officer.

"Aye, awa' an' tell ye mammie all about her soldier son," said Jimmy, laughingly. The encounter ended as it had begun, without malice or any ill feeling.

Another source of unexpected entertainment came via the wireless.

The German High Command had, for a long time, believed in broadcasting all sorts of propaganda. Most readers will remember or have read about the efforts of Lord Haw-Haw, to undermine the resolve of the British public during the dark days of the bombings of British towns and cities.

Now in Holland it was our turn to be wooed by the gentle art of propaganda. The person to whom the task fell was a lady by the pseudonym of Mary of Arnhem. Unlike the obnoxious Haw-Haw, with his nasal snarling voice, Mary of Arnhem had a nice cultured voice with a friendly approach.

Each evening we would turn to the medium band and pick up the pre-war Dutch radio station of Radio Hilversum, to hear the latest news from Mary about the progress of the war, as seen through the German eyes, Towards the end of her broadcast she would entreat us to stop being the lackeys of the Russians and Americans and ask ourselves why we were in Holland enduring the rigours of this cold winter, when we would be far better off in our home towns looking after our wives and families.

She would then pick out a town or city well known to one or other of our divisional battalions and mention pubs and dance-halls which had been damaged by bombers. Always very factual and almost convincing. No false claims like her male counterpart, just small true facts.

Some of her favourite sallies were reserved for the Leicesters. Her special preference was for a certain Capt. Saunt of, I think, it was 'B' Company.

Capt. Saunt was a dashing officer who had been a thorn in the flesh ever since they had arrived on the 'Island'. More so now following the attack at Zetten which had caused so many casualties to the Germans. Mary had a special welcome waiting for him, should he ever have the misfortune to be captured. She would entreat his lads:

"Instead of blindly following your Capt. Saunt as he tries to gain a Victoria Cross, why not lay down your rifle and come and join your friends who gave themselves up at Zetten? They are now enjoying good food in a pleasant warm camp in Germany. The chips are as good there as any you will find along Belgrave Gate in Leicester."

We became very adept at interpreting the meanings behind her messages, especially after any sort of heavy engagement with enemy patrols or strongpoints.

Whenever Mary belittled a unit or some activity with which they had been concerned, we knew that it had hurt either the pride or personnel of our foe. She did, however, score one notable victory against us.

A patrol from the Hallamshire Regt. advanced from the area of Valburg to test out the position of the enemy line. Despite diligent searching and prodding for most of one night, there were no obvious signs of occupation of any of the houses in a small hamlet from which it had been thought that enemy patrols had commenced a number of night raids.

Upon their return, it was decided that a platoon of some 29 men would occupy these houses, so as to render them useless as a springboard for any future Jerry malpractices.

During the hours of darkness, the 29 men left the Hallam's HQ and made their way forward into the darkness of the night. They never came back. Not a shot was heard, not a cry. Not a flare was fired. They had just disappeared.

We waited to hear what Mary of Arnhem would make of this.

On the first night's broadcast – nothing.

The second night also gave not a hint of what might have befallen our Yorkshire friends.

Surely, we thought, Mary couldn't keep this titbit to herself any longer. She must know the answer to the mystery, but not a word about it on night three.

On the fourth night, I would think that the whole of the 49th Division listened in to every word she uttered. General news from all fronts and the usual Nazi propaganda hand-outs compiled the whole programme which ended with the usual, "Good-night boys. Enjoy your sleep – while you can." Then almost as an after-thought: "By the way, boys I wonder what ever happened to those men of the Hallamshire Regt?"

We looked at each other and shrugged our shoulders. "They've got the whole bloody lot in the bag, every man jack of 'em," said Jackie Brooks. Everyone nodded in agreement.

For the first week, Mary added a sentence or two each night, just to whet our appetite. Every mite of propaganda was wrung out of this episode, but she was careful never to let slip just how the capture was achieved.

It was not until after the war had finished that we heard just what had transpired.

The Germans had observed the patrol on the first night and lay doggo. On the second night, they laid an ambush around the hamlet, then as the Hallams rendezvous at the large barn was complete, the SS closed on the barn. An officer speaking in perfect English, said simply, "Gentlemen, you are completely surrounded. We have a machin-gun at every window. For you the war is over."

They had fallen into the perfect trap — and into a prisoner of war camp in the Fatherland:

Mary kept us well informed about the luxuries they were enjoying in their warm and well run campsites, whilst we existed in cold, flooded hovels with inadequate food rations, misguidedly fighting to free the ungrateful Dutch.

This was received with much derision and many suggestions which were simply physically impossible.

From the first time that man took up his club to do battle with his enemies, graffiti has recorded his thoughts, etched on a convenient wall with whatever materials came to hand.

Prehistoric man recorded his on the walls of the caves in which they lived. We recorded ours on the walls of the houses and farmhouses of Holland.

Strange as it may seem, there was very little filth or obnoxious material written in the houses in the forward areas. The 'in thing' was to produce upon the wall a type of poster which was used to advertise the cast of a music-hall show, such as one could see on any hoarding in the streets of Britain.

The front door of the vicarage at Ressen opened into a cream coloured hall and it was there on the left-hand side that I first saw one of these posters. Done in plain black crayon or charcoal, it spelled out the kind of fare that we could sample each and every night. The main theme being the weapons and nicknames given to units and persons taking part in the nightly battles all around us.

Presenting TONIGHT & EVERY NIGHT
"THE ISLAND FOLLIES"

* * *

General Rawlings Internationally famous Circus with its performing POLAR BEARS
Crocodiles, Alligators, Weasels, Buffaloes, Kangaroos
Capt. Saunt and his famous Tigers

*

'THE HALLAMS' and their amazing disappearing act

*

'SPANDAU JOE' and the merry 'EIGHTY-EIGHTS'

*

'MOANING MINNIE' and the 'NEBEL WERFERS'

*

'BILL BOFORS' and his coloured patterns in the sky

*

Listen to the rhythmic beat of 'JOE CANUK' with his backing group 'R. TILLERY'

*

COMPERE   'MARY OF ARNHEM'

    These are just a few which spring to mind. Each unit included snippets of local interest in their own inimitable style.

    With some of the creations, great care and real artistic prowess was in evidence. I recall one glorious multicoloured production with its beautifully patterned Edwardian lettering picked out in gold. Framed in painted velvet curtains, with the old time footlights at the base, it was a joy to behold. A masterpiece, painted by some unknown soldier of one of the Yorkshire Regiments on to the plaster wall, in the hallway of a farmhouse near to Valburg.

    I often wonder whether it still lies under the wallpaper, a testimony to the subtle humour of those young men, or whether it was ravaged by war, or simply obliterated by the application of a coat of emulsion.

    I doubt whether I could find the farmhouse now. Gone is the Flying Fortress which pointed the way to the Battalion Command Post.

TWENTY-FOUR – THREE DAYS' LEAVE IN BRUSSELS

"Watch what you're doing, Weggy, we can't afford to break another needle." I detected a note of alarm in Harry's voice.

"Just concentrate on the sewing, Harry lad, I'll look after the motive power," I replied as I endeavoured to keep up a steady rhythm on the sewing-machine handle.

"You're jerking that bloody handle as if it's a starting handle on a three-tonner," said Harry.

"Don't start getting hot under the collar," I joked. "Look, if we break this needle, bang goes your chance of a collar on your shirt, this is the last one."

Harry guided the material with extreme care and attention. His nose almost touched the table as he peered anxiously at the delicate needle bobbing up and down as it joined together the khaki material. He finished the run and lifted the foot. As he straightened up he gave a little sigh of relief.

"Another one done. Yours next, I hope it lasts," he said as he inspected the thin sliver of steel yet again. Then, with a reproachful look at me, "We can't just nip down to Singer's for another packet."

This was the scene which had been repeated a dozen times during the past two weeks, the attaching of handmade collars to collar-less shirts.

It all started when the first batch of Fusiliers returned from their 3 day leave in Brussels.

They were furious. The Belgian girls and the Women's Forces of the British Army didn't want anything to do with the troops from the front line, who were easily recognized by their battledress tunics being tightly fastened at the neck.

A recent Army Order had given permission for troops in the rear areas, when off duty, to wear open-necked battledress tops, with a collar and tie.

The drab khaki battledress had for so long been a bone of contention with the British Tommies. Compared to the off-duty uniforms of the Americans and Canadians, ours had the least appeal to the young ladies at home and more so overseas. So this latest order was received with wide acclaim by the 'Corps wallahs' in the rear.

Front line troops were to continue to be issued with the angola collar-less shirts, unchanged in style from the type used in the South African Boer

Wars. One cannot fight in a tie. Not only does it impair circulation, but it can easily be used for strangulation in hand-to-hand fighting. That is the official reason.

For the lads going on leave to the brightest jewel in Europe something must be done. We couldn't have the young mesdemoiselles turning their noses up at the Royal Scots Fusiliers.

At the baths units, some of the bright lads connived to swap their shirts for Canadian issue shirts, but the baths people soon put a stop to this practice.

The answer was forthcoming from a twenty-five-year-old Lancashire lad in the signal section. We would make our own collars and sew them on to our existing shirts.

"Where the devil are we going to get a piece of khaki material to match the rest of the shirt?" asked Jackie Brooks.

"Cut the tail off your other shirt and use that," said the ever resourceful Harry Chubbs.

"Who are we going to get to sew 'em on? With my sewing my bugger'll be off by the second day," said Jackie.

"I'll have a go," said Harry. "I've seen a little hand sewing-machine in one of the houses up the road. Come on Ken, let's see if it's still there."

Harry and I walked down the little street in Valburg to the house he had visited previously when looking for fuel. The sewing-machine was still in the cupboard in the living-room. I was surprised to see it was a Singer make, it was not much bigger than a child's toy model, but — it worked.

Harry's mother had been a tailoress for many years and so he was conversant with the implements of the trade. My mother was also a machinist of no mean repute, so between us we were able to design or copy from a civilian shirt, which also came to hand that afternoon. I cut out and basted the collars, whilst Harry undertook the arduous task of the machining by hand.

The first one or two were painfully and sometimes a little blasphemously, sewn together. I must say quite unashamedly, that we turned out a pretty professional job. We even managed to produce our own ties. Nothing spectacular, just a straight tubular tie, which when knotted left only the minimum to be tucked into the open-necked blouse and was held there by a safety pin attaching it to the shirt. The material for the ties came from the more worn shirts which were slightly paler in colour. Some we procured from the stretcher bearers and needed to be boiled to remove the blood.

My turn for leave came at the end of February. I was to be accompanied by a young reinforcement who had quickly made himself at home with the rest of us old veterans. Willie Colquohoun was barely nineteen years old, but we got along fine together. He spoke with that lovely soft throaty dialect of a fairly well educated Scot and much to my liking, he had a great sense of humour. A little boyish as times, Willie was a good companion and I looked forward to the three days together.

The newly modified shirt was duly ironed with an old-fashioned flat iron hotted up on the petrol fire, the tie was pressed as were the lapels of the battledress blouse. A Glengarry was proffered by a comrade and gratefully accepted. We were going to do this in style.

Boots were retrieved from the bottom of the big pack and the toecaps polished to the nth degree. No wellies on this job.

We travelled to Nijmegen with the despatch rider in the signals jeep. At 'B' Echelon we were quickly seen by the MO for an FFI. Sgt. Lightbody produced the necessary pass and travel warrants and we were away in a 15-cwt truck to the railhead on the outskirts of the town.

Because of the tremendous damage in and around the main station in Nijmegen, a siding somewhere to the south-east of the town had been turned into an army railhead. This was the end of a complex railway system which had been hastily pressed into service, to bring supplies of every kind to a point as near to the front lines as possible. It was now also being used to ferry personnel to and from leave, thereby leaving the roads free for the ammunition and petrol convoys still coming through from France and southern Belgium.

The RTO (Rail Transport Officer) was housed in a temporary wooden shed on a sandy clearing beside the track. Silver birches and oak trees surrounded the site and I was instantly reminded of the beautiful Swithland Woods in the Charnwood Forest area of my native Leicestershire. Oh happy times, spent as a child as we picnicked on day outings with my parents, to gather bluebells and to run over the small humps and banks of slate and shale. Now the slate was exchanged for sand and childhood had slipped quietly away.

Passes stamped by the RTO, we boarded the train. Not the general purpose wagons of previous rail journeys, 40 Hommes/8 Chevaux. This time it was passenger coaches, not Pullman by any means, but coaches with slatted seats. This was luxury travel.

We travelled slowly with many stops in a westerly direction. Over the unmistakable steel bridge at Grave which had been captured intact by the Americans in September and on to Breda.

At Breda, we reported to a Canadian Transit Camp housed in a warehouse beside the railway. Here a hot meal was ready for our arrival. Well cooked and served up, it was equally well disposed of.

We were destined to stay the night at the transit camp, so we adjourned to the games room for a game of table-tennis followed by darts.

As we came out of the room, Willie saw the sign *Baths Unit — downstairs*.

He was away down those stairs like a ferret down a rabbit hole. I arrived at the unit a minute or so later, to hear him trying to cajole the attendant into a shirt exchange, but to no avail. Like me, he would have to spend his three days in Brussells wearing his Chubbs-West collar-attached shirt.

We did, however, enjoy the showers, probably because we had longer than the usual 3 minutes (one for soaping and two for sluicing). Then it was early to bed, in the two-tier wooden bunks, to catch up with some welcome sleep.

The train departed next morning shortly after eight o'clock. We made our way south via Antwerp and Louvain, to arrive in Brussells just before midday.

After reporting to the Canadian Army RTO, we were directed to our accommodation some ten minutes' walk away down an unassuming street in the typical Belgian style. Apartment buildings lined the street on both sides, paint peeling from doors and shutters, the four storeyed houses looked uncared for and neglected. We found the required number and rang the bell.

Somewhere at the end of a long wire, a bell jangled. A key was turned and the ancient door creaked open. A small wizened old man dressed in black stood before us, a green baize apron tied around his waist as though he had been disturbed in the task of cleaning the family silver by the jangling bell. We were intruders, of that there was no doubt.

"Soldat Anglaise en vacance," said Willie as he proffered the card. The old man stood aside and we entered. The door slammed to behind us.

"I hope he's on our side," I said to Willie as we followed the old Belgian up to a garret at the top of the house.

"If he's not, he'll probably hold us here as hostage till the end of the war," grinned Willie.

The room was about ten feet square. Simply furnished with two single beds, a wall closet, a marble topped wash-stand and two chairs with rush woven seats. It smelled damp and musty.

"Big Stan said we always stayed at The Metropole," said Willie disappointedly.

"If this is The Metropole, this must be the maid's room," I replied.

"We should be so lucky. If it is the maid's room, she'll no doubt be an old crone, like yon wee man," countered Willie; then, spotting the broken window, "I'll toss you for who gets the bed against the door."

"Heads," I cried and bagged the bed against the door.

The afternoon was spent finding our bearings around the vicinity of the hotel which had been commandeered for use as a leave centre for officers and for use by all ranks as dining-hall and restaurant.

We dined amongst unexpected elegance. Deep rich red velvet curtains contrasted warmly with the cream walls and the gilt painted scrolling. Cut glass chandeliers hung from the high ceiling, where smiling cherubs blew their gilded horns, as they gazed down with unseeing eyes on yet another change of clientèle.

The heavy linen table-cloths, immaculate and spotless, awaited our arrival. Waiters dressed in their customary black suits and bow ties, served the soup.

The main course was followed by a geateau, the likes of which we had not seen since pre-war days. Grapes too, large black juicy ones. These were and still are, my favourite choice. In wartime Britain they were unobtainable.

Here in Belgium, one could buy kilos of them in the shops.

In less than twenty-four hours, we were living in a different world. War was a whole world away.

We walked for a while, looking at the shops. Black-out restrictions had long been lifted. Shops were full of all kinds of merchandise. Lingerie of most exquisite design, delicate lace and embroidery, confectionery and bon-bons. Florists and greengrocers vied with each other in their window displays to entice customers into their premises.

To 'do a show' would have been the perfect ending to a perfect day. We were unlucky. Advance booking was necessary, so we settled for a film show, after taking the precaution to book for the ENSA show on the following night.

Errol Flynn was at his swashbuckling best, but I have forgotten the name of the film we saw that evening. Perhaps I was enjoying the black grapes too much — and spitting the seeds into Willie's glengarry.

The wide boulevards of the Belgian capital were now cleared of the accumulated garbage which had been dumped on the central reservation astride the tramway routes during the later weeks of the German occupation and for some weeks after the liberation. On my last visit to Brussells in October, this garbage was stacked from six to eight feet high, rotting and rat-infested.

The retreating Germans had commandeered all transport in the city and the resourceful inhabitants had no alternative but to deposit their waste as far away from habitation as possible. The Town Major's office had made this refuse disposal their top priority on assuming command. We could see on our second day, how successful the operation had been.

Our sightseeing promenade took us to all the well-known landmarks. The Bourse, the Royal Palace in the main square, a couple of museums and of course the 'Manikin Pis'.

Despite snacks at the NAAFI and YMCA canteens, we were more than ready for the dinner to which we looked forward so much. We were not disappointed.

The ENSA show also lived up to our expectations. A good bill of entertainment, with sufficiently partly-dressed girls to appease our male appetite.

Wandering into a small side street café on the way home, we were engaged in some very interesting conversation with old soldiers of the First World War. These Belgian veterans were kind in their compliments of the British Tommies, who for them had made a welcome return to the 'cockpit of Europe'. We drank many beers and many toasts before we left in the early hours of the morning.

Bang, bang, bang, bang.

I was awake in an instant. It seemed only minutes since we had got into bed.

Bang, bang.

"Early morning tea," came the sarcastic voice of Willie. I opened the door. Outside the old retainer stood holding a water jug and basin.

"L'eau, m'sieur." The look on his face spoke volumes. He had got his own back on us for getting him out of his bed to let us in some four hours previously.

"Christ, it's only six o'clock, Ken."

"Aye, and the morning tea is just a jug of ice cold water to wash and shave with," I replied.

We lay on our beds for another hour or so, but couldn't sleep. The old man had won this round.

Photographs and souvenirs for home were the top of the list of the third day's programme.

The Belgians had lost very little time in producing a whole selection of good quality souvenirs with Divisional and individually well-known units being pictured on them.

I found some chic underwear for Margaret and handkerchiefs with Polar Bear motifs for other relatives. A small scarf for mother, etc. Willie made similar purchases.

Being a canny Scot, my companion was loath to part with his money to the local photographers, not believing that they would honour their promise to forward the resulting copies to us.

We walked around for two hours until we saw a sign in a café window.
English soldiers – photographs whilst you wait.

We entered the café and rang the bell.

Madame entered from the rear room, beckoning as she came. Three or four young – well, rather young – ladies followed her. Business was starting early today.

"Photographs, Madame." Madame shrugged her shoulders at the ladies. All looked rather peeved.

"Henri, Les Anglaise," she shouted upstairs.

A slim dapper Belgian descended the stairs. With his neatly trimmed goatee beard and pince-nez spectacles, he looked exactly as one would expect a French or Belgian fashion photographer to look.

"How long will it take for our photographs, m'sieur?" asked the impatient Willie.

"Twenty minutes, m'sieur," he was assured.

"How much, combien?" queried the careful Scot. The price was favourable.

"We go to the backsides – follow me messieurs."

We waited in the back yard as he set up his large tripod and camera. He explained . . . .

"Zis is a new system, I make the photograph and print him all in the same camera." Our interest was aroused.

"In nineteen thirty-eight, I have an American from a big photographic company, he come to buy my patent. I don't trust 'im — not enough dollars." He rubbed his fingers in the manner that the continentals do when discussing money.

Standing shoulder to shoulder, Willie and I tried to fathom out what was going on under the large black cape. He took six photos and after some twenty minutes, there in his hand were six very good black and white prints.

As we adjourned to the café for a beer, he poured out his story to us. I am sorry that I was never well versed on that particular subject, otherwise I would have realized we had just witnessed the very beginnings of Polaroid photography. Years after the war I read that Eastman or Kodak had bought out the patents of a polaroid camera from a Belgian. Was it, I wonder, our dapper little friend?

In the afternoon, we had studio portraits done in the NAAFI studios and they were sent on to our home addresses. A copy of mine appears at the front of this book.

The evening's entertainment was a dance in the NAAFI buildings. Despite our hob-nailed boots, Willie and I performed reasonably well and spent most of the evening in the company of two ATS girls. The young willowy blonde partnered Willie and I was saddled with the plump old lady of twenty-five. Suffice it to say that we danced the night away, then at the finish, Willie insisted that we escort the girls back to barracks.

We talked of home and families as we walked the two miles or so to the barracks. On reaching the barracks, we found that the two girls had to enter by different gates. I took Mary to her gate and returned to the corner where we had agreed to meet after Willie had taken Carol to her gate.

Twenty minutes . . . no Willie Colquohoun. Thirty minutes . . . no sign of the blighter. I decided to walk back as we were overdue. On a whim I called at the café, just in case he'd gone there.

"Non m'sieur, votre ami — not tonight." I decided to wait and ordered a beer. I shouldn't have done that. I left the café well after three o'clock in the morning.

I hammered the door for some minutes, before the old man would answer. I think he had disconnected the bell. When he appeared at the door, his face was as black as thunder. He kept on repeating something about, "Je parley avec La Comtesse — La Comtesse." I replied that the Comtesse could visit a taxidermist for all I cared and went to bed. Willie was already there.

Two hours or so later, the episode of the water jug of the previous morning was repeated. This time threats of "La Comtesse" were also included.

Breakfast in the elegant dining-room was a prolonged meal. We wished to savour the moment. It may be many months before we ate again in such surroundings — it may be never . . . .

As we talked with one of the waiters, it became increasingly clear that we had been the guests of a most remarkable lady. None other than the Comtesse de Mont Blanc. A confirmed Anglophile, she had defended the British against all German threats despite her great age.

Returning briefly to our billet to collect our kit, we were just leaving when the old retainer came to the door. As he opened the door with one hand, the other hand was held in a cupped fashion.

"I think he's expecting a tip, Willie," I said.

"Right, I'll give him one then," said the Scot, much to my surprise. He bent down and shouted in the old man's ear "Never count your chickens till they're hatched, laddie."

Three paces down the street and a discreet cough was heard from above.

I looked up quickly and saw an old lady dressed all in black sitting in a wheelchair on a small balcony. Beside her was a younger woman in attendance.

"Crikey, it's the old toff," I said quietly, "we'd better throw her up a right fourpenny one." Out of the side of my mouth I gave the command: "One, two, three, right turn — hup two three, down two three."

We threw the dear old Comtesse probably the finest salute she had ever received in her long life. As we stood there to attention, we received in return a gesture of the right hand, known in England as a royal wave.

Our hearts softened and instinctively we both bowed to her. Little did we know that we were repaying the Comtesse de Mont Blanc for the great support she had given the Allies for over four long years.

Yes, a little old lady who so much resembled the old Queen Victoria.

The journey to Brussells had been quite uneventful. The journey back from that gay city was unforgettable.

Everyone was in high spirits. In some, the spirit level was higher than others, especially the Canadians who formed perhaps three-quarters of the passengers on the train. With their higher rates of pay, they had been able to fortify themselves with bottles of spirits of all descriptions. These were quickly opened and the contents duly sampled.

Tales were exchanged as we settled down to the long journey ahead. Enamelled army mugs were unstrapped from small packs, to receive the generous tots of whisky and gin from our Canadian comrades-in-arms.

Someone was recounting his experiences with one of the ladies of the night. Just as interest was beginning to build up, a faced passed by the window of the carriage — on the outside of the train.

We all dashed to the end of the corridor and looked out of the window. To our right, came the lurching, swinging figure of a French Canadian. Bottle in hand, he edged along the wooden running board which ran the whole length of each carriage. Grabbing a hand-hold wherever possible he reached our door.

"Bon vacance, mes amis, bon sánté," he cried as he passed the bottle through the open window.

Someone took the bottle from our inebriated friend as others endeavoured to pull him through the window head-first. After a struggle, he was safely delivered on to the floor of the corridor. He was helped to his feet and stood there swaying as he asked most politely for the return of his bottle. Still full of *bonhomie*, he lurched off to look for his friends further along the train.

Ten minutes later he was back again, on the outside — going in the opposite direction. We waved to him as he passed by and carried on with our conversation.

Another ten minutes and cheerful mustachioed faced Pierre was back again, mouthing felicitations in French through the glass window.

"Christ, there's another one out here," exclaimed Willie as he looked out of the opposite window.

Further inspection from the window in the corridor revealed not one, but three more on the far side. Two going in one direction and one in the opposite direction.

Things were now getting ridiculously out of hand.

Brakes were slammed on and the train shuddered and screeched to a halt.

Red-capped Military Policemen ran down the trackside as the train stood belching steam in the open countryside. But the Redcaps were not quick enough. Friendly hands had pulled the jay-walkers aboard.

After a fruitless search, the train moved forward once more towards Antwerp.

Twenty minutes later, knock, knock, knock, knock, came the sound from the roof of our compartment. Someone stood on the seat and looked out of the air vent in the ceiling of the carriage. A pair of eyes met his gaze.

"C'est le train pour Breda, m'sieur?"

"The goddam Frenchies are at it again," said the Canadian as he regained his seat. We dashed to the window once more, but not a sign of anyone along the running board. They'd taken to the roof.

Shortly afterwards the train screeched to a halt again. An irate British officer with an RTO armband, stormed up and down outside.

"Any more of this bloody silly carrying on and I'll have the engine uncoupled at Antwerp," he warned. There *was* more of that bloody silly carrying on.

The long line of carriages drew slowly to a halt as the train arrived at the main station in Antwerp. Heads quickly popped out of the opened windows to check on whether the threat would be carried out. It was . . . .

Obscene abuse was hurled at the Belgian railwaymen as they uncoupled the engine. More abuse was hurled at the driver as he steamed away towards the sheds. They knew not, or cared not, what we said.

We sat in that train for an hour and a half, knowing full well that at any time a V1 rocket might fall, slap bang in the middle of Antwerp and wipe us all out.

The Germans were not only firing their latest rockets at London, they were also aiming them at Antwerp. If they could prevent the Allies from using the great port of Antwerp, or disrupt the important railway yards in the vicinity, they could impede the necessary build-up of vital supplies for the spring offensive which we all knew would be coming.

Here, in the engineless train, we were sitting ducks — fortunately the Germans were not duck shooting that day.

A great cheer heralded the return of the engine. The sound of the buffers clanging together and the jolt as the engine took the strain came as a great relief. Our sojourn had had a most sobering effect on the vast majority of the returning leave party, but not all.

A quarter of an hour later, a familiar face was seen at the window. Smiling faces urged him on to the open window at the end of the carriage.

"Entrez, mon ami," said the burly Corporal as he pulled Pierre through the window.

I never saw the Corporal's right hand move. One moment the erring pedestrian was standing in the swaying corridor, the next moment he was laying pole-axed on the floor.

"We'll wake him up when we get to Breda," he said as we resumed our seats.

The last dregs of the whisky were wrung from the bottle and we all joined in the uproarious sing-song which lasted for the remainder of the journey to Breda.

There were many handshakes and heartfelt good wishes as we detrained and went our respective ways.

The transit camp beds were most welcome that night. The official reason for leave in Brussels was to give the troops three days of rest and recuperation from the strains and stresses of war. We, like most others, had taken the opportunity to let our hair down and live every minute to the full. We were used to going without sleep.

There were no cafés, no accordion bands, no dancing girls in their scanty costumes, no 'ladies of the night', nor were there any juicy black grapes. Not where we were going.

The loss of sleep was a pretty fair exchange for three unforgettable days and nights in the bright, friendly, embracing capital city of Brussells.

There were tales to tell, though not all of them, to our grandchildren.

TWENTY-FIVE — DRYING OUT

Someone once wrote, war is mud and discomfort . . . and being frightened . . . and losing one's good friends suddenly.

To some readers this may seem an over-simplification, but I would agree with the writer's sentiments. As an infantryman, one is faced with each of the above experiences on numerous occasions. No matter how one adapts or becomes hardened to battle conditions, the unexpected act or surprise move can deliver a body blow to one's morale.

Sometimes it takes great strength of character to overcome the effects of such experiences.

The thaw of late February carried on into March, and with it came the floods. Bad as they had been during the winter, the water now rose to a height which gave grave doubts to our continuance of tenure to the 'island'. Indeed, it took high level discussions between the British and Dutch governments before the matter could be resolved.

The British High Command wanted to breach the dykes of the old Zuider Zee and so drain away the flood water on to the newly reclaimed land. Agreement could not be reached, so the Queen of the Netherlands, in exile in England, was asked to give her assent.

Queen Wilhelmina replied that if such action would speed the removal of the German Army from her country, it was a price the Dutch nation would have to pay.

The RAF bombed the dykes and twenty-five years of work of reclamation was lost in a matter of hours.

Inch by inch, the flood waters receded. We still held the 'island' — and we still held the Waal bridge.

No longer need we patrol by rowing boat, or use ladders as improvised bridges to cross ditches and irrigation channels.

The 'ladder patrols' as we came to know them, quite often became hair-raising night operations. The ladders used were mainly of the type used in the orchards for picking fruit — light wooden pole ladders to facilitate their easy portage, quite safe and sound when used in an upright position, but very unstable when used in a horizontal position. I lost my rifle because of a rotten ladder.

Jimmy Logan dashed into the room and grabbed the rifle standing behind his bed roll.

"They want a signaller on a 'ladder patrol' — see you later," he shouted as he left hurriedly. Unfortunately the rifle he had taken wasn't his, it was mine, as I found out later.

The patrol, after 'listening out' for the appointed time, was on its way back when they were spotted by a Jerry patrol. In the ensuing exchange of fire, the enemy patrol came menacingly close to the ladder bridge. A rearguard action by Jimmy held them at bay sufficiently long enough for the rest of his party to cross. As he ran across the frail structure, there was a resounding crack and down into the muddy waters went Jimmy — and my rifle. He retrived the broken ladder and pulled it away to make it unusable, but the rifle stayed at the bottom of the ditch. He crawled to safety and radioed for a 'stonk' to disperse the enemy patrol. For this action he was recommended for the Military Medal.

For losing my rifle, I was told I would have to pay £9 for a replacement. Despite protestations from both of us, we were reminded that a soldier is responsible for his kit at all times and part of my kit, to wit, one rifle Lee Enfield Mk 3 was missing.

Now that the roads were beginning to dry out, more vehicles were being used. We sensed that it was only a matter of time before some Brass Hat would decide to push forward and clear the rest of the 'island'.

Before this could happen, more information was necessary about the composition of the units facing us. It was only to be gained by capturing prisoners in a 'snatch patrol'.

However, enemy mines in the Haalderen sector had made patrolling very difficult. It was therefore decided to attempt an amphibious landing behind the German lines. Following a successful landing, the craft would retire and the patrol would return by land after completing its task. 'D' Company were chosen to carry out this operation on 10th March.

Embarking at Nijmegen in four assault landing craft, they proceeded upstream along the river Waal to a point some 1,200 yards behind the enemy lines. Nos. 17 and 18 Platoons touched down at 05.45 hrs. with the former quickly gaining its objective, a white house on the bund beyond Haalderen. After driving off two counter-attacks, they were compelled to withdraw when the house ultimately caught fire.

Meanwhile, No. 16 Platoon had met fiercer opposition as they attempted to clear six houses on the bund. Reaching the third house, the Platoon came under machine-gun fire from the fifth house and called for an artillery stonk. On reaching the last house, the Platoon consolidated.

At 08.00 hrs. the Company was ordered to withdraw, using a route taped out by prisoners through a suspected minefield. The successful operation had resulted in 36 enemy killed or wounded and 10 prisoners taken. 'D' Company casualties were three killed and eight wounded. For his leadership of this outstanding enterprise, the Company Commander Major Rowell was awarded the

DSO (Distinguished Service Order).

I had stayed on duty at 'A' Company HQ whilst this raid was in progress, then as the 'D' Company lads came through our outposts, I handed over to Arthur Thompson and got my head down for a few hours' sleep.

Shortly after I had returned on duty, the field telephone rang.

"Is that you Ken?" The voice of Nat sounded tired and strained. I answered in the affirmative.

"I thought I ought to let you know the news mate, Pottsie and Sgt. Little copped it on the raid this morning." I swallowed hard and felt my stomach muscles tighten.

"Pottsie, dead?" I could scarcely believe it. "Not Pottsie, our old pal from the old No. 17 Platoon days?"

"Yes Ken. Sorry to be the one to tell you, I knew he was a pal of yours."

"The last thing I heard, they'd got some in the bag and were on their way back — what happened?" I questioned.

"Oh, the raid went according to plan, but after Little had taken the first strong point, he asked Potter to give him covering fire and ran forward. They were caught by Spandau fire. The lads are going out later to bring them in."

I felt angry. Most of us in the Signals knew that the Sergeant had transferred from the MT section to a rifle platoon in order to follow the example of his forebears who had won medals for gallantry. His bravery in Normandy had gained him the Military Medal. Not satisfied with that, he had made no secret of the fact that he wanted to gain a bar to that medal. Rightly or wrongly, I felt that Pottsie had been killed unnecessarily through the overzealousness of the Platoon Sergeant. The thought of my pal lying out there in the rain made me feel very sad.

On the following day, the Colonel made his mid morning rounds. He came into the lean-to building at the side of the bund which housed our Company HQ. Clearly he wasn't his usual cheerful self.

"Bad news about Sgt. Little and Fusilier Potter," I said.

"Yes, we lost a couple of good men last night, West, two very experienced men."

"Yes, I'll miss Potter," I said, "we were pals in Normandy when I was with Sgt. Hill's Platoon."

He looked at me with compassion as he said, "I'm sorry that you lost a friend."

"I think we all lost a friend, Sir."

"Yes, I suppose we did," he added sadly. "Please ring Major Rowell and let him know that I'm on my way." He touched his cane to his Tam-o'-Shanter and strode away to the jeep awaiting him in the side road at Haalderen.

Sgt. Little, MM and Fusilier Potter were buried during the afternoon in the temporary cemetery just by the crossroads on the Bemmel to Ressen road. They could rest in peace there. No matter how often that crossroad was stonked, the cemetery was never hit. They were safe in the arms of the Lord.

Crump — the unmistakeable sound of a landmine being triggered off assailed our ears.

"I suppose that's another ruddy goat," said the Major, "get someone to check it out Sgt.-Major."

We were being plagued by goats. No one knew from whence they came, although we did rather suspect that they were being introduced into the area by the Germans and encouraged by them to stray across our lines.

As they foraged for food, they were blundering into trip wires and minefields which we had laid during the early winter, around the perimeters of the villages we were occupying. Each time a wire was broken and the alarm sounded, a search was needed to check out who had caused the alarm.

Stray dogs had caused much havoc in the early days, but most of them had now been shot. Goats were now declared to be enemy number one.

A signal message recorded that, 'All goats will be shot on sight. Nil returns required.' This meant that a daily report must be sent in to record the goat tally for the previous day.

'A' Company had the answer to this — 'Hedy Lamarr'.

Capt. La Marre was a 'Can-loan' officer. Because of the shortage of British infantry officers, the 49th Division had been reinforced by Canadian officers on loan for the duration of the war. Hence the nickname of 'Can-loan'. These officers in their distinctive olive green battledress and their black leather calf length boots, were very popular with the Polar Bears. Not quite so stand-offish as their British counterparts, they mixed well with the men.

Capt. 'Hedy Lamarr' was, as his name suggests, a French-Canadian. Of average height, this black moustached man with the swarthy complexion, spoke with that delightful broken English accent one associates with continental film stars. As a master of the written word he was somewhat lacking, he therefore received much of our mail for censorship.

Following my verbal fracas with Pin-down, I no longer gave him the satisfaction of reading my letters to Margaret. Instead, it was my wont to deposit my affectionate letters to my wife with Hedy for his perusal. I am certain that he didn't always comprehend fully what was written, but they were duly signed and returned for posting.

He may not have been the best reader of English literature, but my word he could shoot. Armed with a German make Mauser rifle, he would depart immediately after the Colonel's morning rounds, invariably saying as he left the Company HQ, "An' now I go . . . . to shoot us some goat."

He would be away until almost dusk, to return with either, "Today I kill us a goat," or he would return dejectedly saying, "Bloody goat — today 'e 'ide 'imself," then wander off swearing in French.

His map reading matched equally his shooting ability and at night he would pin-point with great accuracy on the map or aerial photographs, the exact position of his latest kill.

We were now receiving aerial photos almost daily. These we pored over at night, searching for tell-tale signs of any new movements by our counterparts. The snowy wastes with their pock marked shell bursts were a thing of the past. Now roads and footpaths were revealed together with the ponds and other natural obstacles. We searched diligently for the tell-tale tracks that would announce the arrival of tanks. We saw none.

The March winds whistled and whined. Doors and windows creaked and rattled. The nights were full of noise.

The herring-bone patterned brick roads were drying out too. Gradually the build-up of vehicular traffic during the hours of darkness was helping to solidify the roads as the bricks were pressed more firmly into the sandy soil below. The quarter meter squares of concrete which formed the cycle-tracks through the village, were also drying out. It was a long time since I had been for a bike ride.

Paddy came into the office with the news that he'd found a bike. Outside stood one of the Airborne folding cycles, miraculously with both tyres still inflated. We took turns to have a little ride around. The cycle seemed to be none the worse for its lack of use, having stood in the barn all winter. If we could find another bike, we could go visiting friends.

After much searching of outhouses and sheds, an old upright model was found. The flat front tyre was overlooked as we wended our way towards the Leicesters Signals HQ.

One of the Tigers signallers had trained with Paddy and myself up at Richmond, so we were off to have a chat with our old pal Arthur Lindley.

About half-way along the road to Ressen, we were overtaken by a jeep which then pulled in front of us, making us stop. The three-pipped officer was unknown to either of us.

"Where are you two men going?" he demanded.

"Just having a ride around," said Paddy.

"What unit do you belong to?"

There was no sense in trying to mislead the Captain, so we told him.

"Identification," he said brusquely.

"Not allowed to carry any sir," we lied.

"Give me your names then, we can't have people swanning around on bloody bicycles." I looked at Paddy and nodded.

"Fusilier McKay," said Paddy.

"Fusilier Maclaren," I lied, taking my name from the goal-keeper of Leicester City FC., a Jimmy Maclaren.

The Captain wrote down the names and, turning us about, sent us on our way back to the RSF. We dumped the bikes near to the crossroads and made our way back separately. Paddy to 'B' Company and me to 'A' Company. Meanwhile, the chap in the jeep had reported to Battalion HQ about Fusiliers McKay and Maclaren swanning around on bicycles. Suffice it to say, they were never found. Neither were the bikes — somebody had 'nicked' them.

Boots were now required to be worn. The easy going days of slopping about in wellies were over. Feet had gone soft and needed toughening up again. Clothing was getting worn and tattered. Kit checks were imminent. It came as no surprise for all signallers to be called to HQ for checks.

"Fall in outside with all your kit," John the 'B' shouted. A motley crew of signallers assembled in the village street. "What a bloody shower! Stand up man, hold ye'r head up — " he was at it again.

Boots were checked, then rifles and small arms. Battledress blouses scrutinized for replacement.

"Slacks down," said the unbeknowing W/O1 MacCreadie, J. For a moment he couldn't believe his eyes. There before him were about a dozen men with shirt tails of varied hues. As we suppressed our giggles, the air was rent with the cry of anguish from the astonished RSM.

"What the bloody hell's been going on here?" For a minute or two, no one answered. Then someone proffered an answer.

"We needed collars for our shirts for the leave in Brussells sir — so we cut the tails off the spare shirts."

"Ye did so, did ye? An' who did the tailoring?"

No one answered.

"I asked ye, who did the tailoring?"

"We got them done in Nijmegen," lied Johnnie Lefferty.

"I dinna mean the collars, laddie, I meant the Joseph's coats o' many colours," replied the RSM.

We owned up to that part of the operation. We couldn't tell him the full story of how, when the tails had been removed, there were so many cold bums walking about we had to protect the nether regions with whatever was available.

I think Paddy started it off by bringing in a piece of pillow case ticking. Being a former Rugby forward, he had a rather wide beam, so we sewed the opened pillow case on with the stripes horizontally inclined. The shirt tail reached the back of his knees.

Others used curtaining or cushion covers with hand embroidery patterns. I sported the tail off the original shirt from which the pattern for the collar had been copied. Off-white, with vertical dark blue stripes, quite natty I thought, compared to some of the others. As ever, John the 'B' had the last word.

"Right then laddies, all ye arse-end charlies will hand in yon shirts — and ye'r AB 64s part II. Ye'll all be deducted three shillings and ninepence for misuse of government property, i.e. shirt angola — soldiers for the use of — ONE. Dismiss!"

As for the shirts, many of those found their way back to Harry and lived on again to adorn the neckline and not the buttocks.

The third week of March saw us back in Nijmegen for what was to prove the last visit by the whole Battalion. Warmly welcomed as ever by our family, the few days passed too quickly. We were saddened on the last evening but one, to hear that one of the young friends of the family had met an untimely death on the previous night. A member of the Dutch underground movement, as were quite a number of the young people we had come to know, this nineteen-year-old boy had crossed the Rhine with a small party on some operation. During the night their car had run into a parked German tank on the outskirts of Utrecht. All the young Dutchmen had been killed outright. A tragic accident.

As the young man had called to see us on our first evening three days previously, we shared the family's grief. It seemed somehow ironical that the whole of the Canadian Army sat stranded on the west bank of the river Rhine unable to move and these young teenagers were tripping back and forth across the great river to bring us information about our adversaries. They were brave young men.

Unexpectedly, the move back on to the 'island' was not into a forward area, but to the reserve area between Slijk Ewijk and Bemmel. Something was afoot.

The American airborne troops had held this part of the line, immediately after their brave crossing of the Waal back in September, until relieved by the 50th Division.

The thin lines of assault cable crossed and recrossed the fields, there was miles of the stuff. Some bright spark decided to reel in as much as possible, we spent all one day on this task and in retrospect, I don't think we ever used an inch of the perishing stuff.

A new lot of reinforcements arrived and were distributed around the Companies. Shortly afterwards a strange droning sound was heard. It came from the west.

Suddenly the sky was full of planes — and gliders, a vast armada filling the whole sky as far as one could see. They all travelled eastwards. Just as they were almost out of sight, we saw small specks of colour descending from the planes. The British 6th Airborne Division was landing on specified targets on the far side of the Rhine beyond the German town of Emmerich. With field-glasses we could see the gliders turn and lose height as they approached their landing zones.

The tow planes relieved of their burdens turned amidst the flak towards the Scheldt estuary as they started their homeward journey.

We stood spellbound at this panoply of planes and parachutes unfolding before our eyes. A sight never to be seen again in this theatre of war.

We had witnessed bomber raids of two hundred and fifty planes on Villiers Bocage, also the thousand bomber raid on Caen. They had been cold and calculated raids.

Somehow, the airborne operation we were witnessing, was live and warm and pulsating. We cheered them on their way.

Then as suddenly as it had started, it was all over. Like the wild geese that fill the autumn skies, seemingly for hours, the laggards strive to catch the main body before they come to roost, then one looks again and the sky is clear. One hopes that the lame ones have reached their haven safely.

It was quieter now. We had time to think. Long sobering thoughts. Very few people spoke, but in their minds the message was clear, the 2nd Army springboard was over the Rhine.

How long before we also crossed the mighty river?

Fusiliers Ken West and Willie Colquohoun enjoy a 3-day leave in Brussels

TWENTY-SIX – RED OVER GREEN

"There's summat up," said Arthur Thompson as he read the signal message. " 'O' Group at 14.00 hours – all Sunrays plus signaller."

The message hardly came as a surprise. For the past two days the whole Battalion had been recapping on their offensive training in the reserve area around Slijk Ewijk.

Signallers had been training with new wireless sets, the No. 46 set. These sets were 'ganged sets', in that the operating channels were preset to prevent 'fading' as sometimes happened with our standard No. 18 sets.

The difficult flat terrain of the Netherlands had been a nightmare for the Red Devils at Arnhem, where wireless communications were only possible over very short distances.

On the 'island' during the static war of the winter months, we had witnessed very few problems. In the fluid conditions of an offensive warfare we questioned the effectiveness of our standard sets over longer distances.

The No. 46 sets performed quite well during the training period, but the operators found them to be more cumbersome than the No. 18s. The weights were about the same, but the new sets were slung over the left shoulder and hung on the right waist, rather like a newspaper boy would carry his paper bag. Although they were easy to take off, they bumped and banged against one's legs to impede progress more so than the standard back pack type to which we had become so accustomed.

I don't think it was general practice in the British Army, but in the Fusiliers the signallers were often included in the officers' 'O' groups, particularly where an offensive was planned. The reasoning behind this inclusion of a Company signaller was, to my mind, good sound common sense. Should the Company Commander become a casualty in the fluid situation of the offensive, the signaller was well briefed enough to ensure that the plan of operation could be still carried out. He could, and in some cases did, direct the Company operation until the second in command was able to assume command.

It was a 'full house' at the 'O' group. Gunnery officers were in attendance, Div. Signals, also a Canadian tank man – tanks!

Arthur was right, summat was up!

The plan was outlined by the Colonel. The Division would advance on a broad front to sweep the enemy from the rest of the 'island' and indeed all the ground from Nijmegen to the west bank of the Rhine at Arnhem.

Our Battalion would take the right flank from Bemmel to the bund, with Hulhuizen, Elieren, Baal and Angeren, as the Company objectives. 'D' Company would lead to take Hulhuizen and 'A' Company would go through them and take Angeren.

Tanks of the 11th Ontario Regt. would be in attendance.

Signallers would use No. 18 sets. No. 46 sets would be carried on Company transport, in case of emergency.

'Operation Destroyer' would commence at 07.00 hours on the morrow, 2nd April. Gunners would lay down a barrage from 06.00 hours as a softening up on all objectives.

The old feeling was there again in the pit of the stomach as we assembled with 'A' Company HQ group. Not since the days of Normandy had I experienced the indescribable feeling one gets in those few minutes before the order to start an offensive. Not fear as such, nor bravado, nor expectation of death, and certainly not constipation.

Forced jokes and unnecessary chatter are bandied about, as if to prove that no one is thinking of the job in hand as everyone takes up their appointed places for zero hour.

I walk to the jeep. Who should be standing with the driver but our old newshound friend 'Black Bob'. We exchanged nods.

"Prepare to move," shouted the Major.

Fusilier Nimmo jumped into the driver's seat with the Major beside him. 'Black Bob' prepared to hop on to the rear seat beside the Major's batman. "Sorry, I need that place for West," said the Major, "I'm afraid you'll have to walk."

I received the sort of look from 'Black Bob' that a dog would give to someone who had just kicked him.

I knew instantly that whatever may happen during that eventful day, my name would not appear across the front pages of the *Weekly News*, whenever the story came to be released for publication.

We had gone only a few hundred yards along the back road to Haalderen when, immediately to our front, perhaps two miles distant, a green coloured flare climbed lazily into the morning sky immediately followed by a red flare which climbed above the green. They hung momentarily at the apex of their orbit, then fell slightly faster, leaving a thin wispy trail of smoke as they disappeared behind the trees of a wood.

Our hearts lifted. Major Weir, still looking fixedly to the front, nodded in acknowledgment. The rumours were correct.

Ever since the news of 'Operation Destroyer' had been announced, a buzz had gone around the Company to the effect that captured prisoners had said that if there was an attack in force by us, the Germans would withdraw from the 'island'. This would be signalled by two flares, i.e. red over green . . . .

The sounds of Spandau fire and the occasional crump of the mortars meant that there would be some kind of rearguard action to hold us up as long as possible. Machine-guns were chattering along the bund too.

The jeep bumped and rocked as it moved along the shell pocked road at walking pace towards the little white cottage by the bund. Shortly before reaching there, a bedraggled group of some twelve or fourteen men in field grey overcoats passed us, led by an arrogant blond-haired young NCO with a large black German sheep-dog on a leash. In complete contrast to the man, the shepherd dog looked in the peak of condition, its well groomed coat gleaming, the eyes alert and watchful, its muzzle barely hiding the great fangs in the strong jaws.

I was glad we hadn't bumped into that fine animal on a dark winter's night.

We reached the rendezvous with 'D' Company a little early and took shelter in a café-cum-shop at the end of the village — this was it.

The bowels loosened a little as we waited. Through the shattered doorway came the ever popular Sgt. Duncan. Eyes twinkling and a wide smile across his ruddy countenance, he sniffed.

"Everbody farting fit? That's the idea, my whippets always went better after a good fart," he said. "We'll be off in another three minutes."

Bang! — the resounding shot from a .303 rifle as someone nervously checking his Lee Enfield inadvertently loosed off a round into the ceiling above where 'Black Bob' stood. He must have jumped a foot into the air.

"Now then laddie, no need to fire a starting gun, I'll tell you when to bloody start," joked the Sergeant. He looked at his watch, then at the young men in the room. Momentarily the brashness dropped.

"Come on then lads, follow me." His voice was now softer and more kindly. He cared for his lads.

They moved out on to the road, fanning out behind the leading tank as it advanced towards Angeren.

"Get on to the back of the third tank, West." The Major's voice had an urgency I had not noticed before. "Keep in touch with Big Sunray and work with the tank commander."

Hands pushed me on to the back end of the Sherman tank and I squatted as near to the turret as possible. Engine roaring, the tank soon joined the rest of the vanguard.

The Canadian Lieutenant and I soon worked out a message passing system. If I had a message for him, I would tap him on his left shoulder's pips and shout the message. Anything for me to pass on was signified by a winding motion of his right hand and an imaginary phone held to his left ear.

The delicate inter-communications we had spoken about in the 'O' group were working perfectly on the command tank, the one with the little pennant flying from the wireless aerial — ours.

The leading tank observed movement in some houses and went off with Sgt. Duncan and his lads to investigate. We halted in the middle of the road. Suddenly I felt naked sitting on the back of that tank, sticking out like a nipple on a cold day at a nudist camp.

That's when it started to rain.

No sooner had the rain shower started, when — wham! Down went the conning tower (a nickname we gave to the turret cap). Lousy sods, I thought. It was all right for them in the dry, inside the tank. What about me on the top? I was getting wet through — but not for long.

Pulling and tugging at the camouflaged tarpaulin sheet which all the Shermans carried, I managed to afford some sort of cover and sat there in the dry, holding my earphones hard on to my ears as I listened to the commentaries of the various participants, completely absorbed in the operation as it unfolded according to plan.

The April shower now passed. I tapped on the conning tower to relay the message coming through. The cap opened gingerly, a pair of eyes squinting through the small aperture.

"You can come out now," I said. "It's stopped raining."

"Christ! I'd clean forgotten about you Jock," said the Lieutenant. He looked about him and down went his head. Another head appeared, looked at me in disbelief and down he went. A third head popped up following the same routine, but this one spoke.

"You're a bloody cool customer, Jock. Sitting up there with all that stonking going on."

I looked around the area of the tank. Five black tell-tale holes confirmed that while we'd sat there, we'd been stonked by mortars or some light shells, the nearest no more than ten feet away. I'd sat there oblivious to the explosions. Concerned only about keeping dry, I thought that was why the Canadian lads had covered up.

The reason for my rapt attention during this stonking, was the hold up to our left. The 4th Battalion Lincolns had met stiff resistance from a small group holding a waterworks or pumping station, thus barring the advance towards Zand and Huissen. Machine-gun emplacements and a bazooka well entrenched behind the grassy mound surrounding the works, had repelled all attemps to dislodge the occupants. A call had gone out for the assistance of rocket-firing Typhoons.

Whether the rocket-firing 'Tiffies' had arrived too soon, or whether the Lincoln's Platoon did not withdraw far enough, I'm not sure.

The 'Tiffies', loosing their rockets, screamed over our heads and then turned away to repeat the run. They came in again and successfully knocked out the machine-gun posts. Unfortunately in this second strike, they also caused many casualties amongst the Lincolns. Perhaps they had gone in to winkle out the enemy after the first strike and had been caught in an exposed position. That is sheer conjecture on my part. The fact that almost fifty per cent of the Platoon were casualties is not, and we were saddened by the news.

As we were the nearest unit to the Lincolns, we were asked to mop up the waterworks. This we did, also bringing aid to the wounded of both sides, before moving on to a small hamlet to our left. Here the rest of 'A' Company reported their present positions and we established HQ in a small house almost completely untouched by shelling or mortaring.

In the April sunshine one suddenly realized that it was spring. Buds were beginning to appear on the bushes and small trees, hardy perennials were throwing up their shoots bravely from the uncultivated soil. We looked for tulips, but we found none and were a little disappointed.

Back in the house, a message from Arthur Thompson. A search of the houses had revealed that one of the houses had been recently evacuated by the Germans. Up in the roof an observation point had been found. Through the single hole in this roof, just one tile's width, one could see the whole of the 'island'. With field-glasses one could see every vehicle which crossed the big Waal bridge at Nijmegen. No wonder we had been stonked so accurately whenever a vehicle had moved.

I looked once more through the window at the once neat little garden and wondered what colour the roses might be.

Suddenly I put the roses from my mind. Around the end of the next house but one, came six figures with their hands clasped on top of their heads. I looked for the smiling Tommy who usually walked at the rear of such a party. No smiling Tommy Atkins. These laddies had decided that they had done enough for the Fatherland and were giving themselves up. At that moment the wireless set crackled into life.

"Messsage for all Companies. With effect from 14.00 hours a prisoner-of-war reception area will be established at map reference .... acknowledge." I recognized the voice as that of the adjutant.

At that precise moment the Company runner shouted through the front door.

"Come on Westy, the Major wants you. We're off again towards Hussein." I heard his footsteps fading away as he ran back towards the tanks.

"Acknowledge, 'A' Company," came the voice of the adjutant.

" 'A' Company acknowledging. We have six prisoners for you now," I replied, looking at the six men coming into the front garden.

"Hello 'A' Company I say again . . . . " repeating the message.

"Hello, Sunray minor. I say again, I have six prisoners now coming up the path to the front door," I repeated.

"Hello 'A' Company, don't you understand, man? Reception of prisoners cannot commence until 14.00 hours." This was getting stupid.

"Hello Sunray minor, I have been ordered by my Sunray to rejoin the tanks to continue the attack. I have six Germans knocking on the front door to surrender — shall I ask them to call again later, Sir?" I said sarcastically.

"Don't be so bloody sarcastic — what's your bloody name? Do you know who you're talking to?" I never bothered to answer and went rifle in hand to the front door.

"Kamerad, Tommy," said the first man without taking his hands from his head.

"Ja," I replied in my best, and only, German.

Pointing my rifle down the road, I signalled them to move with a slight inclination of my head to the left. A few steps of running on the spot gave them the right idea and we trotted away to the road junction to rendezvous with the tanks.

At the T-junction the prisoners were encouraged to trot back down the road towards Hulhuissen where presumably someone would take them to the adjutant's reception area, providing of course, that it was after 14.00 hours.

We embussed aboard the tanks and proceeded in the general direction of Huissen. My eardrums were getting a bit of a battering from all the activity on the air. Everyone seemed to be very close together. Everyone wanted to be the first to Huissen. The Canadians beat us all to it in the end, so we held all the west bank of the Rhine.

For six months we had held on to half of the ground between Nijmegen and Arnhem and apart from a few isolated gains here and there, nothing to show for all that period. Now we had cleaned up the rest of the ground in just over half a day. A funny business, war.

'A' Company moved back to the small hamlet of the six POWs and found comfortable billets, not in the same buildings formerly occupied by the enemy. These were usually lice-infested, straw strewn, and could be easily smelled out.

There's a peculiar smell surrounding the habitat of the Jerries. One's nose is soon able to distinguish it. A rather obnoxious smell.

Signallers and stretcher-bearers enjoying a brief respite — (l. to r.) E. Naylor, K. West, D. Spittlehouse and D. Moore

TWENTY-SEVEN – OVER THE RHINE

A feeling of satisfaction stayed with us for the next few days. A nice feeling of elation, of a job well done, rather akin to the sort one must get as a boy. After the apprehension of continued threats from a bully, the bully gets a thump on the nose and suddenly he is no longer a threat and he runs away.

We knew he hadn't gone far, just across the River Rhine. Not just a river, but the greatest waterway in western Europe, some 850 miles long and, here in Holland, wider than the Thames in London. Quite an obstacle to overcome with tanks and armour, without the aid of a bridge.

We trained as we waited in the vicinity of Bemmel and Slijk Ewijk. Some of us managed to get into Nijmegen for baths and a film show. The town was now almost emptied of fighting personnel. Most of the armour had cleared from the side streets. Well-known unit signs had disappeared. Only the 'Nijmegen Home Guard' seemed to be in residence.

This derisory name had been given to the 49th Division (the Polar Bears), because of its prolonged stay on the 'island' defending the Waal Bridge for the six long winter months, from mid-September to the end of March.

Other units and Divisions had passed through this fine old university town on their way to the Reichwald Forest battles and Kleve and Goch and Emmerich. We were supposed to have had a 'cushy number', sitting on our backsides as they fought our battles for us.

The Canadians didn't think that way. They knew that it was necessary to hold the bridgehead. Not only would it provide a springboard to launch an attack on western Holland in the spring, but it would also need an unknown number of Germans to keep watch on, thus tying up men and armour for months.

It also provided a cornerstone around which to pivot.

In the vicinity of Emmerich, Canadian forces had determinedly thrown a pontoon bridge across the Rhine and after bitter fighting had linked up with the 6th Airborne. They now swung westwards towards Didam and the river Ijsael.

To our front we could see more clearly the 'Boston Stump'. Across the river Rhine, we could see on a clear day the gaunt silhouette of the bell tower of the great church in Arnhem. Standing out above the battered remains of houses, it had remained tauntingly inaccessible throughout the winter months.

Now in the clear spring days of early April, it seemed nearer, and we could see the damage that had been caused when the German guns had knocked off the small spire from the top of the tower. Now it seemed to taunt us even more, as if daring us to recapture it from present holders.

To those of us who came from the Midlands or the counties of Yorkshire and Lincolnshire, we recalled those happier days when we journeyed through the fen lands of Lincolnshire to the seaside resorts of the east coast. We would stand with noses pressed against the railway carriage windows, searching for the first sight of the giant 212 ft hexagonal tower of St. Botolph's church in Boston. This great edifice had dominated the landscape around the ancient inland port of Boston ever since the fourteenth century and had become well known throughout the land as the 'Boston Stump'. It now beckoned to us menacingly.

Historians have recorded that the artillery barrage which preceded the attack of Field Marshal Rommel's army at El Alamein in the Western Desert, to be the greatest concentrated barrage in the history of the British Army.

The 36-hour barrage which preceded the second battle of Arnhem was reported at the time to be only second in ferocity and concentration to the one at El Alamein. The sheer noise of the blasts of the artillery pieces and the whine of the shells overhead, made speech wellnigh impossible. Crunching and clanging into the streets of houses in Arnhem, they were creating intense damage to the property. What it was doing to the morale of the defenders we knew not. Hour after hour the unrelenting gunfire continued, making our ears ring and the head ache.

A wireless black-out had been imposed and messengers were kept on their toes, delivering signals and reports. Normal conversation was impossible, every sentence had to be shouted. We wouldn't be sorry when it all finished.

The order to load up came quite unexpectedly. A couple of hours' notice and we were on our way with the noise of the barrage still ringing in our ears, through the familiar roads of Bemmel. Sadly we saw how much damage had been done since we had first become honorary citizens way back in October. The Signals HQ was now reduced to a hulk of a building, not surprising really, when one recalled how on a dark night in February, one of our patrols had stumbled across a lone Jerry on his way to the Kasteel right in the centre of Bemmel. Subsequent interrogation had found that the enemy had been spying on us for months from a secret hide-out in the castle turrets.

We carried on past the knocked out Guards Div. tank and through Haalderen and Hulhuissen to Doornenburg, where as we debussed we could see the results of a few days' hectic work by the Canadian engineers.

A class 40 Bailey bridge now spanned the Neder Rhine. All sorts of vehicles were lined up ready to cross. Jeeps, 15-cwt trucks, Bren carriers, scout cars and even Sherman tanks. I crossed in a Bren carrier belonging to HQ Company. Even at the slow speed imposed, the bridge swayed rather alarmingly and at times the carrier was too near the side for my liking, but we reached the other side without any losses or mishaps.

Crossing the great river had been a bit of an anticlimax. I think we had all expected a D-Day type of amphibious crossing with the 'bayonets fixed, ramps down, charge lads' full bloodied frontal attack so beloved by newscasters and film makers. Wading through chest high water may look great from a comfortable cinema seat, but it takes a hell of a while to dry out from a good soaking. I'll settle for an anticlimax any time.

Signposts showed that we were now in the neighbourhood of Pannerden. After passing through Zevenaar and Duiven, we took up a position along the river Ijssel opposite a partly built autobahn leading towards Rheden and Velp.

There were many civilians still in the area, which pleased our Dutch liaison officer who had been with us since October, following his transfer from the 1st Dorsets in the now defunct 50 Div.

Henk (Lt. H. J. Kruisinge), had become a firm friend of the Battalion and very popular with all ranks. On the 'island' there had been very few civilians around, so, his main tasks had been the interrogation of prisoners and to assist his fellow countrymen who came through our lines and those of the enemy with amazing regularity. Here, north of the Rhine, he lost little time in establishing contacts with the recently liberated Dutch people. He seemed to take on a new lease of life.

Under cover of darkness we established contact with the forward Canadian unit with which we were to liaise. We soon ironed out a rota for the night duty. The Canadians would take the first part of the night and we would continue until dawn.

Although the farmhouse we occupied was rather large, we were cramped into the front room, with the Signals HQ down in the cellar. The rest of the house was jointly occupied by the Canadians and the civilians. I found myself a spot on the floor beneath the table, then, putting the 38 set on the table along with the customary half mug of tea for later use, I retired for the night.

Crruump .... An almighty sound awoke me in an instant. In the semi-darkness I heard North American expletives rent the air.

"Stay here with the wireless, Jock. I'll take some guys and sort those sons o' bitches out," said the Sergeant. They ran out of the house towards the bund to search for the perpetrators.

Just over an hour later the Canadians returned to report that they'd chased three Jerries along the bund, but did not wing any with their rifle fire.

The explosion had been caused by a bazooka type missile being fired at the house from the bund. Fortunately for those of us in the front room, the missile had hit the large chestnut tree in the front garden and had exploded. Shrapnel had shattered the window and the room was splattered with broken glass, but there were no casualties, except Toby.

Toby was my old faithful brown enamelled mug. A piece of shrapnel had pierced the side of the mug almost at the base. The cold tea which I had stored for the middle of the night, now dripped down on to the back of my hand from the edge of the table. I got to my knees and held my brown friend as the tea ebbed from his mortal wounds.

In the morning he was laid to rest with due ceremony, his grave marked by a cross with the inscription 'TOBY' — RIP. The Canadians, for a change, thought that WE were crazy.

Around midday, Henk came to the farmhouse to inform the civilians that they must evacuate the farm. The impending attack on Arnhem was beginning and the area must be cleared in case of enemy reaction. Much argument accompanied the loading of the horse-drawn farm cart, but about two hours later the old horse pulled the cart filled with the family's belongings and tied down with a large white sheet, up the slight incline through the orchard towards the road.

The cart had just reached the safety of the road when . . . sswwiiisssh . . . . The sound was like that of an express train passing at top speed, followed immediately by a tremendous explosion. Someone had evidently seen the departure of the civilians or perhaps it was just coincidence.

"They're firing that bloody railway gun again — down the cellar quick." The Canadian Sergeant was moving even as he spoke.

We had just reached the safety of the cellar when the express train came again. This time it scored a direct hit on the top floor of the farmhouse. The force of the shell exploding in the top of the house, penetrated right down to the cellar, cracking the arched roof from corner to corner with an inch wide diagonal scar. As the dust settled we awaited the third shell. We all knew that the Jerries always shelled in threes. Not this time however. Perhaps they were getting short of ammunition.

When the realization dawned on everyone, they left the little cellar one by one — everyone except me. Paddy returned after a few minutes to see where I had got to.

"Come on now O'West, let's be having you."

I tried to get up but my legs wouldn't function. Try as I might, I just couldn't get to my feet. I felt as though I had been hit on the head with a sledge-hammer.

Paddy gave me a hard look and then grabbed me under the armpits and dragged me to the steps. Leaning me briefly against the wall, the burly Irish rugger player threw his arm around me like a lock forward and half carried me up the steps to the fresh air out in the orchard.

"No use staying down there, Kenny lad, you'da gone bomb happy. You probably caught part of the blast. Come on let's have a walk and check the lines, they're nearly all knocked out."

We busied ourselves with the line repairs and my head cleared and the shaky legs soon lost their shakiness. Paddy grinned as I explained my feelings in the cellar.

"It happened to me in Normandy," he said. "I caught the blast from a mortar in a slit trench. Dere I was lying in the bottom unable to move, when up comes a bloke an' he says, says he, poor old Paddy he's had it, better shovel the old bugger in, says he. I was out o' dat trench like a flash. I'm not dead, says I — sure de bloke t'ought he'd seen a bloody ghost."

I chuckled at this story which was new to me. I didn't believe it at the time, but it was perfectly true.

The attack on Arnhem was expected to come from the south by either the Canadians or the Polar Bears forcing a crossing from the 'island'. The Germans in expectation of this had dug their defensive positions facing the river Neder Rhine. The streets of the town had been systematically barricaded by roadblocks to allow only the minimum of roads to be used for through traffic.

The Canadian Army in full knowledge of this had planned an attack not from the south, but from the east, forcing a crossing of the River Ijssel at Westervoort, then infiltrating the suburbs with infantry and tanks; they would link up with the pincer movement coming from the west at Oosterbeek, thus cutting off the enemy in Arnhem.

Towards the end of the massive artillery barrage, we had surreptitiously moved round to the east bank of the river Ijssel to await the assault crossing of that river.

The assault was carried out by the 56th Brigade of the Polar Bear Division near to the railway bridge at Westervoort. The amphibious vehicles known as Buffaloes were used very effectively and successfully. Engineer sappers soon had a pontoon bridge across to ferry the scout cars of the Canadians and later the Sherman tanks needed to support the infantry.

The Royal Scots Fusiliers were to play their part on the second day, when on reaching the town centre, we would be called upon to clear the remaining northern area of the town.

We climbed into the high sided Buffaloes under cover of darkness. The track down to the water's edge had been churned up by the continuous chain of vehicles as they emerged from their return trips, to be filled yet again with troops on dry land before clanking their way down to the river where they waddled across with about 15 to 20 men aboard. As we crossed we could see the giant railway bridge with some of its spans blasted down into the river bed. The Engineers could be heard working on it feverishly as they battled to get more tanks and supplies over the damaged structure.

Once on the other side, we made our way steadily towards Arnhem until we reached the suburbs. A little ahead of our time schedule we brewed up and attacked a packet of hard tack. We moved off cautiously through the side streets towards the town centre. Our rendezvous with the tanks was brief. We were required to proceed from the area of the station and clear the roads leading to the main road to Utrecht. If necessary we must proceed house by house and only call for tank support if really pinned down.

'A' Company worked their way along the street, taking cover from time to time from the odd mortar or shells which clanged down metallically, echoing in the empty town, which had been evacuated by the civilians after the Airborne had left in September. Not voluntarily, but by order of the Germans who had then systematically looted the town. All furnishings and even doors and windows had been removed to towns in the Saar and Rhur to replace and repair the damage caused by the Allied Air Forces.

In the afternoon, it became obvious that the tanks had found a way round the defences and had linked up with their countrymen coming in from the west. Apart from a few small skirmishes, we had encountered very light opposition and our casualties were very light. The only one in 'A' Company being Cpl. Dawson who, on hearing a noise from a house, jumped through the window in pursuit only to find that it was a cat trying to get out of a cupboard. On his way back through the windows the Corporal caught his arm on some jagged glass and suffered a severe cut, slicing through tendons.

By the time the food came up to us, we had collected a small gathering of young boys. Some were orphans, others had come in from nearby villages to forage for food, we felt so sorry for them and wanted to give them food. Our officers made us turn from the boys and eat our food, telling us that we must eat so that we would be able to continue the fight for the freedom of more people. The boys would be taken to the rear and given food later. Even so, most of the youngsters were given sweets or a bit of chocolate as they were sent on their way.

We rested the night in the north-eastern part of the town. A few prisoners had been taken, but in the main the Germans caught with their defences facing the wrong way had scrambled to get out of the trap we had laid. Some had been successful but not all.

The second battle of Arnhem was over. A brilliantly conceived planned operation, 'Quick Anger' had been executed with precision and skill by the Canadian Army of which we were a part, in just 36 hours.

Historians have recorded that it was a model operation and that it demonstrated perfectly the tactics required to capture a heavily defended town by an encircling movement.

The first battle of Arnhem by the Red Devils of the 1st British Airborne Division had been a bloody, bruising battle. Planned to last only three days, it lasted for over ten days and nights with bitter hand-to-hand fighting. Fearsome losses were inflicted on either side. The total casualties were counted in their thousands. In the British Military Cemetery in Oosterbeek lay some 1,700 young men, the cream of the Airborne forces.

We did not gloat over our victorious operation of Quick Anger, the two battles were not comparable.

Theirs was the glory and rightly so.

We felt that we had just completed the battle that they had started in September 1944 and we hoped that we may have avenged them on 14th April 1945.

TWENTY-EIGHT – AWA' DOON THE ROAD TAE AMSTERDAM

Suddenly the file of riflemen in front of me turned the bend in the road and ran shouting and screaming up the road and out of sight.

I felt the adrenalin pumping inside me as I trotted in their wake, laden down by the heavy No. 18 set on my back.

So this is what a bayonet charge sounds like, I thought. I reached the bend in the road and looked in the direction in which the screaming dervishes had vanished. There in front of me was a hill, not a large hill I grant you, but definitely a hill. On the top of this hill were the small section of our forward Platoon dancing around and singing the well-known school ditty 'I'm the king of the castle'.

Every schoolboy in Britain knows that Holland is a flat country bisected by canals and inland waterways. Colourful windmills dominate the picturesque landscape festooned with field upon field of tulips of all colours of the rainbow. There aren't any hills in Holland, at least not in the school books of my era.

In wartime Holland, the waterways and canals were all there in profusion much to our chagrin at times. The windmills were there too, but mostly devoid of their colourful sails. Early in the occupation by the Germans, the ingenious Dutch millers had devised a signalling system by setting the sails of the mill in various positions which, when understood by the underground movement, could pass messages about troop movements and Gestapo operations across the whole country in a matter of an hour or two. So sails came off.

The beautiful tulips it was said, had been used to supplement the meagre food rations, though I had always believed the tulip bulbs to be poisonous to human beings.

Of course there had not been any hills in this flat land, most of which was below sea level and reclaimed in a relentless battle with the North Sea.

No hills that is, until today. We had been fanning out from the suburbs of Arnhem towards Velp, searching for any remnants of the defending enemy forces.

We were now in the beautiful Veluwe district which starts to the north of Arnhem and covers a large area of undulating ground. Thick woods of silver birch, oak and beech are a veritable haven for wildlife and in peacetime are much frequented by nature lovers as they walk, cycle or ride their horses along the miriad of paths which criss-cross the sandy terrain.

The unexpected discovery of a hill just around the corner had been too much for the merry lads of 'A' Company. Throwing all caution to the wind, they had charged up the small mound like a group of kids on a Sunday-school outing.

They were still playing 'King of the Castle' when the Major appeared on the scene, Webley pistol in hand.

"What's all this damned nonsense?" he demanded. Sheepishly the lads stopped their dancing.

"It's the hill, sir," someone said.

"What about the damned hill?" asked Major Weir.

"Well, it's the first one we've seen in Holland, we didn't know they had any," said the spokesman.

"I thought you'd put in a bloody bayonet charge on our objective," replied the Major. "It's not a damned Sunday-school outing — bloody fools," he ended.

He surveyed the scene at the T-junction of the road from Rozendaal to Velp. A large beech tree had been felled across the junction and deep entrenchments had been dug out beneath the fallen tree. A well-placed machine-gun could have wiped out the merry lads of 'A' Company as they ran up the slope in youthful exhilaration. Fortunately no one was at home that morning.

"Check the area for mines and booby traps. If it is clear, we will make it Company HQ." With that he returned his pistol to its holster and helped in the checking of the trench. Everything was quite safe, so we set up HQ in this most delightful spot. Patrols were sent out and the Company consolidated its position ready for nightfall.

The main meal of the day arrived during the early evening by 15-cwt truck. We no longer had to fend for ourselves, as the situation now called for us to be on instant readiness to move forward at short notice.

With the food came the realization that we must sleep in trenches once more. It wasn't a pretty thought. After months of being mollycoddled under cover of a roof of some sort, we must now readapt ourselves to the cold hard fact of sleeping rough out in the open. We didn't relish the thought as we looked at the damp sandy sides of the hole burrowed under the beech tree.

The issue of a rum ration, the first since the flooded days of the 'island', cheered us a little as we settled down to the two hours on and four hours off duty stags.

It was a cold night, with a slight ground frost in the morning. We arose stiff and uncomfortable. We had become soft during our winter's hibernation.

"The Nijmegen Home Guard look decidedly dejected," said Arthur Thompson in an unusually eloquent statement.

"Too many nights at the Wintergardens," joked the Major's batman,

"I'm about ready for a bowl o' porridge." It was another hour and a half before that treat arrived.

Arthur had his usual promenade after breakfast and returned shortly afterwards to report that he had found some Airborne canisters in the woods to our left. We walked over to them and found that they had contained food desperately needed for the beleagured paras, but they had fallen into enemy-held ground and now lay broken open, with the contents having supplemented someone's meagre rations long ago. We searched hopefully for fragments of parachute silk to replace our now bedraggled scarves but found none.

During our search along the paths beside the road, a tall well-built man with thick dark hair came towards us. He wore a white armband on the left sleeve of his black overcoat. In hesitant English he asked the way to the Headquarters. Placing one hand on top of the other fingers we indicated the T-junction to him and he carried on.

Half an hour later, as we were about to abandon the search, another man came down the road from the direction of Rozendaal. A thin, averaged-sized man, dressed in a grey suit, wearing a pair of gold-rimmed spectacles and a Dutch steel helmet, he half walked and half ran towards us, brandishing a revolver.

"Hef you seen a big man wiz strong haar," he demanded agitatedly.

"Yes mate," said Arthur. "He's just gone down to our Headquarters."

"You should 'ave shot 'im." He gasped for breath. "He's der biggest Nazi in der whole district — when I get 'im I shoot 'im."

"Who are you?" I then asked.

"I am der Burgomeister von der next village," he replied, "an' I have a message from der airborne for your General."

"You'd better come with us," I said and took him to the Major at the T-junction and explained the situation.

"Are you a General?" asked the Burgomeister.

"No," said Major Weir, " but you can give me the message, I'll see the General gets it." The Burgomeister cut him short.

"Then you are no good. I promise the airborne officer on the Bible zat I only give zis message to a General." We saw John Weir stiffen as he answered curtly.

"I promise you that I will take it personally to the Commanding Officer," and held out his hand.

"And is zis Commanding Officer a General?" the man persisted.

"No, but he is the senior Colonel in the Brigade."

"Zen I am sorry sir," he said politely, "I cannot break a promise to a brave paratrooper. I must ask to see a General. Will you take me please?"

The Company Commander, realizing that the man was adamant, called to the Sgt.-Major to escort the gentleman to Battalion HQ and ensure that he be taken directly to the Brigadier. "And make him put that damned gun away before he does any damage with it," said the Major as he turned away.

"Ye're no' getting in yon jeep till ye pocket yon gun."

Meekly the gun was reholstered and the jeep sped away.

Within minutes of the Sgt.-Major returning, an 'O' group was called at Battalion HQ. Half an hour later the jeep returned minus the Major. Driver Nimmo handed the Sgt.-Major a message. I stood by him as he opened it.

"Christ man, I dinna ken what was in yon message tae the General," he said confidentally, "but it's certainly stirred the shyte up. We're awa' doon the road tae Amsterdam at two o'clock." Then cupping his hands to his mouth, he shouted "Pack up lads, prepare tae move oot at 14.00 hours."

Promptly at two-o'clock on that bright sunny afternoon we walked down the road towards Rozendaal. There, hidden under the trees along the road, we saw the waiting Sherman tanks. Major Weir was waiting too.

"Come along lads," he said cheerfully, "hop on to any tank, they're all going the same way — to Amsterdam. What are you waiting for Thompson?" he asked.

"I'm waiting for a number 27, sir," said Arthur cheekily, "perhaps there'll be another along directly."

"You'll take a number 5 and like it," replied the Major with a smile as he pointed to the fifth tank in the line.

We moved off into the centre of the road and started to overtake the walking riflemen of 'D' Company. From either side of the road came ribald comments about the layabouts of 'A' Company cadging another lift, but we replied to the effect that only the élite were chosen to lead the attack on the city of Amsterdam.

As soon as we reached the old main road to Ede, the tanks were deployed into the woods which lined the straight road. At first the Canadian drivers proceeded cautiously at walking pace, but gradually the pace quickened. The silver birch and oak saplings were brushed aside. Those directly in the path of the tanks were flattened as the 40-ton monsters ploughed their way through, only to spring back into an almost vertical position once they were freed of the pressure. We all entered into the spirit of the new experience, cheering and encouraging the drivers in their devilment.

The wood was thicker now and the trees were also more mature. Our driver was picking his way through the smaller saplings, but the tank in front of us ploughed on in a dead straight line until it met a well matured oak.

The tank stalled at the trunk, then after withdrawing a few yards, charged the oak tree like an enraged bull. The tree shuddered but stood firm, the tank with its engine at full revs started to climb the trunk as the tank's tracks ploughed into the soft earth striving for greater traction.

The angle of the hull of the tank became too great for the riflemen to remain their hold and one by one they slid off the back of the Sherman with the maple leaf emblem. Their shouts of glee now changed to howls of anguish as the lumbering monster reversed from the oak, threatening to bury them in the ground beneath its tracks. Fortunately there were not any casualties and they were soon aboard again following in our wake, taking care this time to assess the girth of the trees in their path.

The evening sun threw delicate reflections amongst the small bushes and especially on to the silver birches. The refreshing smell of the leaves that carpeted the ground brought back memories of camps we had attended as boys at our favourite camp site at Little Dalby in the heart of the Quorn hunting country in my own Leicestershire. We could not hear the birds above the roar of the engines, but they must be there, and I looked for robins and thrush and blackbird in vain. The noise of war had scattered them. I also expected to see bluebells in the pretty little glades as we passed. This however was not Swithland Woods, nor were there any delicate bluebells to sway as we went past.

Crack . . . crump . . . . crack . . . crump.

My reverie was rudely interrupted by the sound of heavy metal objects hitting heavy metal targets. Our tank slowed immediately to a stop. The tank commander shouted to us to debus as the leading tank of the column had been knocked out by an anti-tank gun at the edge of the woods. We formed a protective screen round the Sherman and waited.

The light was beginning to fade now and so the tanks decided to harbour for the night and let the infantry sort out the offending gun crew. I crossed the road to where 'A' Company HQ were assembling. In a small clearing the Sgt.-Major was checking the roll and soon we were all accounted for.

"Dig in, we'll no' be going any further tonight," came the order.

I found a shallow ditch and soon had the shovel working through the sandy soil at a steady pace. It didn't seem the same somehow digging without my old mucker George and I remembered the times we had slogged away at the Normandy shale for hour after hour to get a miserable trench barely two feet deep. Here, within three-quarters of an hour I was down far enough for shelter for the night and enough height for a firing point if necessary. Almost as I finished, so did the argument to our right front between a Spandau and a couple of Bren-guns. The Spandau stopped firing first, so we took it for granted that our lads had removed the immediate danger to the leading column.

We sat with the men of the Ontario Regt. and ate our meal beside their tanks. We talked quietly and dispassionately as fighting men do about friends who have just been killed. They had lost Charlie, a well-liked Lieutenant, together with the driver, by those two well-aimed anti-tank shells. The other members of the tank's crew were badly wounded and were on their way to receive the best medical treatment possible at the field hospital.

We talked of many things, one of which was the recent death of F.D.R. The news of Franklin Delano Roosevelt, the American President, had come just before we began the attack on Arnhem. The sudden news of his death was a shock and some of us wondered just how much this would affect the post-war world political scene.

News came about the advance on the morrow. The RSF would lead the attack at dawn, supported by our Canadian friends, the Calgary Regt. in their Shermans. 'A' Company would start the ball rolling at 05.00 hours.

In the conversation that followed, we were told by a Canadian Captain that as 147 Brigade were to lead, they had asked for the Royal Scots Fusiliers because of the fine example they had shown when clearing the 'island'. He spoke of the splendid courage shown by a signaller who, despite the mortaring and shelling going on about him, had sat on the back of one of their tanks coolly relaying messages about the battle back to his Battalion HQ and then, as the shelling stopped, cheekily informed the crew who had 'battened down', that it was safe to carry on.

Could this be the beginning of a legend, I mused? I couldn't break the illusion, not on this night, not for those great guys from the Canadian plains — but I have often asked myself what really happened at the Little Big Horn with General Custer and all those Indians . . . .

In the semi-darkness I changed the battery in my 18 set in readiness for the long day ahead, and attempted to net on the 'netting call' from HQ signals.

The call to move off came quietly from Major John Weir and we set off on foot along the cycle track on the left hand side of the main road to Ede. I found to my horror that my wireless set was u/s, dead, flat as a pancake! Frantically I rechecked the battery — completely flat and useless, I'd been given a dud the previous night. Quickly I ran to the Major and reported the bad news. He was furious.

"All bloody night to prepare, West, and we're out of touch with Battalion HQ in the first two hundred yards. Get Thompson up here quick, and get that bloody set of yours working and catch me up." He marched off into the dawn.

I turned and walked back to look for the singals carrier for another battery. Operation 'Dutch Cleanser' would have to proceed without me for the time being.

Within thirty minutes I was ready once more, having got a good net on to the Battalion network, I set out at a trot weaving my way through the back-up Company and the supporting vehicles. I reached the edge of the woods and stopped. There before me was a vast expanse of heath, at least a mile across to the far side and half as wide again. I looked for 'A' Company. The small copse bestraddling the road some four hundred yards in front of me showed no signs of movement, the building to the right of the road appeared to be a restaurant, whilst to the left stood a large wooden barn; both were deserted.

I looked further and then saw a thin line of dots walking in line abreast. They were about two-thirds of the way across the heath and pressing on steadily. I tried to raise Arthur on the wireless and succeeded after some minutes, whereupon I reported my position and asked for instructions. I was told to get a lift on the first available vehicle.

The Commanding Officer's carrier was the first to come along, he too had been called up to join the CO and was awaiting the signal to go forward.

"We might as well have a brew up while we're waiting," said the driver and set up the petrol burner at the rear of the carrier. In a matter of minutes he called that the tea was ready and walked to the front of the vehicle; mashing can in hand he waited for me to hold out my mug.

Ping — a bullet hit the can. We looked at the small round hole in the base of the former sponge pudding tin, turned black by the numerous mashings in all kinds of situations. As we stared in disbelief, the tea discharged itself from the aperture in a manner rather reminiscent of the Mannikin Pis monument in Brussels. This was too much for Donaldson, he let fly with a stream of abuse and obscenities in the direction from which we thought the missile had come. Neither of us had the sense to catch the liquid in our mugs, or for that matter, to take cover from the unknown marksman.

We were still bemoaning the loss of the tea when the order came to link up with the CO and 'A' Company.

Donaldson had the carrier at top speed long before we reached the copse, I looked at the barn and could see that it had been used for stabling horses and showed recent use.

Past the copse we swung off the road and followed the tracks of the 'A' Company carrier which showed up clearly in the soft ground.

"If we follow their tracks we can't hit any mines," said the driver, "keep your head down in case yon sniper's still got one up the spout." That thought had already entered my mind and the body had instinctively responded.

Despite the fact that we were speeding along as fast as the tracks would take us, it seemed ages before we reached the other side and parked the carrier amongst the sand dunes beyond the heather. Donaldson looked at his watch, it was only 8.30 a.m. I thanked him for the lift and reported to the Major.

As we deployed amongst the dunes, we looked back over the heath. Fate had been kind once more.

The Company had crossed the Ginkelse Heide, the main training ground of the Dutch army in pre-war days, in just over three hours. They had quickly overcome the token resistance at the copse buildings and from entrenchments in the sand dunes, completing not only their own objective but that of the Battalion.

Information from the prisoners taken, indicated that the rest of the defending forces had withdrawn to the barracks on the outskirts of Ede, just beyond the screen of trees at the end of the dunes. Machine-gun fire and mortar fire from that direction announced their intention to hold on to the barracks.

In response to a call to our RAF friends, came the welcome sound of a flight of rocket-firing 'Tiffies' winging their way to the selected target. The noise of the rockets screeching down on to the barracks block was rapidly followed by the sound of the tanks blasting away with their 65mm and 75mm guns as they ringed the buildings. The battle was short and sharp and by early afternoon it was all over.

Meanwhile, we had the satisfaction of hearing on the BBC one o'clock news that 'A famous Scottish Regiment this morning captured its objective to the north of Arnhem before breakfast.'

What it didn't say was, that the breakfast didn't arrive until four o'clock in the afternoon. We were more fortunate with the evening meal which reached us in the suburbs of Ede at about eight o'clock in the evening.

It was then that we realized that it was 17th April, seven months to the day when the Airborne had dropped to start the first battle of Arnhem, and it was on to the blazing hell of Ginkelse Heide that they had dropped on the second day in the face of murderous fire.

It was fitting therefore that we should see a number of jeeps with men wearing the famous red beret, scurrying about the town and being cheered by the population swelled by hundreds of people who had been evacuated from Arnhem.

The following morning we set off along the road towards Lunteren. Newspaper reporters and Canadian news-reel men were out in force to record the scenes for posterity. It was rather nice to be the centre of attention.

Canadian reconnaissance units had flushed out the enemy on the previous evening, but the awaiting populace of this lovely undamaged village were out in force to welcome us as the liberators. Teenage girls ran to place garlands of laurels around our necks as we marched along singing the old Boers trekking song which had become a big favourite of ours. I have pleasant memories of being kissed over and over again by two girls, one on each arm, as we made our way to the centre of the village.

The Burgomeister was standing under the largest red, white and blue tricolour of Holland that I'd ever seen. We halted as he made a speech in English, haltingly and a little unsure, but most sincerely he thanked us for giving them their freedom. He kept referring to the Canadians here today, so we had to inform him that we were indeed British.

"This cannot be," someone said. "If you were English you would be singing 'Tipperary' — all English soldiers sing 'Tipperary'."

So we sang 'Tipperary' — again and again and again. In fact we were still singing it when we marched out of the far end of the village.

I don't know where the Major had been during all this time, but he suddenly roared up in his jeep.

"Right, before we go any further get rid of all that damned foliage, the war's not over yet laddies."

I removed the small flower from the tip of the barrel of my rifle and placed it in my buttonhole of my pocket. The laurel wreaths were hung on a gate post and we continued towards Barneveld. Here too, the Canadians had already passed through and we rested the night in a small hamlet just outside the town.

Operation 'Dutch Cleanser' was planned as a full scale offensive by the Canadian Army to force a wedge from the Arnhem area to the Zuider Zee (now known as the Ijsselmeer), thereby cutting off some 120,000 Germans in western Holland. The attack led by the Royal Scots Fusiliers on Ginkelse Heide was, I believe, the last major attack by the 21st British Army Group in the Second World War.

The Canadians with their armoured cars and scout cars, tore holes in retreating German defences and it was most difficult to keep check on what towns and villages were actually occupied by our forces. The next day or two were spent on this mission.

Capt. Rushmore MC, rejoined the Company after a long spell recuperating from wounds, and he and I soon reached a good rapport. He was a cheerful friendly man with a nice informal manner, the sort of officer that one has instant respect for.

"Can you come with me West, please — and bring your wireless? I'll be in the jeep." This was my first meeting with the Captain.

Fusilier Nimmo was behind the wheel, the Captain sat beside him and on the rear seat sat a Bren-gunner. I climbed in beside him. Funny, I thought — a Bren-gunner? We drove out of the hamlet for about three miles and entered another village. Nimmo looked at the captain.

"Straight on to the crossroads," he said nonchalantly. At the crossroads we stopped and he decided quickly to take the road to the right. On reaching the extremity of the village, we returned to the centre crossroads and on to the far boundary. About turn once more and back to the crossroads. The village was completely deserted.

The Captain turned to me and said casually, "Report to Battalion that this place is clear." Then to the driver, "Back home for tea now Nimmo, please."

As we walked into the 'A' Company HQ, the Captain asked me to help him with his report. "Thanks for your help West, it could have been nasty you know."

He slipped the Sten gun from his shoulder and walked across the room to stand it against the wall. The Sten slipped through his fingers and ... bang! The butt hit the floor and a round of 9mm was loosed off. The bullet penetrated his right hand at the base of the second and third fingers leaving a nasty wound on the back of his hand.

I ran across the room, but already he was calmly taking a handkerchief from his battledress with his left hand to wrap around the wound.

"Blast! This is where I came in," he said, "sorry about that West. I was just beginning to settle in, the start of what could have become a very good friendship — ask Nimmo to run me down to the Regimental Aid Post will you?"

I called the driver of the jeep and the two of them sped off towards Barneveld. A wave of the left hand and he was gone. The Captain's stay had lasted less than 48 hours and I never saw him again.

By now the Canadians had reached the Zuider Zee, according to the rumours, thereby completing the encirclement of the one hundred and twenty thousand Germans in the Rotterdam and Amsterdam areas. We awaited the call to embus on the tanks once again. The order never came, instead we were moved quickly towards some woods to the north of Barneveld where two or three enemy machine-gun posts were causing a disturbance. The air was alive with rumours. Some said that there was a truce being arranged, others said that the Germans had been given 48 hours to surrender, we were not sure whether these machine-guns existed or not.

We soon found out.

From two points along the base of the wood the sound of Spandau fire could be heard. A section of riflemen was sent towards them and were met by a fusillade of shots. As they fired the Bren in reply, an officer ran up to us and told us that a cease fire had been ordered.

"Tell the Corporal to stop firing and get the Boche to pack it in as well." He turned and trotted off to convey the good tidings to others.

"Stop firing Corp, there's a cease fire — official."

"Well get someone to tell those silly buggers over there," he shouted back, "I'm not going to get shot being the bloody hero."

We derived a plan to loose off a shot from time to time in the direction of the wood and the Spandaus obligingly fired bursts in reply. It took an hour or more for them to use up all their ammunition, then two heavy bursts from the Bren brought them out with their hands up. Five youngsters who looked no more than seventeen years old.

I let someone else advise the adjutant of the prisoners.

We had barely returned to 'A' Company's house when I was summoned to Battalion HQ.

Nimmo took me in the jeep and I reported to the orderly room in the old farmhouse. Sgt. Lightman told me that the CO was out in the yard at the back of the house with some news.

Colonel Eykin was chatting to a small group of men by the haystack in the corner of the farmyard.

"Ah West. Good man, I think you're the last," he counted and nodded. "Yes, all here. Well chaps, I've some good news for all." He looked at each one and smiled. "You're all going on home leave tomorrow."

It was our turn to look at each other, in surprise. We had seen others off for a quick seven days leave, but all thought that we would have to wait a long time yet.

"Before you go, I would like to tell you something in confidence," continued the Colonel. "A truce has been arranged with the Germans, to prevent more suffering to our Dutch friends. Food is to be distributed to the Dutch people who are starving. The Germans must not interfere, otherwise we shall go in and blast them out. I believe it is the beginning of the end. Possibly by the time your leave is over, the war in Europe will be over. I ask you not to raise your families' hopes, but if the war does finish, I ask you to return on the correct day so that your comrades can proceed on their leave. If you are late, they will be delayed."

He then shook hands warmly with each one of us and thanked us for all the good work and the good times we had shared. His final words were, "I don't know where we may be when you return, but wherever we are, you will all be most welcome. Let us hope and pray that all this ghastly business will be over. Thank you chaps and have a good leave, you all deserve it."

Barneveld Church

TWENTY-NINE – HOME LEAVE

I didn't need an alarm clock to waken me in the morning, I had barely slept at all during the night. The prospect of seven whole days at home with my beloved wife Margaret had kept me awake for most of the night.

I had packed my kit as soon as I had returned from the meeting with the Colonel and sorted out the few souvenirs and presents that had been most carefully preserved during the past hectic weeks, now I was washed, shaved and ready for the journey by road to Nijmegen.

On our way we passed through Arnhem. Only now with the obstacles removed by the sappers' bulldozers could we see in full the appalling damage. Three-quarters of the buildings in the town had been either blasted out of recognition or had been damaged by shelling or the subsequent fires.

The indigenous population was now returning and were already beginning to pick up the threads of their lives which had been so rudely interrupted in our endeavours to bring them their freedom.

A short stop at the Wintergardens in Nijmegen gave me the opportunity to dash down the Groesbeekseweg to see the Beukering family. A brief wonderfully happy reunion, culminating with an invitation to the wedding of Iet and her fiancé in early May. I promised to attend, if at all possible, then ran back to catch the truck to the railhead.

We sang happily as we settled down for the long rail journey to Calais. For a change, we didn't care which way the train went as long as it was westwards towards the Channel port.

At Calais we entered the transit camp for documentation and to receive our pay and rail passes. There were thousands of men milling around this huge camp, with great long queues for everything, including the latrines. After twenty-four hours in this camp we were ready for the 9.30 a.m. ferry the next morning.

The crossing was uneventful and the sea like a mill pond. As we approached Dover harbour, there was a reminder to all ranks that it was an offence to take into England any revolvers or pistols. There followed a series of hundreds of small splashes in the wake of the former cross-Channel ferry, as souvenirs for the family were dumped by those who lost their nerve.

Once through the customs, we were quickly on our way to the capital, passing first through the hop fields of Kent with everyone threatening to do justice to the resulting year's crops at some future date.

Victoria Station was the scene of great activity as we trooped off the train, everyone dashing to the barrier to get their leave passes stamped. Some were already embracing their loved ones who had managed to get on to the platform.

The stairs to the underground were chock-a-block with a huge sea of khaki-clad men laden down with their equipment as they surged forward eagerly towards the platforms from where a great number would cross the capital to the mainline stations of King's Cross and St. Pancras.

At the bottom of the steps stood the colourful figure of Ras 'Prince' Monolulu with his ornate headress of ostrich feathers and his long flowing jibban.

Prince Monolulu was known to all racegoers as the flamboyant racing tipster renowned for his resonant shout of "Iiiive gotta horse, Iiiive gotta horse" from Ayr to Royal Ascot.

This morning his call had been altered to "Iiiive gotta tip, Iiiive gotta tip ...... these lads are gonna win the warrrr." Then with his horse's tail fly whisk he led the way to King's Cross, singing as we went, the popular song of the day, "There'll always be an England."

No one paid on the tube as he led us, still beating time, on to King's Cross-St. Pancras tube station. We left him still beaming with a great smile on his ebony face and shaking hands with as many of the lads as possible. I dived into an empty phone booth and sent a telegram to Margaret in case the letter I had sent from Holland had not arrived, then adjourned to the YMCA canteen for tea and wads as I awaited the departure of the next train to Sheffield, calling at St. Albans, Bedford and Leicester.

I heard the tram clanging its way down the steep hill of London Road and ran across the road to catch a lift to the city centre. There at the clock tower I caught the bus to my in-laws where we had made our temporary home. It was late in the evening before Margaret arrived from Chester, where she was now working with her uncle at an army camp.

The long warm embrace made words unnecessary, we were content to be together, oblivious to the world. We had waited long months for these treasured moments to come true. It was after midnight before we retired for the night to enjoy the sheer bliss of our love.

The days were passing all too quickly, visiting family and friends and of course calling at the factory to see my old workmates.

I called at the office first, to see Peggy, an old friend of ours with we had spent many happy hours at the Free Christians Hall at Saturday night 'hops'. Peggy didn't seem to be her usual bouncy self and I pulled her leg about not missing her fiancé Harry.

One knows when one has literally put one's foot in it! I had, right up to my neck. Poor Peggy broke into tears and turned away. Someone told me gently that Harry had been reported killed in action. He had been one of the lads of the Lincolns, who had been caught by the 'Tiffies' at the waterworks on the 'island'. I didn't realize that he was with the 4th Battalion until that moment.

After consoling her, I was able to tell Peggy the full facts of how Harry had met his death just four short weeks ago. It wasn't easy and I fully realized just how painful was this duty of informing next of kin, a task usually undertaken by an officer of the company to which the deceased had belonged. Perhaps this was worse because Harry had been a personal friend.

Meanwhile on the wireless the news from the front was very optimistic, the Americans were advancing on a broad front but there was very little news from Holland.

I suppose I must have had this on my mind as we walked along Gallowtree Gate one morning. Here in the centre of Leicester the shops were clean and, despite wartime rationing, still had much on offer. No bomb damage here, it all seemed so far away the carnage of war — until the delivery van backfired.

Instinctively I did a shoulder roll to my left and finished up in a kneeling alert position in the doorway of Thos. Cook & Son. Corporal Hands of Budbrook Barracks would have been proud of his pupil's reaction.

I was slightly embarrassed as an old lady asked after my welfare as I regained my feet. Margaret had been completely taken by surprise by my sudden departure from her side and asked "What on earth happened? One minute you were walking along arm in arm with me and the next you'd vanished."

"I must have stumbled on something," I replied.

Later whilst having tea with my family I told them the true story, much to their amusement. For years afterwards the family would ask, when they knew I had been into town, "Did you drop in at Thos. Cook's again?"

The announcement about the cease-fire came quite unexpectedly. A short communiqué was read to the effect that the Germans would sign the treaty of unconditional surrender on May 6th and that the 8th May 1945 would be celebrated as Victory in Europe Day, VE Day. All troops would be given two days celebratory leave, except those forces from the British Liberation Army in Europe who would be required to return on the date stamped on their pass.

I could have spit. I was due back at Victoria on 8th May. Everybody could have a holiday except those who had done the fighting. Just like the Generals to think up one like that.

There were still two days to go, two days to enjoy to the full. On the last day but one, we cycled out into the countryside. Down the short steep hill by the cricket pitch and into Barkby. The conker trees now coming into blossom, the hawthorn buds had burst open and soon the May blossom would be sending its sweet fragrance wafting across the fields from the hedgerows. We turned towards Beeby along the gated road. The gates were still there, but in the hedgerows now, taken from their hinges never to return.

The Nissen shelters along the roadsides were full of bombs and shells, the progress of the war machine could not be slowed by the continuous opening and shutting of field gates. The gravelled surface of the road too had changed, a layer of tarmacadam had been added, making cycling easier.

We stopped at the pump in the hollow to refresh ourselves and carried on to the fields we knew along the road to South Croxton. In spring these fields were carpeted with an abundance of yellow belled cowslips, interspersed with pale blue delicate lady-smocks. Proudly in my childhood I had taken a bouquet of these lovely English flowers back to my mother to confirm each year the arrival of spring.

Alas the fields of cowslip and lady-smock were gone. The brown earth had been winter ploughed. The roots of my beloved flowers buried beneath the surface as the field was being prepared to produce a crop of potatoes. The cycle rides to Beeby would never be the same again.

On the morning of the last day, VE Day, Margaret and I cycled across the city to say goodbye to my family. Even as we arrived, preparations were well in hand for the party to be held in the middle of the road beside the Hamilton brook. All my family were there, with the exception of my eldest brother, Arthur, who was still serving in Italy. Ernie, invalided from the Army, Alan working in munitions, Betty on leave from the Women's Land Army, Doris, the youngest and still at school. Dad producing pigs' hocks and other unrationed items as if from a magician's hat. Mother masterminding the whole scene, was one of those remarkable women born before the turn of the century who, during the difficult nineteen-thirties was an unofficial midwife, nurse, sitter-up, layer-out. A stalwart of the district, no one sent for the doctor until they'd first checked with Mrs West to see if it was chicken pox or measles. A doctor cost two shillings and sixpence a visit. A visit from Mrs West cost nothing and she usually brought along a couple of new-laid eggs for the invalid.

Sadly we could not stay for the festivities though I was sorely tempted, Margaret reminded me of my promise to the Colonel and to emphasize the point she accompanied me to the station complete with her own baggage ready for the trip north back to Chester.

At Victoria no one wanted to know us. It was a case of a lone Redcap calling miserably, "Straight on the train you blokes, an' 'urry up."

As we passed through the metropolis the sky was ablaze with colour, it looked as though the whole of London was on fire. From every street corner and every piece of derelict land, huge bonfires burned. The bomb battered Londoners danced around the fires and only stopped to cheer us as we passed by in the train, then recommenced their private celebrations. We were caught up in the excitement of the night and sang and danced along the corridors and in the compartments, but once clear of the built up areas, the realization that the party was over for us began to sink in and we were soon bemoaning our luck on coming home a day too early.

The usual formalities and the customs officials at Dover were very conspicuous by their absence and it was a very subdued party which embarked on the ferry that night.

Calais was much the same, no formalities and straight on to the train at the end of the jetty and we were on our way. We quickly settled down for the night, or rather early morning. One man on each luggage rack, two on each seat, one on the floor of the compartment and one in the corridor outside.

The sudden braking of the train woke us from our slumbers, it must have been about seven o'clock. We looked out of the windows to see what was happening. We were parked in the sidings of a French town.

"Ask that Froggy where we are," said someone.

"Armentières," came the reply. "We're stopping for an hour, got to change the engine."

Across the road on the other side of the train came the sound of the accordian band and people singing. On checking we saw the locals were still whooping it up from the previous night's celebrations.

"Me old man was always tellin' me about the mademoiselle from Armentières," said a L/Cpl, "let's go and see if it's true."

With that we all left, without as much as a by-your-leave, and joined in the singing and dancing in and out of the cafés alongside the railway. A very enjoyable time was had by all and we turned a deaf ear to the calls to board the train, until the driver in exasperation started to pull away. We quickly rejoined the train. The Lance-Corporal remarked that his old man was right about the mademoiselle from Armentières and that during the brief stay, the Anglo-French victory had been consummated.

This and other like topics were discussed on the return journey to Nijmegen where we arrived late at night.

It was only at midday the next day, that I suddenly remembered the date. It was the day of Iet's wedding. I tried to slip out of the camp but was caught half-way to the main road and duly hauled up before the officer in charge.

I showed him the invitation and was well on the way to convincing him when a truck from 147 Brigade arrived to take our party back to our units. This, I thought was my chance. I worked on the driver all the way into Nijmegen, but despite all attempts to bribe him he wouldn't agree to my entreaties. Dead regimental, this fellow. He'd signed for nine men and he was going to deliver nine men, besides which he'd got a date with a Dutch girl that night, which he'd every intention of keeping. So I missed the wedding of Iet van Beukering. I was very annoyed and quite upset. How could I write and tell her I had been in the town on that day, but couldn't attend because of a load of red tape? I would apologize later, I told myself.

THIRTY – THE FLOWERS O' THE FOREST

Almond trees in blossom are a beautiful sight to the eyes of the beholder. To see so many, in such lovely surroundings, was so very unexpected. The bright pink of their blossom contrasted so vividly with the variegated greens of the evergreens and the conifers. The dark leaves of the copper beeches brought out extra dimensions to the gardens in this lovely unspoilt town of Baarn.

Situated between Amersfoort and Hilversum it had been veritably untouched by the ravages of war, inhabited by rather well to do families, the houses were in keeping with the general standard of middle upper class dwellings.

In less than two weeks, the whole scene had changed from the black lifeless branches of the trees, to a fairyland of colour and life. It was as though someone had been waiting for the ending of this terrible war to start a new era of beauty and colour, of new life and new hope for those who had survived.

Birds were singing, sparrows, thrushes, blackbirds, all joined in a happy chorus of song. Nests were being built ready for the new expected fledglings. The sun shone for everyone. It was spring and the sap rising.

Humans too joined in the celebration, they sang and whistled as they attended their daily tasks, it was even rumoured that the company cook had smiled, once.

A large flagpole dominated the entrance to the large white house standing in about half an acre of ground. Only days before it had seen the dreaded red flag with the black swastika in the centre, flying from its halyard, now the tricolour of the Netherlands flag flew proudly at the top.

Inside the house, the Battalion Command Post was billeted together with the signals section. I found myself a nice spot under the bay window overlooking the main drive.

One of the first people I bumped into was the Colonel.

"Hello West, back already?" he enquired. "Did you have a good leave?"

I assured him that I had, but thought darkly about the clot of a driver from 147 Brigade who had returned me with such speed the previous night, when I could have been at the wedding reception.

"We could do with you and some of the other married chaps," went on the CO. "There are some children who need to be entertained this afternoon –

the RSM will give you the details."

Shortly afterwards the unmistakable voice of John the 'B' was heard exhorting all married gentlemen to assemble on the drive.

"We have been asked to visit some youngsters in hospital who have not yet seen any British soldiers — so it is our job to fly the flag, to show them some SMART soldiers. Be back here in half an hour shining like a tanner up a sweep's arse — with as many sweets and bars o' chocolate as you can scrounge. Dismiss."

We duly reported with an assortment of sweets and chocolate safely in our pockets and about thirty-six of us climbed into the waiting 3-tonners.

The hospital was somewhere near to Hilversum. A large house had been converted into a sanatorium and we were ushered into the main room of the office block.

We were introduced to the administrator who in turn introduced his staff. He explained that news of the liberation had reached the hospital quickly, but of course they had not seen anything of the Tommies who had done all the liberating. The patients would dearly like to meet us and in our honour they had organized a small concert.

There may have been only about fifty people in the hall but we were given a tumultuous reception as we were escorted to the seats of honour at the front where normally the officers would sit.

The programme commenced with a solo pianist playing a selection of Chopin on the concert grand. This was followed by a former contralto of the Dutch Royal Opera singing a selection of well-known arias. Another solo performance by the pianist was followed by a baritone joining the contralto for two delightful duets.

We of course applauded like mad, which pleased the hosts so much that they suggested that we might like to sing something typically British. We hadn't expected this, but we settled for 'There'll always be an England'. Very few of the lads had been on a stage before but I thought we had performed fairly well — but not well enough for an encore.

We sang 'Tipperary', in which they all joined in and 'Pack up your troubles' — then the trouble began. They wanted us to sing a typically army song of the present day. After much demurring we settled for the Liverpudlian song 'Maggie May'; as only one bloke knew the verses it livened the afternoon up a bit, he was flat and we bashed through the chorus a bit sharpish.

The call now was for one last song from the brave Tommies, so we put all we'd got into our finale, a superb renditioning of 'Roll me over in the clover'.

As we drank the weak, milkless tea, it became quite obvious to us all, that there were not any children at this hospital. It was a sanitorium for the terminally ill. All around the grounds amongst the beautiful silver birches were dotted small wooden chalets, each occupied by one or two adults. We spent a couple of hours walking round and talking to the inmates, some of the lady patients, unable to speak in our language, leaned forward to shake hands and with tears of joy running down their faces to kiss us in gratitude. It was most touching and we soon had given all the sweets away. Unfortunately for the men, we had left hundreds of cigarettes behind and all most of them wanted to do was to talk of Arsenal and Tottenham Hotspurs who had played in Rotterdam and Amsterdam shortly before the war, and to smoke an English fag.

The excitement of our visit was obviously tiring them, so we reluctantly returned to Baarn. To the credit of our lads there wasn't a fag to go round on the way back, not even a knob-end, and the cheeky chappies who asked how the baby sitters had gone on, were soon put in their places.

The next morning saw me off again to 'A' Company who were guarding a cache of prisoners about a mile from the town of Baarn. As we approached the POW camp we could see hundreds of field grey clad men in a field, the place was swarming with them. Unshaven and unkempt they did look a sorry mess, but it was obvious that field kitchens were being organized and their stay would be only temporary.

In the next field were more bicycles than I have ever seen in my life. Row upon row, I should think that every prisoner taken by our lads must have been in the possession of a bike. There must have been thousands in that compound. It is true to say that there were more troops defending the bicycles than were looking after the Germans.

Around the perimeter of the fence were dozens of Dutch people, all clamouring to barter watches, cameras, binoculars, anything to exchange for a bicycle. Occasionally a bike would come sailing over the fence and away would pedal a delighted Dutchman, his transport difficulties overcome for the time being. Although I would not have thought it possible at the time, I have read that over ninety per cent of all Dutch cycles were returned to their rightful owners after the war, some from as far away as Italy.

Once again 'A' Company HQ was situated in a farmhouse and some of the lads were actually sleeping in tents. Most of the rest of the day was spent collecting revolvers and hand pistols from the POWs and emptying the magazines of ammunition.

The next morning was enlightened by the visit of a little Dutchman in a long light coloured mackintosh and a large trilby hat, he looked around him very agitatedly and someone said unkindly, "It ain't that bloke still looking for that bloody Nazi is it?" It wasn't.

"Vere iss your Kapitan?" asked the little man, "kvick!"

We took him to the Major, who listened earnestly and then emerged from the front door and held his hand out expansively to the little man, offering him the freedom of the garden.

The little man walked quickly to the large fir tree about fifty yards from the house, leaning against the tree he took a sighting on some part of the house and then carefully measured ten paces from the tree. He stopped about a foot and a half from the Company latrine which had been dug in the garden.

Excitedly he motioned for a spade and dug feverishly until about two feet below the surface he unearthed a box. He opened the box and took out a bag about nine inches in circumference, then carrying it heavily he placed it at the Major's feet. When he opened it up, he gave a huge sigh of relief, for there in the bag were hundreds of silver guildens. Mostly they were the two-and-a-half guilden pieces, but I think there were some larger coins, perhaps five guildens, I'm not sure. What is certain is that buried in the ground not half a yard away from our latrine was this man's life savings. He had, he said, buried it for safety on a dark night in 1940, as the Germans had invaded Holland, only to find to his horror that we had dug our 'bog' on the same spot, but not quite.

He stayed for a time and chatted with us and then, declining an invitation to run him home in the jeep, he wandered off pushing his bicycle along with the waterproofed bag held tightly in the wickerwork basket on the handlebars, pausing briefly at the gate to raise his large trilby in thanks.

Two days later we were back at the old pastor's house in the small hamlet down the road from Barneveld. The son we had met before, but now his sister had rejoined the two males on her return from a relative living at Apeldoorn.

The pastor was a nice old chap, but was as deaf as a post. He did however play the harmonium very well and since his parishoners were still dispersed, it was his wont to conduct a small family service each evening at six o'clock. He would commence with a prayer, sing three hymns and then end with another prayer.

We noticed on the first occasion that as he sang, the son and daughter would carry on talking, etc., then when he turned round they would mouth the words and carry on with the conversation as he returned to the harmonium. The son explained.

"He's completely deaf, but it keeps him happy if he thinks we are joining in with him. He's so lonely since our mother died."

We carried on chatting and miming alternately and the fact that the hymns were being sung in Dutch didn't really matter, as mime is internationally understood anyway.

At the end of the family service, the old pastor turned and thanked us and shook hands, before departing to his study to prepare his sermon for the first service to his flock in a free country.

The group of young people stayed and talked well into the night about their hopes for the future and of their plans to restart their neglected education.

"Have you seen the Company notice-board?" asked little Ernie Naylor, the Company runner. "It's a sure sign that the war's over. Battalion Church Parade on Sunday, best battledress, boots polished, belt and gaiters to be blancoed — it's back to the bullshit again lads. An' there's another two notices above that, too high for a short-arsed bloke like me to read — besides, there are some big words like therefore and forthwith in it, too hard for a simple Yorkshire lad like me." It was imperative that we should investigate this new bulletin immediately.

A small knot of people stood before the board surveying the three notices. We lifted Ernie up to enable him to improve his education.

The first notice was a proclamation from the General Dempsey of the British 2nd Army,

> *With the cessation of the war in Europe, it will be necessary for the redeployment of some units .... Therefore those units which have been serving under the command of the 1st Canadian Army will now return to the command of the British 2nd Army forthwith.*

The second notice was a copy of a letter from the GOC 1st Canadian Army, General H. D. G. Crerar, in which he thanked all members of the 49th Division for the support they had given him and that how sorry he was to lose them. He ended by wishing all of them good luck for the future.

"So ends a beautiful bloody friendship," said the diminutive Company runner, as we dropped him to his feet.

"Amen to that," we all chorused.

Our eyes now turned to the notice in the middle of the board. It re-affirmed what Ernie had told us earlier.

> *All ranks will attend a Thanksgiving Service at Barneveld Church on Sunday at 10.00 hours.*
> *Best battledress will be worn, boots will be highly polished. Brasses will be highly polished. Webbing belts and gaiters will be blancoed. Caps T-o-S will be worn. Battalion will parade by companies, HQ Company leading followed by 'A', 'B', 'C', 'D', 'S', in that order. The Commanding Officer, Lt.-Col. D. A. D. Eykin, DSO, will take the salute at the march past following the service.*
>
> .... *signed*
>
> *Victory Parade*
> *A victory parade will be held in The Hague, in the presence of Her Royal Highness Queen Wilhelmina of the Netherlands.*
> *Each Company will provide ten men of not less than five feet ten inches in height. Decorated men will be given preference. Medals will be worn. Companies will be informed of times of departure.*
>
> .... *signed*

"It's no use looking at the bottom one, Kenny lad," said Ernie, "the only way you and me will get there is for me to sit on your bloody shoulders."

"Not much chance of me blancoing," said Freddie Nottis, the stretcher bearer, "I chucked mine away before we left for Normandy."

Freddie had underestimated the Army's efficiency. Bread we may be short of, but blanco, no! On the Saturday morning we were issued with blocks of Blanco Khaki/Green No. 3.

By midday the hedges and bushes around almost every house in Barneveld was festooned with British Army webbing as it basked in the warm sunshine to dry. Dirt and lacquer was scraped from the brasses on the belts and the burnishing began.

All day we worked on our kit. Dubbin was removed from the boots and the 'cherry blossom' was waxed into the toecaps with warmed spoons. Aided by a little spittle and great application of polishing rags, they were quite presentable by nightfall.

Sunday morning was as clear and bright as only a May morning can be. The air was still and the scent of the blossoms hung above the village like a fragrant bouquet.

News of the parade had reached the villagers and they were out, all ready in their Sunday best clothes, chatting animatedly as they made their way to the centre of Barneveld.

Lined up in columns of three, we were checked by the Sgt.-Major until he was satisfied that all was correct. The order of 'right turn' was given and we marched off to the assembly point on the outskirts of the town. I should have fallen out here and joined HQ Company, but opted instead to stay and march with the lads of 'A' Company.

As we marched off to the skirl of the Pipe Band, the happy Dutch people broke into spontaneous applause. The sound of the 'doodlezacs', as the pipes were called and the swinging of the pipers' kilts, was a sight and sound that very few of them had ever witnessed before and it set the scene for a memorable church parade.

In church, Paddy and I 'fiddled' it so that we stood together for the service. As we looked around the church we could see HQ Company to our front, 'C' Company were at the front to the left and opposite us was 'D' Company.

I looked along the ranks opposite and saw the sun glisten on the steel frames of a pair of spectacles. The head turned slightly and a slight smile of recognition flickered in my direction. As I nodded back, I could see the narrow stripes of red, white and blue of the Military Medal ribbon on the left breast of his battledress blouse. I was glad that Louis Hill had made it.

For ninety per cent of the campaign, Sgt. Hill had played the dual role of Sergeant and Commander of No. 17 Platoon, my old Platoon. These he had carried out with much aplomb.

I looked for others. Barnsey was there, George was there, looking almost naked without his fag. Two or three other faces I recognized, but no more. The rest of No. 17 Platoon were young reinforcements. At twenty-two years of age I felt quite a veteran compared with these lads in their late teens.

John Boult placed his hands on the keyboard of the organ and the whole church was filled with a resounding chord. The congregation stood and sang the first verse of the National Anthem, God Save the King.

The Thanksgiving Service on the conclusion of the campaign in North-West Europe had begun.

Our Battalion Padre conducted the service, commencing with the hymn, 'Praise my soul, the King of Heaven', followed by Psalm 98. The lesson, taken from Joshua 24 vs 14-18, 22-24, (Joshua's charge to the people at the end of a campaign) was read by the Commanding Officer.

After an act of thanksgiving and two hymns, the Padre in his short address paid tribute to those who had fallen and read out the casualties sustained from 12th June 1944 to 5th May 1945. I forget the full details, but the total number of recorded casualties remains embedded in my mind, nine hundred and twenty-seven, of whom twenty-nine were officers.

The last hymn was 'Now thank we all our God', and the church was filled again with the sound of male voices as the whole congregation sang this well-known hymn.

There followed a two minutes silence of remembrance.

I saw the faces of Pottsy, little Monty Montague, young Bill's and Lt. Wilson the first Can-loan officer, who we had known for just one brief day. Corporal Donaldson, Paddy Inglishby and his mate. Patterson, three times wounded and the Lance/Jack with the crew cut, in the trench at Juvigny . . . .

Pipe Major Findlay played the lament, 'The Fleurs o' the Forest'. As the first notes of the drones began, I could see an English country lane winding down the small hill beside the cricket pitch. In the distance I could see the top of the village church spire, above the majestic trees in the grounds of Barkby Hall — then came the tears . . . .

Through tear-dimmed eyes, I could see on the front row and slightly to my right, the worn face of Major John Weir, his granite hard jaws biting tightly together as he tried, in vain, to stem the tears which trickled down his cheeks and on to the lapels of his battledress blouse — but a man's a man, for a' that.

As the Padre gave the blessing, there were many sniffs and coughings and clearings of throats. Self-consciously, tears were wiped away by discreet fingers, eyes were averted to avoid embarassment to close friends. One's belt fasteners and boots were inspected for no apparent reason.

The Colonel gently pocketed his handkerchief and walked quietly but with great dignity towards the altar rails, whereupon he bowed, turned smartly about and looking fixedly to his front, marched slowly to the main door of the church, to be followed silently by his men.

In the square outside the church, the Battalion quietly assembled. Gone was the gaiety of the march from the billets. The Dutch too were quiet, as if not wishing to intrude.

"11th Battalion the Royal Scots Fusiliers, will march in column of route. By the right, quick marrrrrch," bellowed Regimental Sergeant-Major John MacCreadie.

The drummers in their tartan trews played their 7 beat rolls to give the pipers time to 'blow up', before they broke into the regimental march, 'Highland Laddie'.

Backs straightened, arms swung in perfect unison. The studded leather-soled boots echoed on the herring-boned patterned red bricked road as they marched through the town, as smart as any contingent of the Brigade of Guards on their way to mount guard at Buckingham Palace.

The route to the saluting base was lined by hundreds of Dutch people, standing to attention in silent respect for this special occasion and looking with quiet admiration at the men who had helped to bring about their deliverance from the dreaded oppressors.

As the dais came into view, we heard the command from Captain Smith in charge of Headquarters Company.

"Headquarters Company, eyes left," a long pause ... and then, "eyes front."

Now it was our turn.

" 'A' Company, eyes left," commanded Major John Weir. Heads flicked to the left as one man.

As each rank passed, they caught briefly the eyes of the Colonel as he stood rigidly to attention with an immaculate salute. A look of mutual respect flashed between them, a togetherness which it is difficult to define. The Colonel knew all his men personally and in that split fraction of a second, one could sense that each man was recognized and acknowledged as an integral part of the Battalion.

The whole of the 11th Battalion of the Royal Scots Fusiliers passed before their Commanding Officer.

They marched proudly and resolutely, with their heads held high and on their heads they wore a sort of floppy beret with a pom-pom on it, the finest head-dress in the British Army — aye:

"An' it's called a Tam-o'-Shanter."

From the time that some 30 Officers and 820 Other ranks of 11th Bn Royal Scots Fusiliers landed in Normandy on 12th June 1944, until VE Day on 8th May 1945, the total casualties were 797.

	Killed	Wounded	Missing
Officers	7	33	2
Other Ranks	164	574	17
Total	171	607	19

HONOURS AND AWARDS

Distinguished Service Order

| Lt-Col | AWHJ Montgomery-Cunninghame | Lt-Col | DAD Eykyn |
| Maj | AL Rowell | Maj | J Weir |

Military Cross

Maj	JR Alexander	Capt	R Dobson
Lt	RN Dickie	Lt	WD Douglas
Lt	TJ Dunlop	Lt	JA McIntosh
Lt	TM Murray		

Distinguished Conduct Medal

| L/Sgt | W Meller |

Military Medal

Sgt	L Hill	Sgt	W Kemmett
Sgt	W Little	Sgt	G Sangster
Sgt	A Shires	Sgt	D Stenhouse
Cpl	J Carter	Cpl	C Halliday
L/Cpl	E Taylorson		

Mentioned in Despatches

Maj	GM Macauley	Maj	J Weir
Capt	J Richardson	Capt	W Ure
Capt	WS Wilson	Lt	A McLean
Lt	WS Watters	CQMS	A McColl
Sgt	E Haigh	Sgt	W Shaw
Sgt	J Smith	L/Sgt	J Wraight
Cpl	J Gilhooley	Fus	S Warren

Croix de Guerre (Gilt Star)

| Maj | GM Macauley |

Croix de Guerre (Bronze Star)

| Sgt | D Stenhouse | Sgt | W Shaw |

Orange Order of Nassau (Netherlands)

| Maj | EK Berwick | Capt | M Wallace |

(Research by Capt GP Dixon and Capt W Ure is gratefully acknowledged.)